HOUGHTON MIFFLIN

Spelling and Vocabulary

Senior Author
Shane Templeton

Consultant
Rosa Maria Peña

HOUGHTON MIFFLIN

Boston • Atlanta • Dallas • Denver • Geneva, Illinois • Princeton, New Jersey • Palo Alto

Acknowledgments

For each of the selections listed below, grateful acknowledgment is made for permission to excerpt and/or reprint original or copyrighted material as follows:

SCRABBLE® and BOGGLE® are registered trademarks of Hasbro Inc. Used by permission of Hasbro Inc. All rights reserved.

Select definitions in the Spelling Dictionary are adapted and reprinted by permission from the following Houghton Mifflin Company publications. Copyright © 1994 THE AMERICAN HERITAGE FIRST DICTIONARY. Copyright © 1994 THE AMERICAN HERITAGE CHILDREN'S DICTIONARY. Copyright © 1994 THE AMERICAN HERITAGE STUDENT DICTIONARY.

Excerpt from *The Book of Giant Stories,* by David L. Harrison. Text copyright © 1972 by David L. Harrison. Reprinted by permission of the author.

Excerpt from *The New Girl at School,* by Judy Delton. Text copyright © 1979 by Judy Delton. Adapted and reprinted by permission of the publisher, Dutton Children's Books, a division of Penguin Books USA Inc.

Excerpt from *A Thousand Pails of Water,* by Ronald Roy. Copyright © 1978 by Ronald Roy. Reprinted by permission of Alfred A. Knopf, Inc.

2000 Impression

Printed in U.S.A.

ISBN: 0-395-85529-2

15 16-B- 03 02 01

Contents

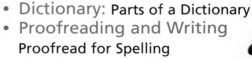

Contents

Contents

Contents

Contents

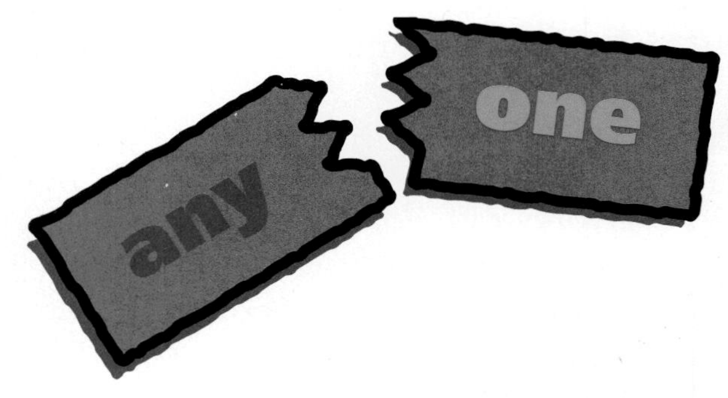

Contents

Student's Handbook

Picture Clues

Consonant Sounds and Letters

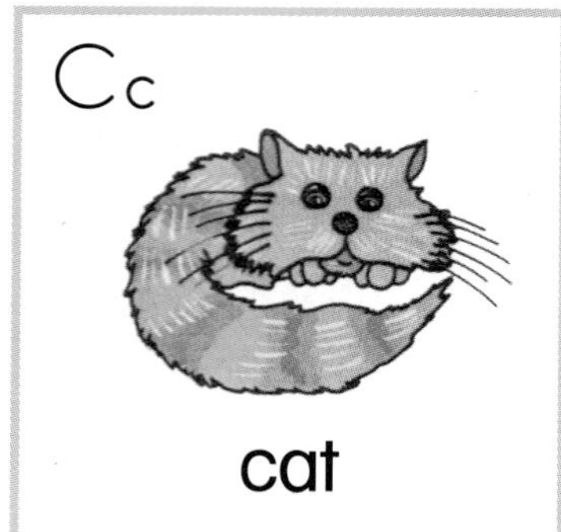

Picture Clues

Consonant Sounds and Letters

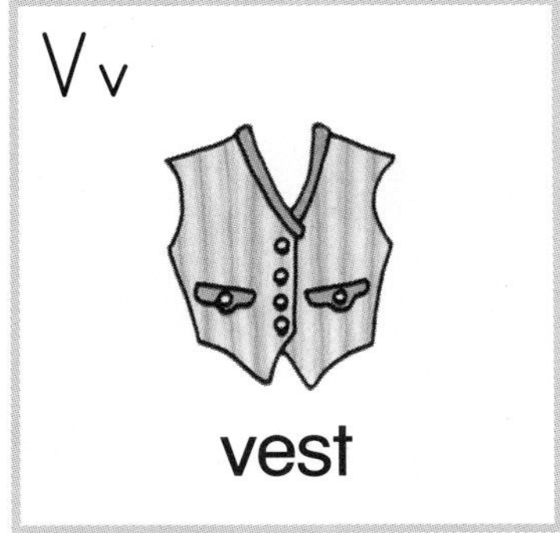

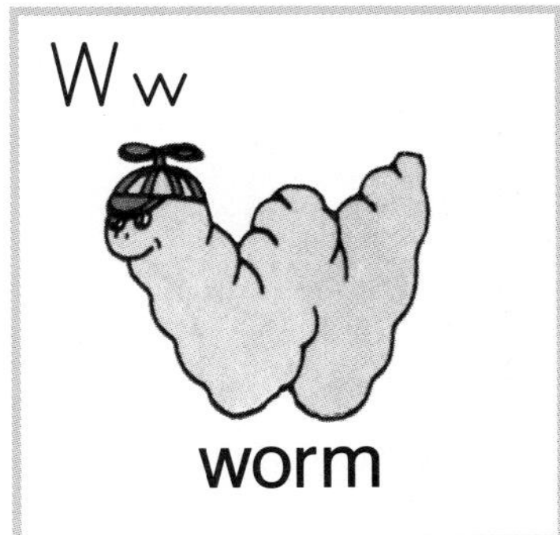

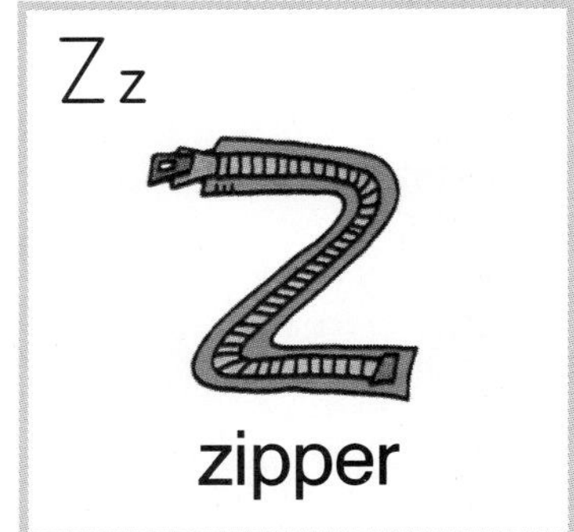

Picture Clues (continued)

Vowel Sounds and Letters

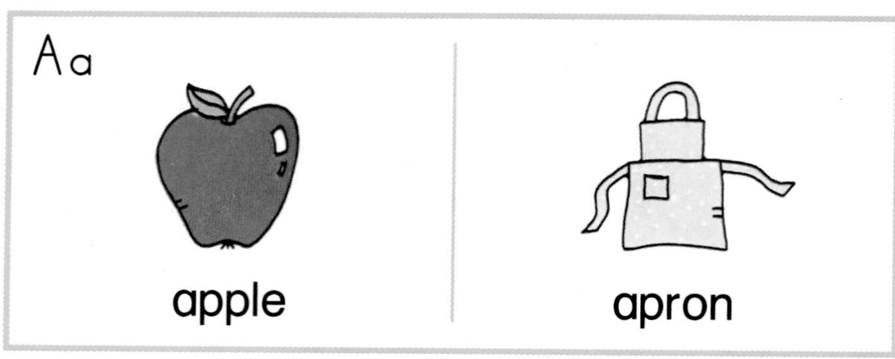

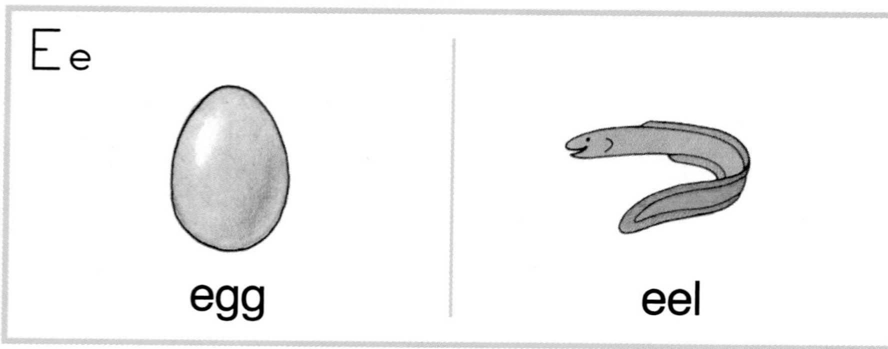

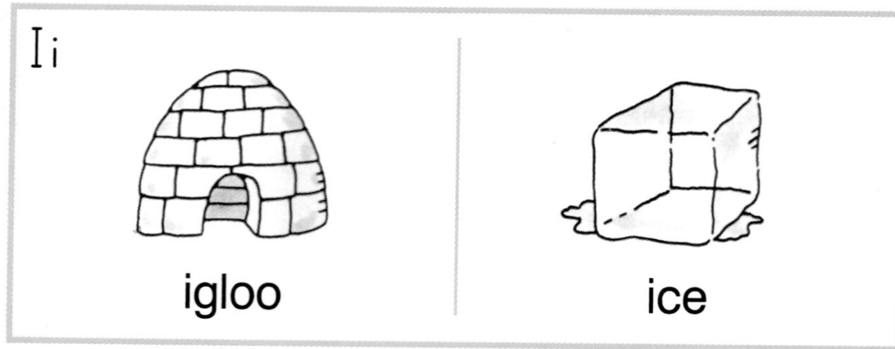

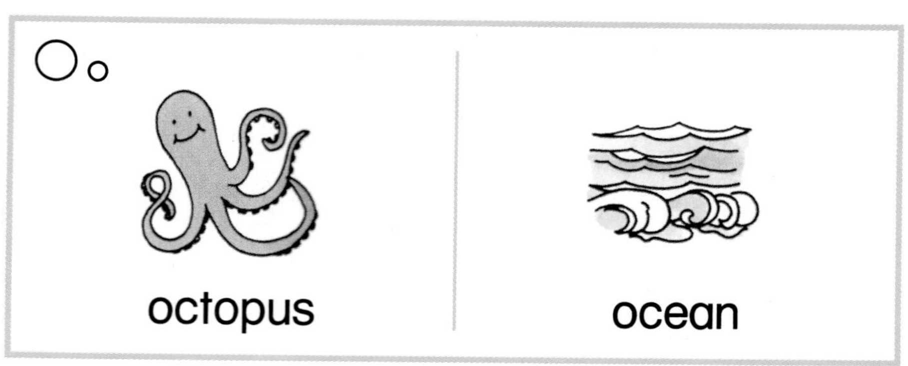

Phonics

1 Picture Clue Review

PHONICS

Write the letter that begins each picture clue name.
If you need help, look at pages 10, 11, and 12.

1. 

2. 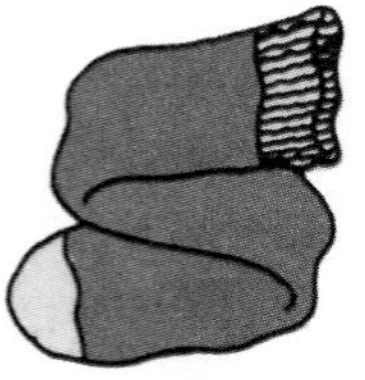

3. 

4. 

5. 

6. 

7. 

8. 

9. 

10. 

11. 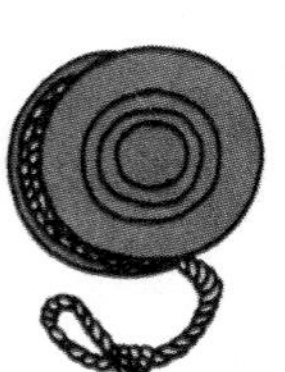

12. 

13. 

14. 

15. 

16. 

1 Picture Clue Review

17. 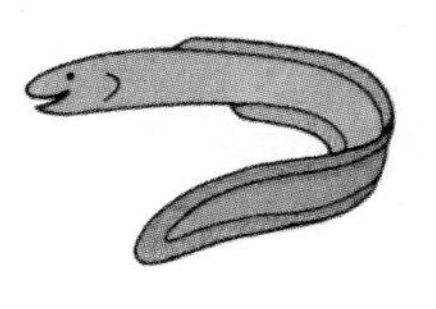

18. 

19. 

20. 

21. 

22. 

23. 

24. 

25. 

26. 

27. 

28. 

29. 

30. 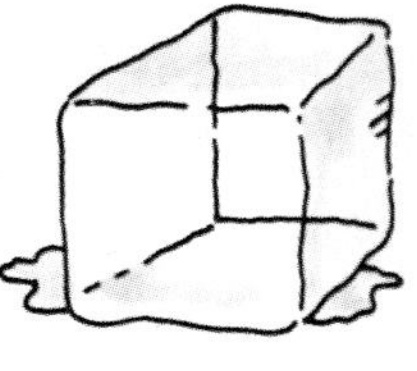

2 Consonants in Words

PHONICS

Think of each **beginning** sound. Write the missing letter to spell the word.

1. 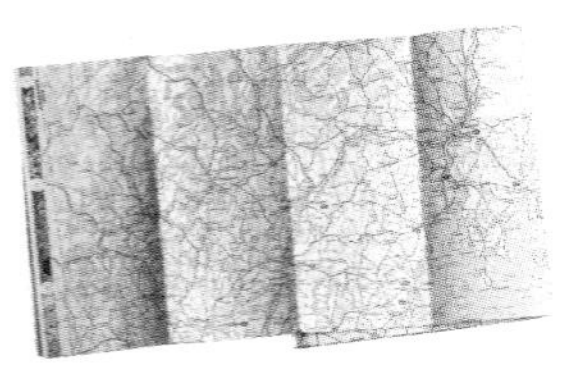

__ap

2. 

__og

3. 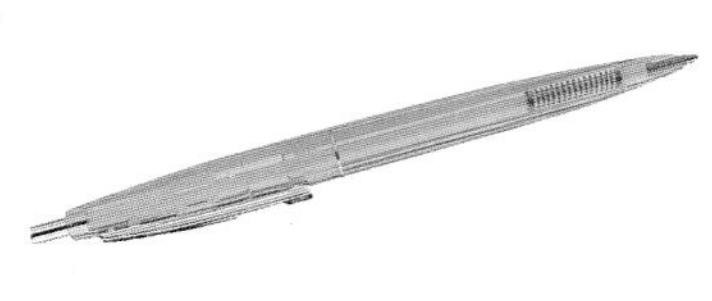

__en

4. 

__ut

5. 

__aw

6. 

__ox

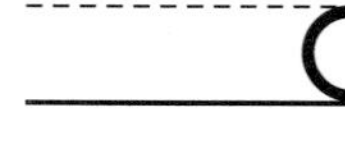

7. 

__eb

8. 

__ar

9. 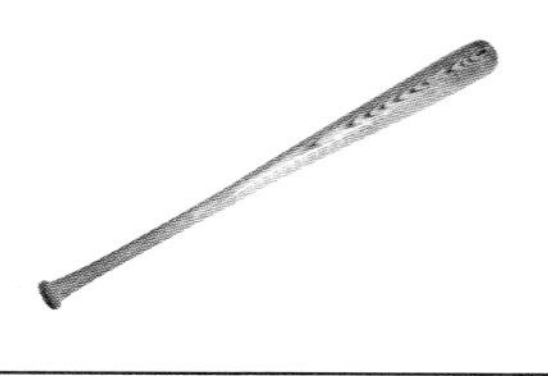

__at

10. 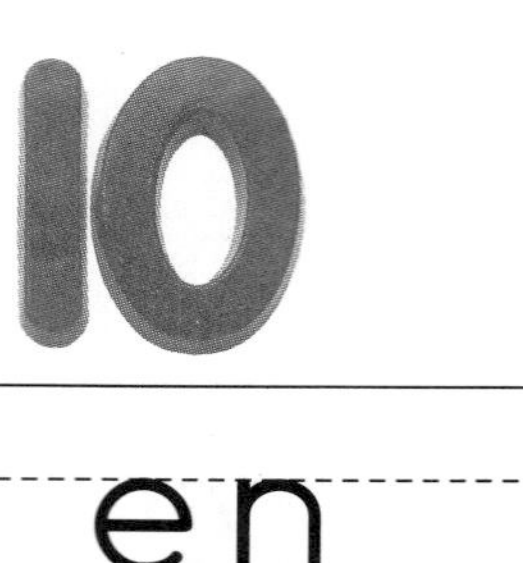

__en

11. 

__ug

12. 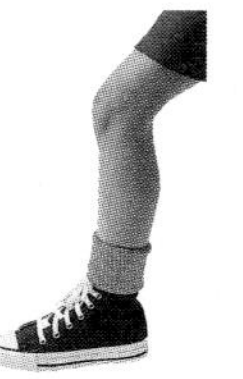

__eg

2 Consonants in Words

Think of each **ending** sound. Write the missing letter to spell the word.

1. 

dru

2. 

nai

3. 

be

PHONICS

4. 

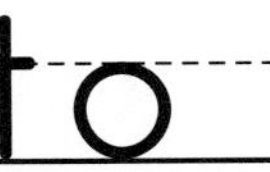

to

5. 

pa

6. 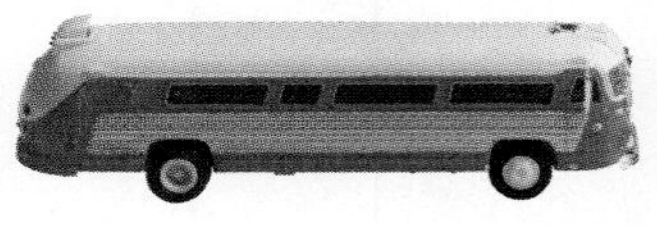

bu

7. 

si

8. 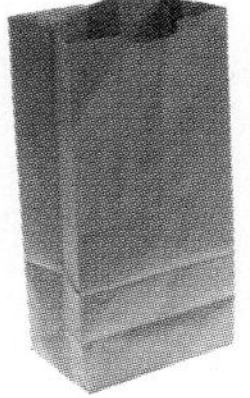

ba

9. 

lea

10. 

tu

11. 

co

12. 

ca

3 Short Vowels in Words

PHONICS

Think of each **middle** sound. Write a, e, i, o, or u to spell the word.

1. 

f n

2. 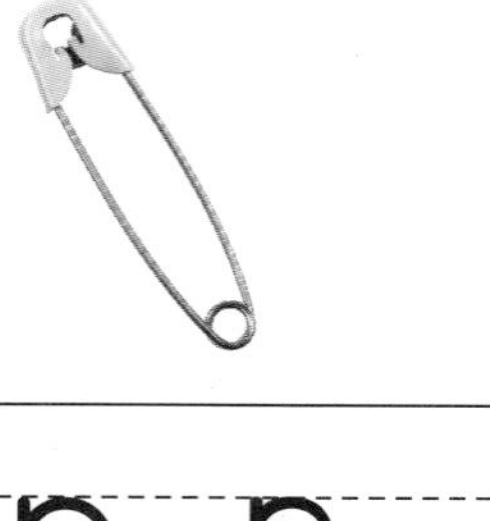

p n

3. 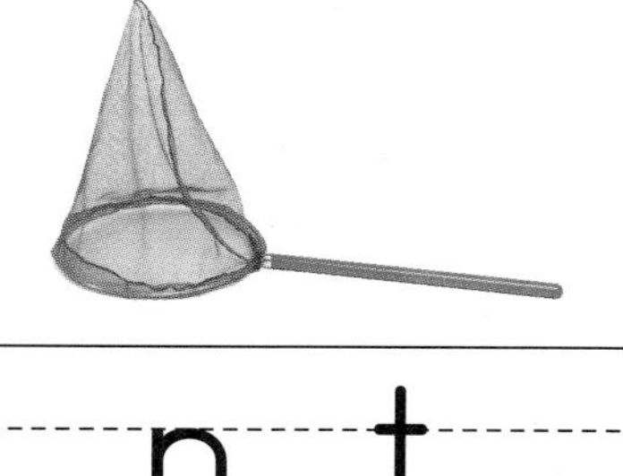

n t

4. 

s n

5. 

p t

6. 

c n

7. 

r d

8. 

m p

9. 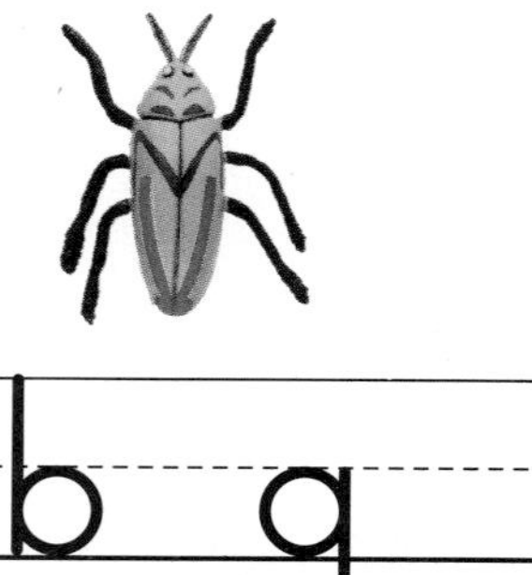

b g

10. 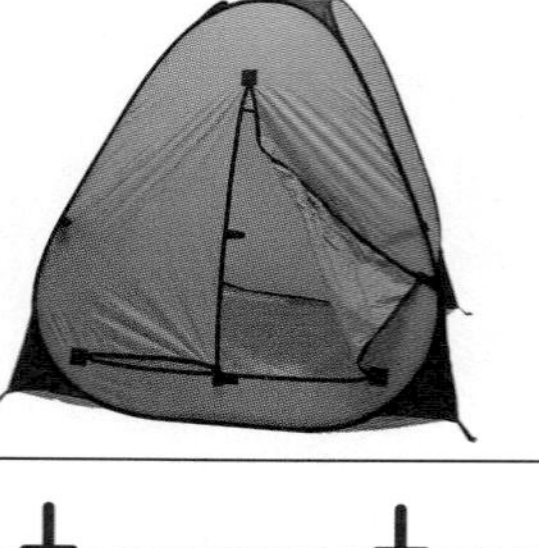

t nt

11. 

b b

12. 

c p

3 Short Vowels in Words

13.

v n

14.

b x

15.

pl g

16.

m n

17.

j t

18.

f sh

19.

r ck

20.

m g

21.

d sk

22.

fl g

23.

w g

24.

l ck

Word List Units

How to Study a Word

❶ Look at the word.

- What letters are in the word?
- What does the word mean? Does it have more than one meaning?

❷ Say the word.

- What are the consonant sounds?
- What are the vowel sounds?

❸ Think about the word.

- How is each sound spelled?
- What other words have the same spelling pattern?

❹ Write the word.

- Think about the sounds and the letters.
- Form the letters correctly.

❺ Check the spelling.

- Did you spell the word the same way it is spelled in your word list?
- Do you need to write the word again?

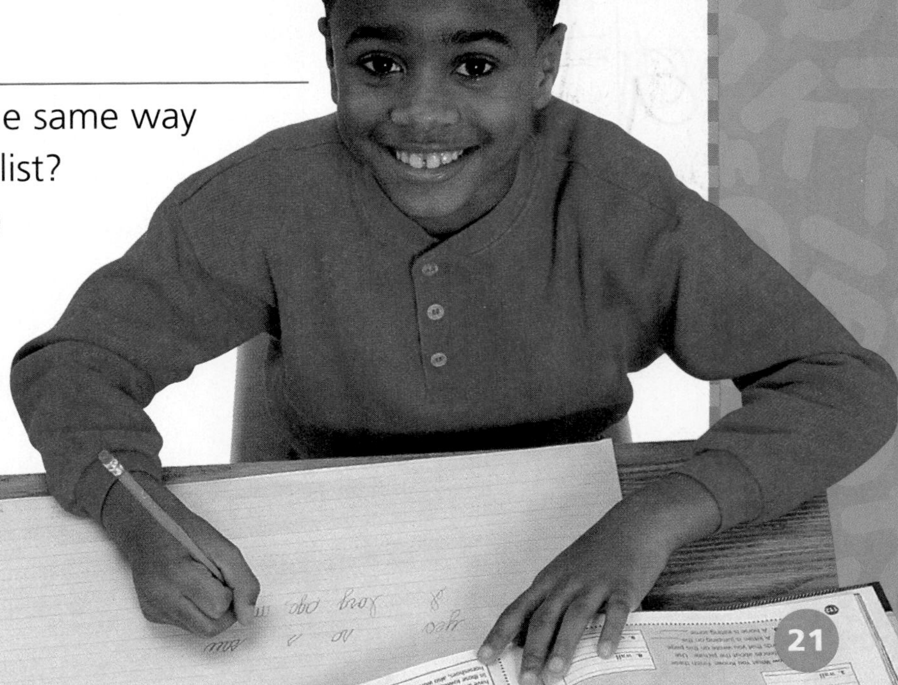

Using Spelling Strategies

Sometimes you want to write a word that you are not sure how to spell. Follow these steps to work out the spelling.

1. Say the word softly. Listen to all the sounds. Think about the letters and patterns that usually spell each sound.

I know that the beginning sounds are spelled **ch**. I've learned that the long **e** sound could be spelled **e** as in **me** or **ee** as in **green**.

I think the final sound might be spelled **k.**

2. Have a go at the spelling! Write the word a few different ways to see which way looks right. Make a chart like the one shown. First, write the word one way. Then write the word another way.

Have a Go!

First try	Second try	Correct
chek	cheek	?

3 Does one spelling look like the right one? If you are not sure, check a dictionary. Look up your first try.

I looked up **c-h-e-k**, but I didn't find it.

4 If the word is not there, look up your second try.

Oh, here it is. It's **c-h-e-e-k**. My second try was right.

5 Finish your chart by writing the word the right way. You might want to circle the parts you spelled wrong to help you remember.

Have a Go!

First try	Second try	Correct
chek	cheek	cheek

Spelling Strategies

1. Listen for sounds and patterns that you know.
2. Think of rhyming words that might be spelled with the same pattern.
3. Use the Have-a-Go chart.
4. Use a dictionary.

UNIT 1

Spelling the Short a Sound

ă
hat

A.

B.

Read and Say

READ the sentences. **SAY** each word in dark print.

Basic Words

1. hat	Tim is wearing a **hat**.
2. bag	I have a pen in my **bag**.
3. as	We clap **as** we play.
4. am	I **am** big.
5. has	She **has** a new doll.
6. sad	Why is Kim **sad** today?
7. bat	I have a **bat** and a ball.
8. ran	Ping **ran** fast.
9. sat	We **sat** in our seats.
10. bad	He had a **bad** day.
11. was	Rob **was** reading.
12. want	The cats **want** to nap.

Think and Write

Most of the words have the short **a** vowel sound. It is the first sound you hear in .

the short **a** sound → h**a**t, **a**s

How are the Elephant Words different?

A. Write the first **ten** Basic Words. Then draw a line under the letter that spells the short **a** sound in each word.

B. Now write the **two** Elephant Words.

Review
13. a **14.** can

Challenge
15. mask **16.** fabric

Independent Practice

Spelling Strategy The vowel sound in **hat** and **as** is called the short **a** sound. The short **a** sound may be spelled **a**.

Phonics Write Basic Words to answer the questions.

1–2. Which two words begin like ?

3–5. Which three words rhyme with ?

Word Meaning Write the Basic Word that means the same or almost the same as each word below.

6. owns
7. unhappy
8. awful
9. raced
10. sack

Elephant Words Think of the missing letter in each Elephant Word. Write each word.

11. w __ nt   **12.** w __ s

Phonics

1.
2.
3.
4.
5.

Word Meaning

6.
7.
8.
9.
10.

Elephant Words

11.
12.

Dictionary

ABC Order The letters of the alphabet are in **ABC order**. You use ABC order to find words in a dictionary.

a b c d e f g h i j k l m

n o p q r s t u v w x y z

Practice Write the missing letters. Use ABC order.

1. o p q 
2. d e f
3. f g h
4. v w x
5. t u v
6. k l m

Review: Spelling Spree

Vowel Swap Change the vowel in each word to make a Basic Word. Write each word.

7. bug
8. is
9. but
10. sit
11. bed
12. run
13. went
14. his

Vowel Swap

7. bag
8. as
9. bat
10. sat
11. bad
12. ran
13. want 
14. has

How Are You Doing?

Write the spelling words in ABC order. Practice with a partner any words you spelled wrong.

Proofreading and Writing

Proofread for Spelling Proofread this play that Alexis wrote. Use proofreading marks to fix six spelling mistakes.

Example: Hilda ~~haz~~ has a funny hat.

HILDA'S FLAT HAT

Hilda: Oh, I em so sade!

Henry: I kan tell. What happened?

Hilda: I sat down in uh chair.

Henry: Is that so bad?

Hilda: My bag wuz on the chair!

Henry: It could be worse.

Hilda: It is! My het was in the bag!

Basic

1. hat
2. bag
3. as
4. am
5. has
6. sad
7. bat
8. ran
9. sat
10. bad
11. was
12. want

Review

13. a
14. can

Challenge

15. mask
16. fabric

Proofreading Marks

- ^ Add
- ⟋ Delete
- ≡ Make a capital letter
- / Make a small letter

Write an Invitation

Write an invitation to a costume party. Tell the day, the time, and the place. Try to use spelling words. Draw a picture to go with your invitation.

Remember to read your writing again one line at a time.

Unit 1 BONUS

Phonics and Spelling

Rhyming Words

Short a Words Make rhyming words that have the short **a** vowel sound. Use the letters in the picture.

v t pl an dr w t ag str t wr ap

an	ag	ap
1.	4.	7.
2.	5.	8.
3.	6.	9.

Work Together On another sheet of paper, write three more rhyming words that end with **ap** or **ag**. Work with a friend.

Art

Costumes All the words in the box have something to do with costumes. Write those words to finish this diary entry. Use your Spelling Dictionary.

Spelling Word Link

hat

cape
gown
vest
crown

June 4

I went to Sam's costume party dressed as a queen. I had a __(1)__ on my head. My long blue __(2)__ was made of silk. A warm __(3)__ covered my shoulders. My __(4)__ had no sleeves.

1. ________
2. ________
3. ________
4. ________

Try This CHALLENGE

Yes or No? Is the word in dark print used correctly? Write **yes** or **no**.

5. The princess wore a **gown** to the ball.
6. The actor's **vest** kept his arms warm.
7. She wore a **cape** on her feet.
8. The king's **crown** was made of gold.

5. ________
6. ________
7. ________
8. ________

Fact File

Long ago in Greece, actors wore big masks made of heavy cloth. The masks told the people watching the play if the actors were feeling happy or sad.

UNIT 2

Spelling the Short e Sound

Read and Say

READ the sentences. **SAY** each word in dark print.

Basic Words

1. pet — My **pet** dog likes to run.
2. leg — He has a cut on his **leg**.
3. ten — Ben has **ten** books.
4. yes — Did she say **yes**?
5. bed — The cat is on my **bed**.
6. help — Who will **help** me?
7. set — Luis **set** the pot down.
8. went — We **went** for a ride.
9. pen — He has my **pen**.
10. wet — Did the man get **wet**?
11. any — Do you have **any** games?
12. said — I **said** no.

Think and Write

Each word has the short **e** vowel sound. It is the first sound you hear in ◯.

the short **e** sound → p**e**t, l**e**g

How are the Elephant Words different?

A. Write the first **ten** Basic Words. Then draw a line under the letter that spells the short **e** sound in each word.

B. Now write the **two** Elephant Words.

A. pet

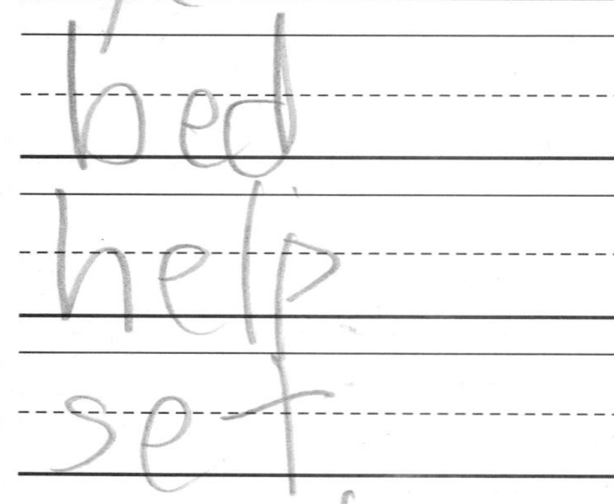

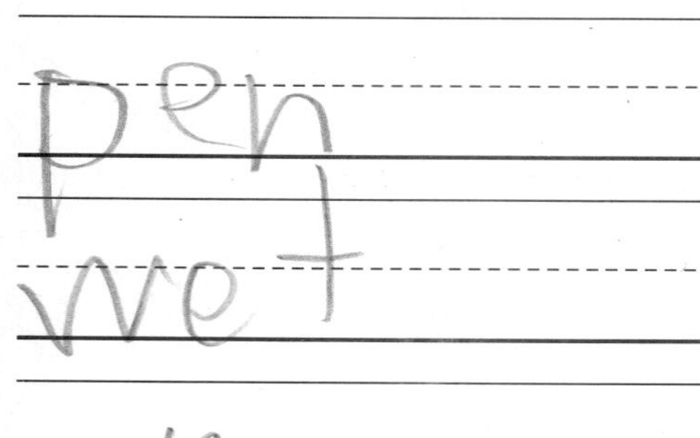

B.

Review
13. get 14. red

Challenge
15. elk 16. penguin

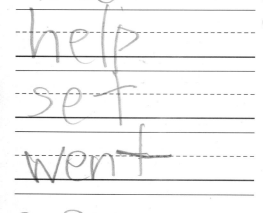

Independent Practice

Spelling Strategy The vowel sound in **pet** and **leg** is called the short **e** sound. The short **e** sound may be spelled **e**.

Phonics Write Basic Words to answer the questions.

1. Which word begins like ?
2–3. Which two words end with two consonant sounds?
4–6. Which three words rhyme with **get**?

Word Pairs Write a Basic Word to finish the second sentence in each pair.

7. Your **hand** is at the end of your **arm**.
   Your **foot** is at the end of your ______.
8. A **bird** sleeps in a **nest**.
   A **person** sleeps in a ______.
9. You **draw** with a **crayon**.
   You **write** with a ______.
10. **Two** comes after **one**.
    Eleven comes after ______.

Elephant Words Think of the missing letter or letters in each Elephant Word. Write each word.

11. __ ny
12. s __ __ d

Phonics

1. ______
2. ______
3. ______
4. ______
5. ______
6. ______

Word Pairs

7. ______
8. ______
9. ______
10. ______

Elephant Words

11. ______
12. ______

UNIT
2

Review: Spelling Spree

Silly Rhymes

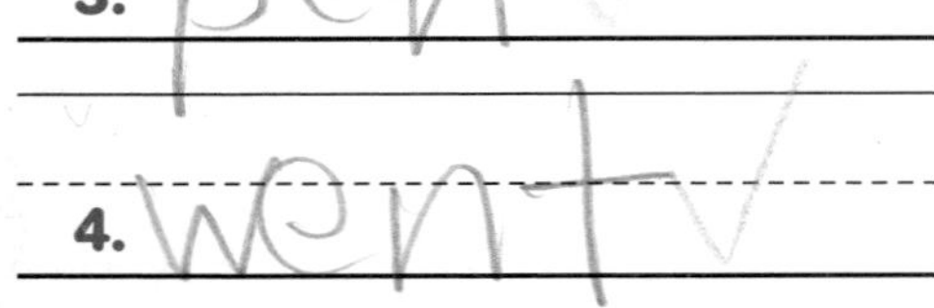

Hidden Words

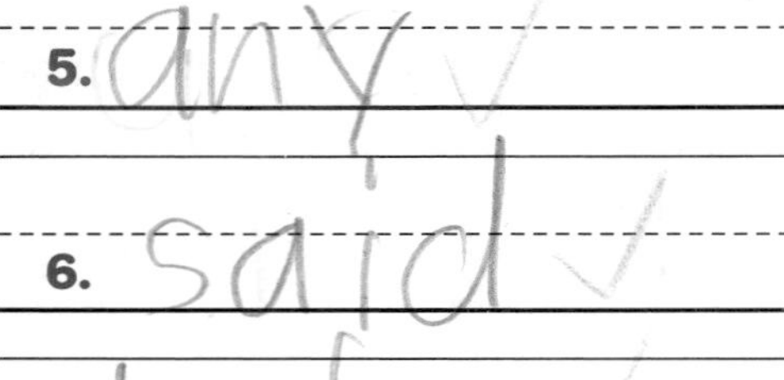

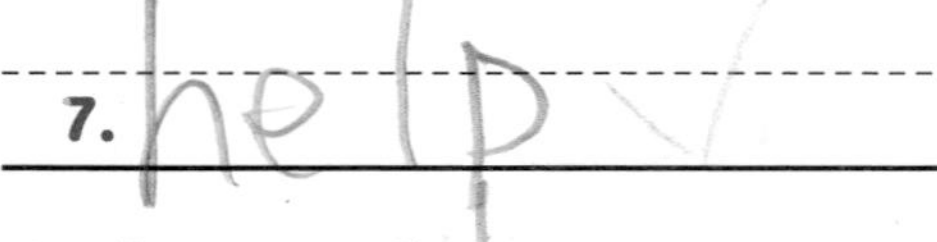

Code Breaker

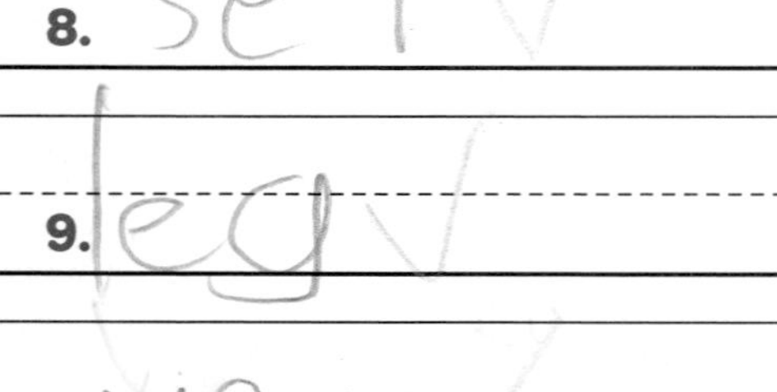

Silly Rhymes Finish these silly sentences. Write a Basic or Review Word to rhyme with the word in dark print.

1. That seal's **sled** is green and ______.
2. Lazy hippos are often **fed** in ______.
3. The smart **hen** writes with a ______.
4. The elephant ______ into the **tent**.

Hidden Words Find the hidden Basic Word in each box. Write the word.

5. eglkanpany 6. aisaidedin 7. ushelpper

Code Breaker Use ABC order to write the letter that comes between the letters in each pair. Use new letters to make Basic Words.

Example: o q + d f + m o = **pen** (p e n)

8. r t + d f + s u = ______
9. k m + d f + f h = ______
10. x z + d f + r t = ______
11. o q + d f + s u = ______
12. s u + d f + m o = ______

How Are You Doing?
Write the spelling words that are still hard for you. Practice them with a family member.

Proofreading and Writing

Proofread: Spelling and Telling Sentences

A **telling sentence** begins with a capital letter and ends with a period.

The pet store sells many animals.

Proofread this letter. Use proofreading marks to fix four spelling mistakes, two missing capital letters, and two missing end marks.

Example: i whent to the pet store last week. (went)

March 18, 1998

Dear Pat,

My pet fish is blue and redd it lives in a bowl by my bed. sometimes it splashes and I git wett! Mom sed I could take Gil to school next week

Love,

Max

Basic

1. pet
2. leg
3. ten
4. yes
5. bed
6. help
7. set
8. went
9. pen
10. wet
11. any
12. said

Review

13. get
14. red

Challenge

15. elk
16. penguin

Proofreading Marks

- ^ Add
- ⌒ Delete
- ≡ Make a capital letter
- / Make a small letter

Write a Description

Pretend that you are a frog. Write two or three sentences about yourself. Try to use spelling words. Share your description.

Proofreading Tip

Check that you began each telling sentence with a capital letter and ended with a period.

Phonics and Spelling

Rhyming Words

Short e Words Make rhyming words that have the short **e** vowel sound. Use the letters in the pictures.

1. ______
2. ______
3. ______
4. ______
5. ______
6. ______
7. ______
8. ______
9. ______

Show What You Know! On another sheet of paper, write two sentences. Tell about an unusual pet. Use words that you wrote on this page.

Science

Unusual Pets All the words in the box have something to do with unusual pets. Write those words to finish this page from a book about animal facts. Use your Spelling Dictionary.

snail
parrot
hamster
lizard

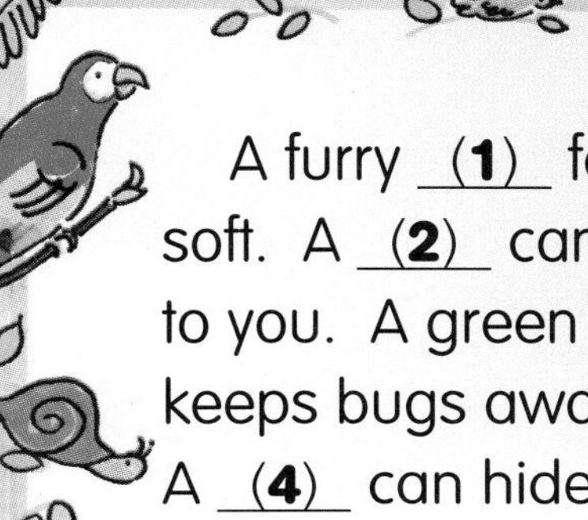
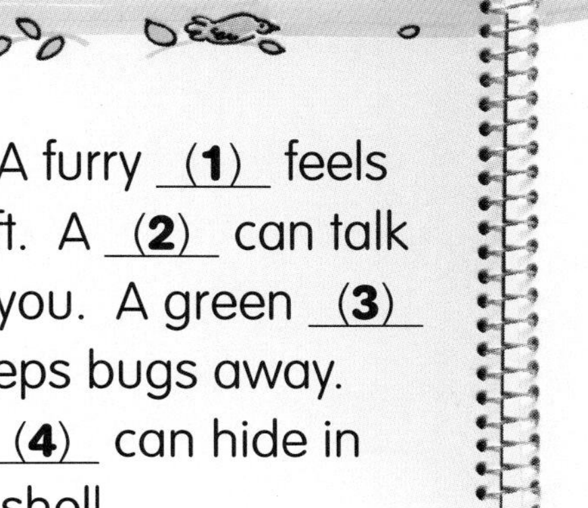

A furry **(1)** feels soft. A **(2)** can talk to you. A green **(3)** keeps bugs away. A **(4)** can hide in its shell.

1. ______
2. ______
3. ______
4. ______

Try This CHALLENGE

Riddle Time! Write a word from the box to answer each riddle.

5. What carries its house on its back?
6. What has scales but cannot sing?
7. What has wings but is not a plane?
8. What wears a fur coat even in summer?

5. ______
6. ______
7. ______
8. ______

Fact File

In China and Japan, many people keep crickets as pets because they enjoy the crickets' cheerful songs. These pets are sometimes kept in small cages.

UNIT 3

Spelling the Short i Sound

ĭ
pig

Read and Say

READ the sentences. **SAY** each word in dark print.

Basic Words

1.	pig	The **pig** is eating corn.
2.	win	Help us **win** the game.
3.	is	That car **is** green.
4.	six	We have **six** apples.
5.	his	Dan has **his** hat on.
6.	if	Be there **if** you can.
7.	hit	Adam **hit** the ball.
8.	fix	Did she **fix** her bike?
9.	pin	Tina gave me a **pin**.
10.	dig	My dog likes to **dig**.
11.	been	The game has **been** fun.
12.	I	Do **I** have to stay home?

Think and Write

Most of the words have the short **i** vowel sound. It is the first sound you hear in igloo.

the short **i** sound → pi**g**, **i**s

How are the Elephant Words different?

A. Write the first **ten** Basic Words. Then draw a line under the letter that spells the short **i** sound in each word.

B. Now write the **two** Elephant Words.

Review
13. did **14.** big

Challenge
15. quilt **16.** picnic

A. pig
win
is
six
his
if
hit
fix
pin
dig

B. been
I

Independent Practice

Spelling Strategy The vowel sound in **pig** and **is** is called the short **i** sound. The short **i** sound may be spelled **i**.

Phonics Write Basic Words to answer the questions.

1. Which word begins like ?

2–3. Which two words begin like ?

4–5. Which two words begin like ?

Word Clues Write a Basic Word for each clue.

6. a farm animal
7. an even number between four and eight
8. what you must do to make a hole
9. what you must do to get first prize
10. what you could use if your button fell off

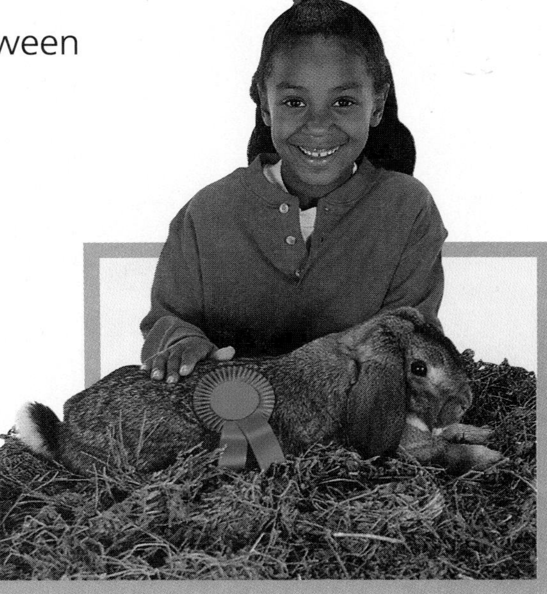

Elephant Words Write an Elephant Word to answer each question.

11. Which word is always spelled with a capital letter?
12. Which word has the short **i** sound spelled with two vowels?

Phonics

1. fix
2. is
3. if
4. hit
5. pin

Word Clues

6. pig
7. six
8. dig
9. win
10. fix pin

Elephant Words

11. I
12. been

ABC Order

1.
2.
3.
4.
5.
6.

Letter Math

7.
8.
9.
10.
11.
12.

Dictionary

ABC Order Words in a dictionary are in ABC order. Look at the first letter of each of these words. The words are in ABC order.

big **d**ig **f**ix

Practice Look at the first letter in each word. Write the word in each group that would come first in ABC order.

1. win pig six
2. six pin I
3. pig fix win
4. is six big
5. hit I been
6. pin his win

Review: Spelling Spree

Letter Math Add and take away letters to make Basic or Review Words. Write each word.

Example: w + p i n − p = **win**

7. d a d − a + i = ____
8. h + p i t − p = ____
9. i + o f − o = ____
10. h a s − a + i = ____
11. b e a n − a + e = ____
12. p a i n t − a − t = ____

How Are You Doing?

Write each spelling word as a partner reads it aloud. Did you spell any words wrong?

Proofreading and Writing

Proofread for Spelling Proofread this sign. Use proofreading marks to fix six spelling mistakes.

Example: Tony gave ~~hizz~~ his prize to Lisa.

The Ames Fair iz great fun!

See the world's biggest pig!

Hit the balloons!

Whin bigg prizes!

Deg into your pockets!

Tickets are siks dollars!

Eye know you will have a great time!

Basic

1. pig
2. win
3. is
4. six
5. his
6. if
7. hit
8. fix
9. pin
10. dig
11. been
12. I

Review

13. did
14. big

Challenge

15. quilt
16. picnic

Proofreading Marks

- ∧ Add
- Delete
- ≡ Make a capital letter
- / Make a small letter

Write a Story

Pretend you saw the world's biggest pig. Write a story telling about the pig. Try to use spelling words. You may want to make a tape recording of your story to share with a friend.

Proofreading Tip **Read each word slowly to make sure there are no extra letters.**

Short i Words Make rhyming words that have the short **i** vowel sound. Use the letters in the picture.

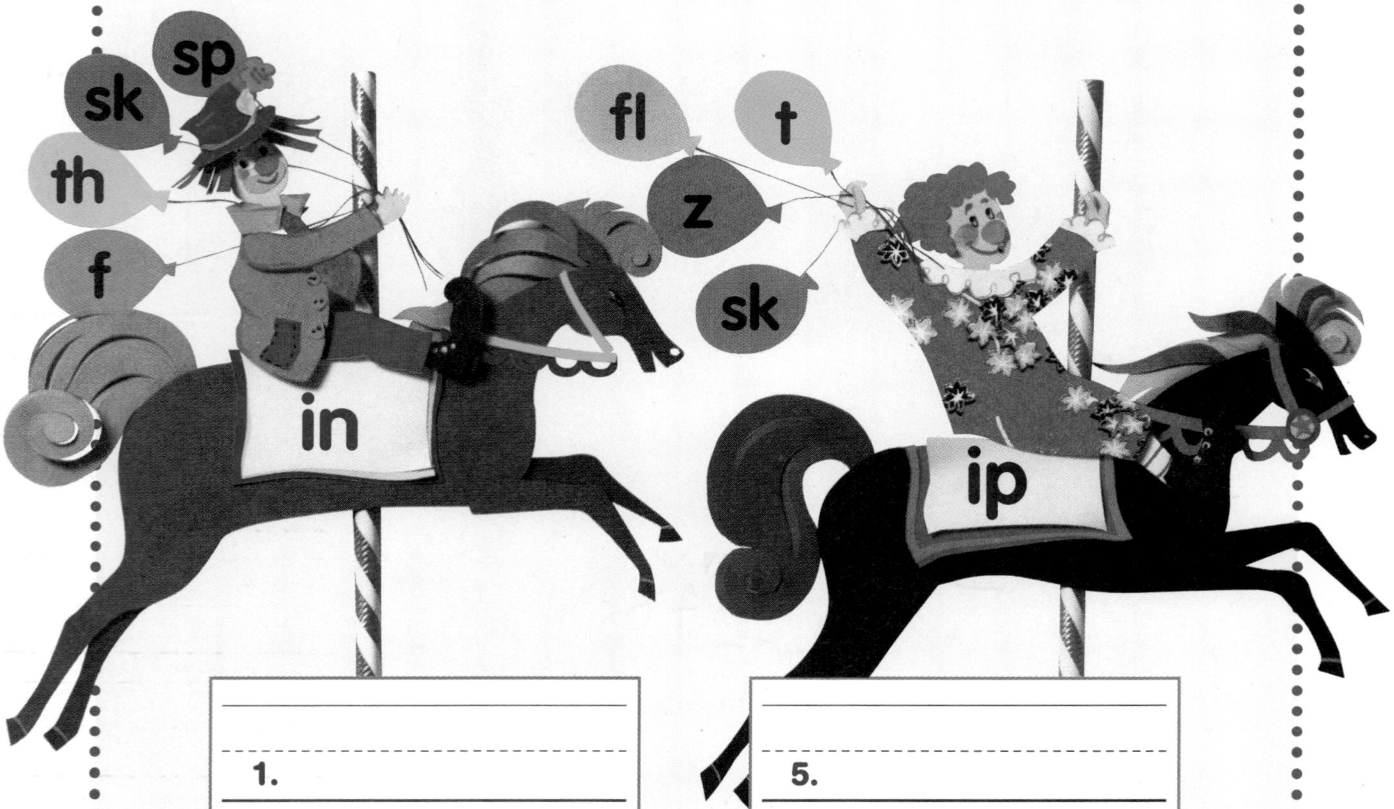

sp sk th f in

fl t z sk ip

1. ____________
2. ____________
3. ____________
4. ____________

5. ____________
6. ____________
7. ____________
8. ____________

Show What You Know! On another sheet of paper, write an ad for a country fair. Use words that you wrote on this page.

Vocabulary Enrichment

Social Studies

A Country Fair All the words in the box have something to do with a country fair. Write those words to finish this program. Use your Spelling Dictionary.

Spelling Word Link

win

ribbon
booth
ring
judge

Horse Show

12:00 **Buy your tickets at the __(1)__.**

12:30 **See the horses jump into the __(2)__.**

1:00 **The __(3)__ will choose the best horse and give the winner a blue __(4)__.**

1. ____________
2. ____________
3. ____________
4. ____________

Try This CHALLENGE

Yes or No? Write **yes** or **no** to answer each question.

5. Is a **ring** a good place to sleep?
6. Would a **judge** pick a winner?
7. Could a **ribbon** be made of cloth?
8. Would you wear a **booth** on your foot?

5. ____________
6. ____________
7. ____________
8. ____________

Fact File

Grandma Moses began painting when she was more than 70 years old. She painted more than 1,500 pictures. One of her paintings is called **Country Fair**.

UNIT 4

Spelling the Short o Sound

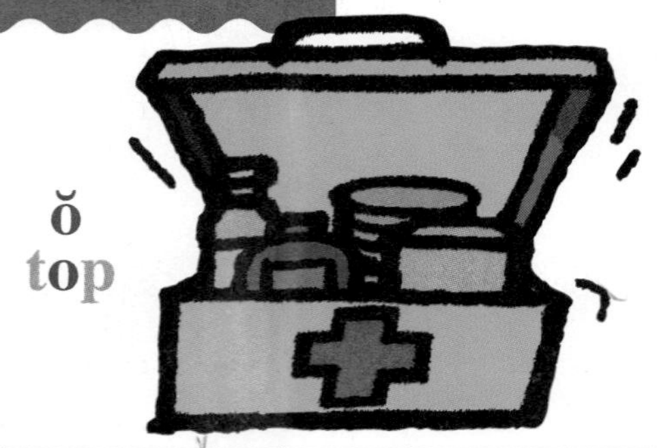

ŏ
top

Read and Say

READ the sentences. **SAY** each word in dark print.

Basic Words

1. job	Jim got a **job** in town.
2. pot	Put water in the **pot**.
3. nod	Did you **nod** your head?
4. top	That box has no **top**.
5. not	They did **not** go.
6. dot	A **dot** is a round mark.
7. fox	That **fox** runs fast.
8. mop	I will **mop** the floor.
9. spot	Is that a red **spot**?
10. hop	I can **hop** on one foot.
11. of	Take my box **of** cups.

Think and Write

Most of the words have the short **o** vowel sound. It is the first sound you hear in .

the short **o** sound → j**o**b, p**o**t

How is the Elephant Word different?

A. Write the first **ten** Basic Words. Then draw a line under the letter that spells the short **o** sound in each word.

B. Now write the Elephant Word.

A.

B.

Review
12. on **13.** box

Challenge
14. block **15.** hospital

Independent Practice

Spelling Strategy The vowel sound in **job** and **pot** is called the short **o** sound. The short **o** sound may be spelled **o**.

Phonics Write Basic Words to answer the questions.

1. Which word rhymes with **Bob**?
2. Which word rhymes with **dot** and has almost the same meaning?
3. Which word begins like (duck)?

4–5. Which two words begin like (flowers)?

Word Groups Think how the words in each group are alike. Write the missing Basic Words.

6. broom, rag, ______
7. bowl, pan, ______
8. deer, rabbit, ______
9. jump, skip, ______
10. bottom, middle, ______

Elephant Word Write the missing Elephant Word.

11. Be careful getting out ______ the bathtub.

Phonics

1. ______
2. ______
3. ______
4. ______
5. ______

Word Groups

6. ______
7. ______
8. ______
9. ______
10. ______

Elephant Word

11. ______

Rhyming Clues

1.

2.

3.

4.

5.

6.

Letter Scramble

7.

8.

9.

Fill-In Fun

10.

11.

12.

Review: Spelling Spree

Rhyming Clues Write a Basic Word for each clue.

1. It rhymes with **drop**. It begins like .
2. It rhymes with **knob**. It begins like .
3. It rhymes with **rod**. It begins like .
4. It rhymes with **got**. It begins like .
5. It rhymes with **ox**. It begins like .
6. It rhymes with **pop**. It begins like .

Letter Scramble Write a Basic Word by changing the order of letters in each word below.

7. top 8. ton 9. tops

Fill-In Fun Write the missing Basic or Review Words.

10. off and ______
11. glass ______ milk
12. jack-in-the- ______

How Are You Doing?

Write each spelling word in a sentence. Practice with a partner any words you spelled wrong.

Proofreading and Writing

Proofread: Spelling and Questions

A **question** begins with a capital letter and ends with a question mark.

Do you work and play safely**?**

Proofread this note. Use proofreading marks to fix four spelling mistakes, two missing capital letters, and two end marks.

Example: who read the list ~~ov~~ of safety rules?

Mia,

Will you help me onn this job. please mop up every sopt of water. I do nawt want someone to slip. could you wipe the table tup too. Thank you.

Jenna

Basic

1. job
2. pot
3. nod
4. top
5. not
6. dot
7. fox
8. mop
9. spot
10. hop
11. of

Review

12. on
13. box

Challenge

14. block
15. hospital

Proofreading Marks

- ∧ Add
- Delete
- ≡ Make a capital letter
- / Make a small letter

Write a Safety Quiz

Write some questions about home safety. Try to use spelling words. Then have a friend or family member answer your questions.

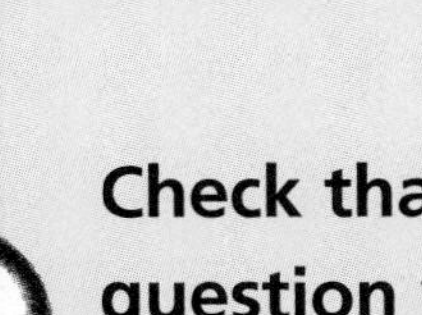

Proofreading Tip

Check that you began each question with a capital letter and ended with a question mark.

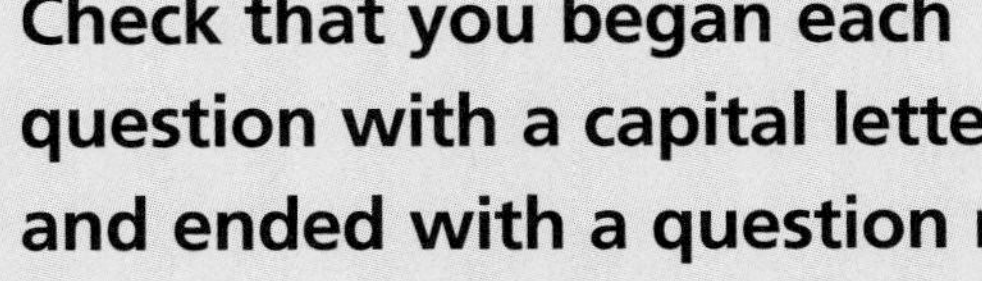

Vocabulary Enrichment

Word Builder

Spelling Word Link

job

Using a Thesaurus Look in a **thesaurus** to find just the right word to say what you mean. Read page 262 to learn how to use a thesaurus.

Write a word you could use in place of the word in dark print. Use your Thesaurus.

1. a hard **job** **2.** **find** the trouble **3.** a **nice** teacher

1. ____________ 2. ____________ 3. ____________

Show What You Know! Look at the pictures. Write a different word for **jump** that best fits each sentence. Use your Thesaurus.

4. Pedro had to **jump** to catch the ball.

5. Becky can **jump** on one foot.

4. ____________ 5. ____________

Health

Safety at Home and at School All the words in the box have something to do with safety at home and at school. Write those words to finish this safety poster. Use your Spelling Dictionary.

Spelling Word Link
hospital
careful
injure
exit
alarm

Fire Drill Rules

→ When the fire __(1)__ rings, stop what you are doing.

→ Walk to the __(2)__ quickly.

→ Be __(3)__ going down the stairs. You do not want to __(4)__ yourself.

EXIT

1. ____________
2. ____________
3. ____________
4. ____________

Try This CHALLENGE

Yes or No? Is the word in dark print used correctly? Write **yes** or **no**.

5. We used the window as a fire **exit**.
6. I could **injure** myself on a rusty nail.
7. The **alarm** made me sleepy.
8. If you are **careful**, you will fall.

5. ____________
6. ____________
7. ____________
8. ____________

Fact File

If you are ever in a room that fills up with smoke, drop to the floor and crawl out. Smoke rises, so the air near the floor will be easier to breathe.

UNIT 5

Spelling the Short u Sound

ŭ
sun

Read and Say

READ the sentences. **SAY** each word in dark print.

Basic Words	
1. sun	The **sun** is hot.
2. mud	Buddy got **mud** on me.
3. bug	An ant is a **bug**.
4. fun	Was the ride **fun**?
5. but	I like red **but** not pink.
6. hug	He gave me a **hug**.
7. bun	She ate a **bun**.
8. nut	An acorn is a **nut**.
9. bus	I take a **bus** to school.
10. rug	The cat is on the **rug**.
11. some	We saw **some** trees.
12. from	You ran **from** the bee.

Think and Write

Each word has the short **u** vowel sound. It is the first sound you hear in .

the short **u** sound → s**u**n, m**u**d

How are the Elephant Words different?

A. Write the first **ten** Basic Words. Then draw a line under the letter that spells the short **u** sound in each word.

B. Now write the **two** Elephant Words.

A. sun
mud
bug
fun
but
hug
bun
nut
bus
rug

B. some
from

Review
13. up 14. run

Challenge
15. thunder 16. puddle

Independent Practice

Spelling Strategy The vowel sound in **sun** and **mud** is called the short **u** sound. The short **u** sound may be spelled **u**.

Phonics Write Basic Words to answer the questions.

1. Which word begins and ends like **bat**?
2. Which word begins and ends like **mad**?
3. Which word rhymes with **us**?

4–6. Which three words rhyme with **run**?

Word Pairs Write a Basic Word to finish the second sentence in each pair.

7. A **bed** is covered by a **blanket**.
   A **floor** is covered by a _____.
8. A **rose** is a kind of **flower**.
   A **cricket** is a kind of _____.
9. A **peel** covers an **orange**.
   A **shell** covers a _____.
10. You use your **legs** to **walk**.
    You use your **arms** to _____.

Elephant Words Write the missing Elephant Words.

11. Every fall we pick _____ apples.
12. They come _____ the old tree in our yard.

Phonics

1.
2.
3.
4.
5.
6.

Word Pairs

7.
8.
9.
10.

Elephant Words

11.
12.

UNIT
5

Parts of a Dictionary

1. "bus"
2. "fun"
3. "hug"
4. "nut"
5. "run"
6. "up"

Hink Pinks

7. "bug"
8. "nut"
9. "hug"

Word Hunt

10. "bun"
11. "sun"
12. "rug"

Dictionary

Parts of a Dictionary A dictionary lists words in ABC order. How would you find the word **run** in the dictionary? You would turn to the end and find the words that begin with **r**.

BEGINNING	MIDDLE	END
abcdefg	hijklmnopq	rstuvwxyz

Practice Write words from the box to answer the questions.

run	hug	bus	nut	up	fun

1–2. Which two words are found at the beginning of the dictionary?

3–4. Which two words are found in the middle?

5–6. Which two words are found at the end?

Review: Spelling Spree

Hink Pinks Write the Basic Word that answers the question and rhymes with the word in dark print.

7. What is a cup for an ant? a "bug" **mug**

8. What is a home for a peanut? a "nut" **hut**

9. What is a tight squeeze? a **snug** "bug"

Word Hunt Write the Basic Word you see in each longer word.

10. bunch

11. sunny

12. shrug

How Are You Doing?

Write each spelling word as a family member reads it aloud. Did you spell any words wrong?

Proofreading and Writing

Proofread for Spelling Proofread this weather report. Use proofreading marks to fix five spelling mistakes.

Example: We will runn in the rain.

TODAY'S WEATHER

Rain will fall frum now until noon, butt then the sky will clear up. The rain may be heavy, so watch out for the mudd! Later the sun will shine. Go outside and have sum fon!

Basic

1. sun
2. mud
3. bug
4. fun
5. but
6. hug
7. bun
8. nut
9. bus
10. rug
11. some
12. from

Review

13. up
14. run

Challenge

15. thunder
16. puddle

Proofreading Marks

- ^ Add
- Delete
- ≡ Make a capital letter
- / Make a small letter

Write a List

Mr. Travis owns a store that sells only summer things. Help him make a list of some things he might sell. Then think of a good name for the store. Try to use spelling words.

Proofreading Tip

Make sure you have written your u's and w's the right way.

Phonics and Spelling

Rhyming Words

Short u Words Make rhyming words that have the short **u** sound. Use the letters in the pictures.

Winter

1. ____________________

2. ____________________

Spring

3. ____________________

4. ____________________

Summer

5. ____________________

6. ____________________

Fall

7. ____________________

8. ____________________

Work Together On another sheet of paper, write three more rhyming words that end with **ug** or **ush**. Work with a friend.

Science

Seasons of the Year All the words in the box have something to do with the seasons of the year. Write those words to finish this letter. Use your Spelling Dictionary.

Spelling Word Link

sun

summer
winter
season
weather

July 19, 1998

Dear Grandpa,

School is over, and I have started my __(1)__ vacation. Today's __(2)__ is too hot and sticky for me. My favorite __(3)__ of the year is __(4)__. I can't wait to play in the snow!

Love,
Taneesha

1. ____________
2. ____________
3. ____________
4. ____________

Try This CHALLENGE

Write a Letter Write a letter to a friend who is thinking of moving to your town. Tell your friend what the weather is like during the different seasons. Try to use some words from the box.

Fact File

In the fall, the days get shorter and colder. The green color on the leaves of many trees fades, leaving bright red, orange, or yellow colors.

6 **Review:** Units 1–5

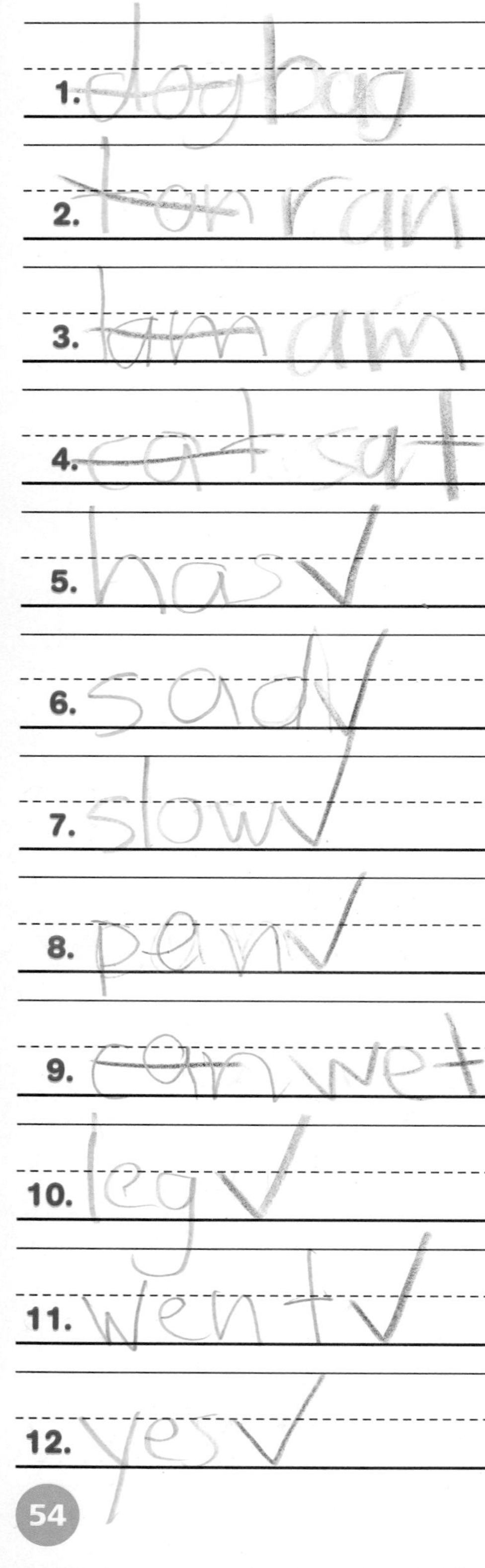

Unit 1 Spelling the Short a Sound pages 24–29

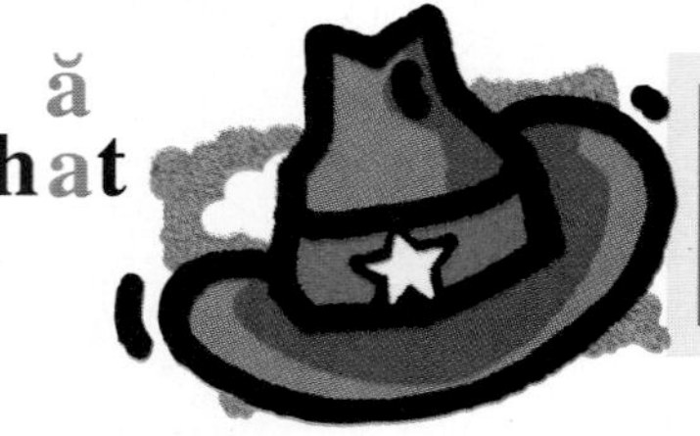

bag	am	has
sad	ran	sat

Spelling Strategy

The short **a** sound may be spelled **a**.

Write the spelling word that rhymes with each word.

1. rag **3.** ham

2. man **4.** fat

Write the missing spelling words.

5. Steven's bike ______ a flat tire.

6. That is why he is ______.

Unit 2 Spelling the Short e Sound pages 30–35

leg	yes	bed
went	pen	wet

Spelling Strategy

The short **e** sound may be spelled **e**.

Write the spelling word that goes with each word.

7. pillow **9.** rain

8. paper **10.** arm

Write the missing spelling words.

The rain clouds **(11)** away. May we go out and play? Oh **(12)**, you may!

Unit 3 Spelling the Short i Sound pages 36–41

pig	win	his
if	hit	fix

ĭ pig

Spelling Strategy The short **i** sound may be spelled **i**.

Write the spelling word that means the opposite.

13. lose **14.** break

Write the missing spelling words.

Jon can __(15)__ the balls hard with __(16)__ new bat. Our pet __(17)__ will chase the balls __(18)__ we don't catch them quickly!

13. win
14. fix
15. hit
16. his
17. pig
18. if

Unit 4 Spelling the Short o Sound pages 42–47

job	nod	top
dot	fox	hop

ŏ top

Spelling Strategy The short **o** sound may be spelled **o**.

Write the spelling word that means the same.

19. circle **20.** cover **21.** work

Write the missing spelling words.

We watched a rabbit __(22)__ into the woods. Suddenly a red __(23)__ came out of its hole. The two animals seemed to __(24)__ their heads and say hello!

19. ~~draw~~ dot
20. blaket
21. job
22. hop
23. fox
24. ~~say~~ nod

25.

26.

27.

28.

29.

30.

31.

32.

33.

34.

35.

36.

Unit 5 Spelling the Short u Sound pages 48–53

mud	fun	but
hug	bus	rug

Spelling Strategy The short **u** sound may be spelled **u**.

Change the letter in dark print. Write a spelling word.

25. r**a**g **27.** b**a**t

26. h**o**g **28.** f**i**n

Write the missing spelling words.

29. A big yellow ______ just went by.

30. It splashed ______ all over my new shoes!

Elephant Words Units 1–5 pages 24–53

was	said	been
I	of	from

Spelling Strategy Elephant Words have unusual spellings. Check them carefully when you write them.

Write the missing spelling words.

Mom and __**(31)**__ just got back __**(32)**__ the zoo. I had __**(33)**__ to the zoo once before when I __**(34)**__ small. Today we saw a lot __**(35)**__ new animals. Mom __**(36)**__ she liked the bears best.

Spelling-Meaning Strategy

Word Families

You know that people have families. Words have families too! Look at this word family.

Anna will **help** you paint.
She is a good **helper**.
Anna is **helpful** in many ways.
She is not **helpless** like a baby.

Think How are the words in this family alike in meaning? How are they alike in spelling?

Apply and Extend

Write a word from the help **family in each sentence.**

1. Mark is the class _______ today.
2. Can he _______ me move the rug?
3. He is _______ when he sweeps.
4. I am not _______, so I will dust.

1. ______________
2. ______________
3. ______________
4. ______________

With a partner, think of words in these families. Make a list for each family.

Check the Word Families list that begins on page 272. Did you miss any words? Add them to your lists.

Literature and Writing

based on

The Balancing Girl

by Berniece Rabe

Mr. Joliet's class helps with the school carnival. The class might have written this story about the carnival. What information helps make the story interesting?

Our school had a carnival. It was really fun, and we made lots of money to buy books for the library! We liked all the games and prizes.

Tommy and his dad ran a fishpond. People paid money to fish for prizes. Margaret won a funny green frog.

Margaret's Domino Push was the best game of all! Tommy won the chance to push the dominoes over. There were one hundred of them! We cheered when the last domino fell over.

Think and Discuss

1. What important things did the class tell about the school carnival?
2. What information about the Domino Push is interesting to read about?
3. Why is the word **we** used in this story?

The Writing Process

Class Story

What special things have you and your class done together? Write a class story about one special thing. Follow the guidelines. Use the Writing Process below.

1 Prewriting

- Make a web. Write your story idea in the middle. Write what you want to tell about it in the other circles.

2 Draft

- Help your teacher write interesting things about your topic.

3 Revise

- Be sure the story events are in order.
- Cross out sentences that do not fit.
- Remember to use your Thesaurus to find exact words.

4 Proofread

- Is each word spelled correctly?
- Does each sentence begin and end correctly?

5 Publish

- Copy your story neatly. Draw a picture for it.
- Make a class book. Think of a title for your book.

Guidelines for Writing a Class Story

✓ Write the story events in an order that makes sense.

✓ Tell about important things that will make the story interesting for your reader.

Compostion Words

was
went
said
win
not
fun

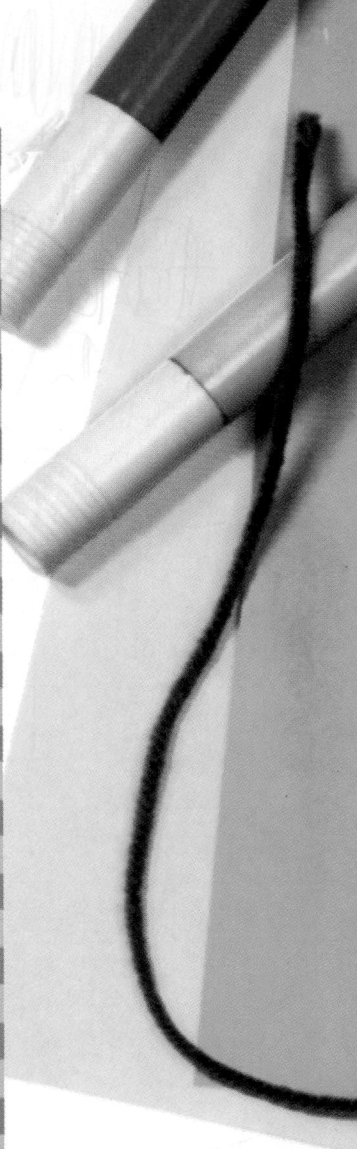

UNIT 7

Vowel-Consonant-e Spellings

ī
five

A.

B.

C.

Read and Say

READ the sentences. **SAY** each word in dark print.

Basic Words

1. five	My class has **five** frogs.
2. late	The bus is **late**.
3. nine	I read **nine** books.
4. made	We **made** a poster.
5. side	Sit on this **side**.
6. ate	Nick **ate** an apple.
7. fine	Do you feel **fine** now?
8. same	We have the **same** job.
9. hide	Did Prince **hide** his ball?
10. line	They got in **line**.
11. give	Did he **give** you a pen?
12. have	I **have** a pet turtle.

Think and Write

Most of the words have the long **a** or long **i** vowel sound spelled with the vowel-consonant-**e** pattern. These long vowel sounds begin and .

long **a** sound → l**a**t**e**　　long **i** sound → f**i**v**e**

How are the Elephant Words different?

A. Write **four** Basic Words with the long **a** sound.

B. Write **six** Basic Words with the long **i** sound.

C. Now write the **two** Elephant Words.

Review
13. gave　**14.** bike

Challenge
15. mistake　**16.** write

Independent Practice

Spelling Strategy The vowel sounds in **late** and **five** are called the long **a** and the long **i** sounds. These long vowel sounds may be spelled by the vowel-consonant-**e** pattern.

Phonics Write Basic Words to answer the questions.

1. Which word begins like  ?
2. Which word begins like  ?
3. Which word begins like  ?

4–5. Which two words begin like  ?

Word Clues Write a Basic Word for each clue.

6. when you might get to school if you miss the bus
7. what you do if you do not want to be seen
8. what you might stand or write on
9. how you feel if you are not sick
10. how many fingers you have on one hand

Elephant Words
Write an Elephant Word to answer each question.

11. Which word has the short **a** sound?
12. Which word has the short **i** sound?

Phonics

1. late
2. made
3. same
4. nine
5. five

Word Clues

6. late
7. hide
8. line
9.
10.

Elephant Words

11. have
12. give

UNIT 7

Review: Spelling Spree

Puzzle Play Write a Basic or Review Word for each clue. Use the letters that would be in the boxes to spell two things found in a school.

1. to cover up __ __ ☐ __
2. to own __ __ __ ☐
3. alike ☐ __ __ __
4. a bicycle __ __ ☐ __
5. good ☐ __ __ __
6. a row ☐ __ __ __
7. not on time __ ☐ __ __
8. handed ☐ __ __ __

Secret Words: __ __ __ __ __ __ __ __

Code Breaker Use the code to write Basic Words.

▲ = a	∩ = g	● = s
☽ = d	∗ = i	⊖ = t
☆ = e	▭ = m	◇ = v

Example:
●▲▭☆ =

9. ∩∗◇☆
10. ●∗☽☆
11. ▲⊖☆
12. ▭▲☽☆

How Are You Doing?

List the spelling words that are still hard for you. Practice them with a family member.

Puzzle Play

1.
2.
3.
4.
5.
6.
7.
8.

Code Breaker

9.
10.
11.
12.

Proofreading and Writing

Proofread: Spelling and Capital Letters
Always begin the name of a person or pet with a capital letter.

Carlos **N**ita **F**luffy

Proofread this math problem. Use proofreading marks to fix four spelling mistakes and three missing capital letters.

Example: Was jason ~~lat~~ late to the school fair?

Ann and sarah made nien bookmarks. They sold fiv bookmarks at the school fair. Their dog sparks ate one bookmark, and they gaev one to their teacher. How many bookmarks did Sarah and ann hav left?

I ♥ Books

Basic

1. five
2. late
3. nine
4. made
5. side
6. ate
7. fine
8. same
9. hide
10. line
11. give
12. have

Review

13. gave
14. bike

Challenge

15. mistake
16. write

Proofreading Marks

- ∧ Add
- Delete
- ≡ Make a capital letter
- / Make a small letter

Write a Daily Plan

Pick a day of the week. Make a list of things you do in school on that day. Tell the time you do each thing. Try to use spelling words. Have a friend read your plan.

Monday List
8:00
8:30
9:00

Proofreading Tip

Check that you began the name of each person and pet with a capital letter.

Unit 7 BONUS

Phonics and Spelling

Rhyming Words

Long a Words Make rhyming words that have the long **a** vowel sound. Use the letters in the picture.

c gr g pl sk t cr scr

ape

1. ______
2. ______
3. ______
4. ______

ate

5. ______
6. ______
7. ______
8. ______

Work Together On another sheet of paper, write three rhyming words that end with **ine** like the word **nine**. Work with a friend.

Social Studies

Schools All the words in the box have something to do with school. Write those words to finish this note. Use your Spelling Dictionary.

Spelling Word Link

write

pupil
absent
locker
gym

Roberto,

Will you walk to school with me on Friday? I am never **(1)** on a Friday because we get to play in the **(2)**. Before we start to play, every **(3)** must put on sneakers. I keep mine in my **(4)** at school.

Dillon

1. ____________
2. ____________
3. ____________
4. ____________

Try This CHALLENGE

Yes or No? Write **yes** or **no** to answer each question.

5. Is a **pupil** a kind of teacher?
6. Would you say "here" if you were **absent**?
7. Would you keep a desk in your **locker**?
8. Could you play basketball in a **gym**?

5. ____________
6. ____________
7. ____________
8. ____________

Fact File

Long ago in the United States, there were few books. Children studied from flat paddles called hornbooks. Most hornbooks showed the alphabet.

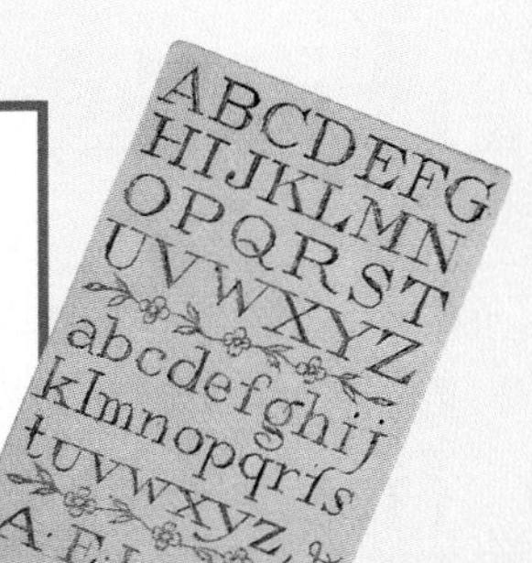

UNIT 8

More Vowel-Consonant-e Spellings

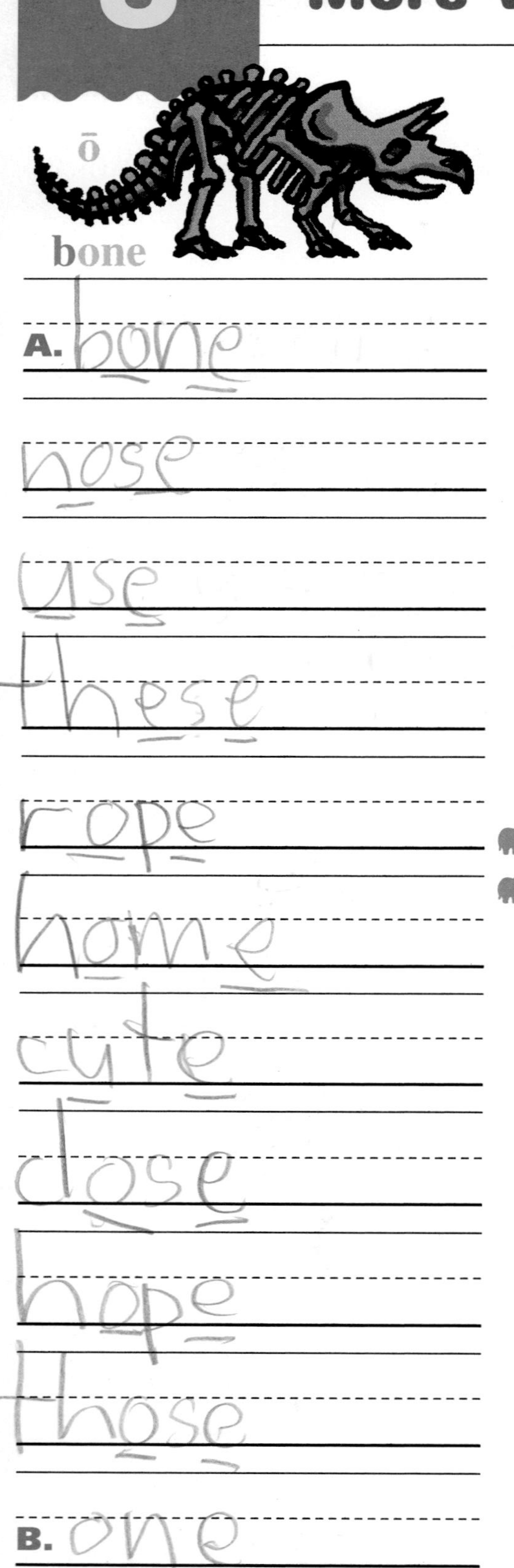

Read and Say

READ the sentences. **SAY** each word in dark print.

Basic Words

1. bone — I fell and broke a **bone**.
2. nose — Star has a pink **nose**.
3. use — Did you **use** the brush?
4. these — Take **these** books.
5. rope — Tie the **rope**.
6. home — A bird's **home** is a nest.
7. cute — Leo has a **cute** puppy.
8. close — Stay **close** to me!
9. hope — We **hope** to see you.
10. those — Look at **those** lions!
11. one — I have **one** hat.
12. goes — The bus **goes** by here.

Think and Write

Most of the words have the long **o**, long **u**, or long **e** vowel sound spelled with the vowel-consonant-**e** pattern. These long vowel sounds begin , , and .

long **o** → b**one** long **u** → **use** long **e** → th**ese**

How are the Elephant Words different?

A. Write the first **ten** Basic Words. Then draw a line under the letters that spell the vowel-consonant-**e** pattern in each word.

B. Now write the **two** Elephant Words.

Review
13. make 14. ride

Challenge
15. globe 16. mule

Independent Practice

Spelling Strategy The vowel sounds in **bone**, **use**, and **these** are called the long **o**, the long **u**, and the long **e** vowel sounds. These long vowel sounds may be spelled by the vowel-consonant-**e** pattern.

Phonics Write Basic Words to answer the questions.

1. Which word begins with a vowel sound?
2. Which word rhymes with **stone**?
3. Which word begins with the same two letters as **clock**?

4–5. Which two words begin like **then**?

Word Groups Think how the words in each group are alike. Write the missing Basic Words.

6. string, ribbon, _______
7. house, apartment, _______
8. eyes, ears, _______
9. pretty, beautiful, _______
10. dream, wish, _______

Elephant Words Write an Elephant Word to answer each question.

11. Which word has the long **o** sound?
12. Which word has the vowel-consonant-**e** pattern but no long vowel sound?

Phonics

1. one use
2. bone
3. close
4. these
5. those

Word Groups

6. rope
7. home
8. nose
9. ~~close~~ cute
10. hope

Elephant Words

11. goes
12. one

UNIT 8

Entry Words

1.
2.
3.
4.

Fill-In Fun

5.
6.
7.
8.

Hidden Words

9.
10.
11.
12.

Dictionary

Entry Words The words you look up in a dictionary are called **entry words**. Entry words are in dark print. They are listed in ABC order.

entry word

nose The part of the head that a person or animal smells with.

meaning

Practice 1–4. Write these entry words in the order you would find them in the dictionary. Use ABC order.

ride	nose	those	cute

Review: Spelling Spree

Fill-In Fun Write the missing Basic or Review Words.

5. a bus _______
6. a _______ run
7. three, two, _______
8. a _______ call

Hidden Words Find the hidden Basic Word in each box. Write the word.

9. anogoeshan
10. cizsnosecz
11. epathoseds
12. khoqucutet

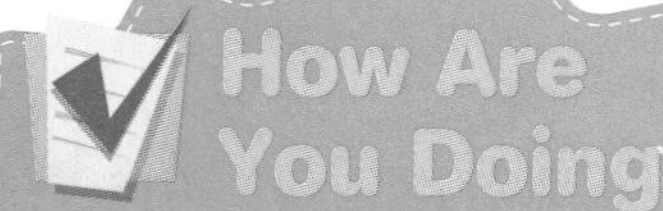

Write each spelling word as a partner reads it aloud. Did you spell any words wrong?

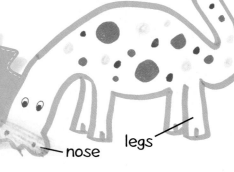

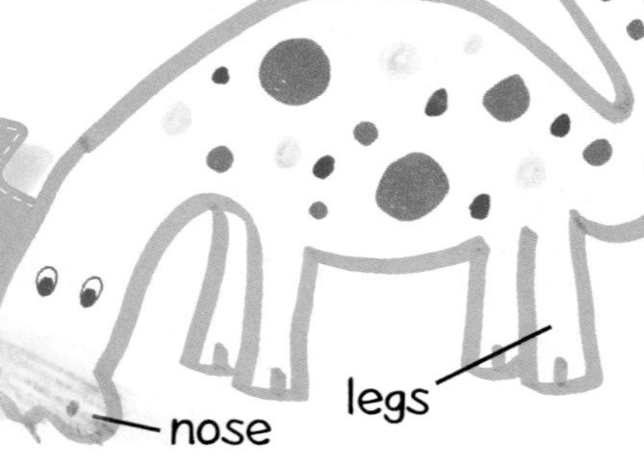

Proofreading and Writing

Proofread for Spelling Proofread this report. Use proofreading marks to fix six spelling mistakes.

Example: They dug ~~wone~~ (one) big hole.

It is hard to find a dinosaur bon^e close to home. People who hoppe to find thes^s old bones mak^e trips to special places. They put ~~roap~~ (rope) around a good spot for digging. They ~~yuse~~ (use) special tools and dig carefully.

Basic

1. bone
2. nose
3. use
4. these
5. rope
6. home
7. cute
8. close
9. hope
10. those
11. one
12. goes

Review

13. make
14. ride

Challenge

15. globe
16. mule

Write a Story

Pretend you traveled back to the time when dinosaurs lived. Write a story that begins like this: **I looked around and saw dinosaurs everywhere!** Try to use spelling words. Draw pictures to go with your story.

Proofreading Tip **Read each word slowly to make sure no letters have been left out.**

Proofreading Marks

- ^ Add
- Delete
- ≡ Make a capital letter
- / Make a small letter

Phonics and Spelling

Rhyming Words

Long o **Words** Make rhyming words that have the long **o** vowel sound. Use the letters in the picture.

one

1. ______________________
2. ______________________

ose

3. ______________________
4. ______________________

oke

5. ______________________
6. ______________________

Show What You Know! On another sheet of paper, write a poem about the dinosaurs. Use words from this page.

Science

Dinosaurs All the words in the box have something to do with dinosaurs. Write those words to finish this newspaper story. Use your Spelling Dictionary.

Spelling Word Link

bone

huge
sharp
reptile
fossil

Dinosaur Bones Found!

Mike Tang went for a walk in the woods last Sunday. He found a __(1)__ of a dinosaur's footprint! Its claws were pointed and __(2)__. Mike could tell from the footprint that the dinosaur had a __(3)__ body. The people who work at the Science Museum believe that this __(4)__ was a good hunter.

1. ____________
2. ____________
3. ____________
4. ____________

Write a Journal Page Pretend you found a large dinosaur fossil. What kind of dinosaur fossil is it? Where and how did you find it? Write a page for a science journal. Tell about your fossil. Try to use some words from the box.

Fact File

Not all dinosaurs were huge! The smallest known dinosaur was the compsognathus. It was about the size of a chicken.

UNIT 9

Words with Consonant Clusters

sw
swim

A.

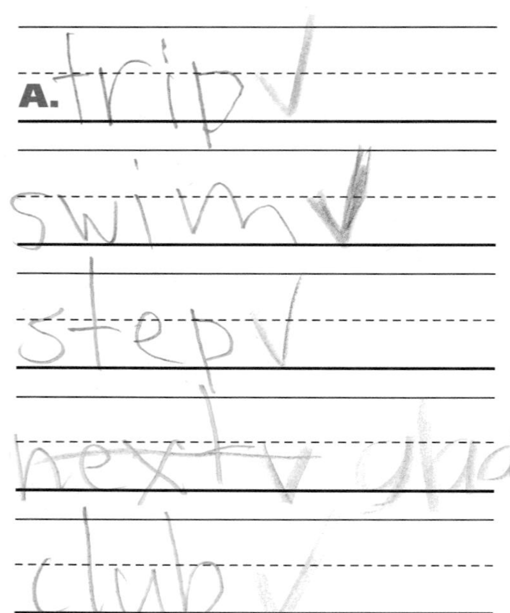

B.

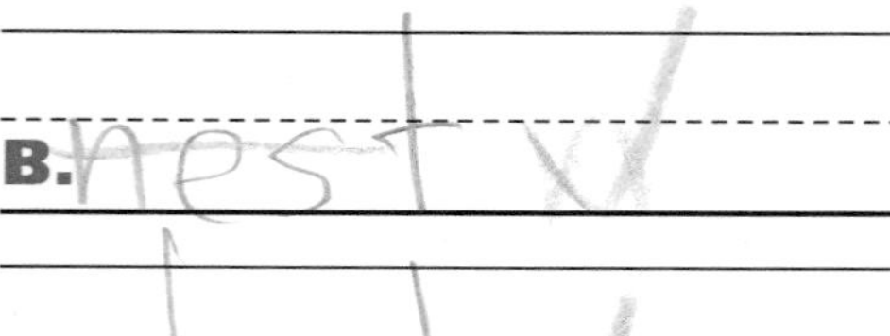

Read and Say

READ the sentences. **SAY** each word in dark print.

Basic Words

1. trip — I took a **trip** to the lake.
2. swim — She knows how to **swim**.
3. step — Please **step** into the bus.
4. nest — Is the bird in its **nest**?
5. club — Did your **club** go hiking?
6. stone — A **stone** is a small rock.
7. next — Is she **next** in line?
8. brave — He tried to be **brave**.
9. glad — I am **glad** you helped.
10. lost — Pedro **lost** his cap.

Think and Write

Each word begins or ends with a **consonant cluster**. A consonant cluster is two consonant letters whose sounds are blended together.

consonant clusters → **tr**ip, **sw**im, **st**ep, **cl**ub, ne**xt**, **br**ave, **gl**ad

A. Write **seven** Basic Words that begin with a consonant cluster.

B. Write **three** Basic Words that end with a consonant cluster.

Review
11. flat 12. slip

Challenge
13. branches 14. storm

Independent Practice

Spelling Strategy A **consonant cluster** is two consonant letters whose sounds are blended together. Some consonant clusters are **tr**, **sw**, **st**, **cl**, **xt**, **br**, and **gl**.

Phonics Write Basic Words to answer the questions.

1–3. Which three words have the short **e** sound?

4–5. Which two words are spelled with the vowel-consonant-**e** pattern?

Word Pairs Write a Basic Word to finish the second sentence in each pair.

6. You bring a **picnic basket** on a **picnic**.
You bring a **suitcase** on a _______.

7. A **player** is part of a team.
A **member** is part of a _______.

8. You go to a **track** to **run**.
You go to a **pool** to _______.

Word Meaning Write the Basic Word that means the opposite of each word in dark print.

9. We **found** our map near the tents.

10. I was **unhappy** that the trail was easy.

Phonics

1. step
2. next
3. nest
4. brave
5. stone

Word Pairs

6. trip
7. club
8. swim

Word Meaning

9. lost
10. glad

Review: Spelling Spree

Cluster Swap Make Basic or Review Words by using a consonant cluster from the box in place of each letter in dark print. Write the words.

gl	fl	cl	xt	br	sw

1. **h**im
2. **m**at
3. **w**ave
4. **p**ad
5. **r**ub
6. ne**t**

Rhyming Clues Write a Basic or Review Word for each clue.

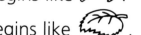

7. It rhymes with **best**. It begins like .
8. It rhymes with **cost**. It begins like .
9. It rhymes with **sip**. It begins like .
10. It rhymes with **pep**. It begins like .
11. It rhymes with **lip**. It begins like .
12. It rhymes with **bone**. It begins like .

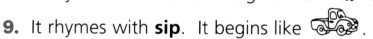

How Are You Doing?
Write your spelling words in ABC order. Practice with a family member any words you spelled wrong.

Cluster Swap

1. swim
2. flat
3. brave
4. glad
5. club
6. next

Rhyming Clues

7. nest
8. lost
9. ~~slip~~ trip
10. step
11. slip
12. stone

Proofreading and Writing

Proofread: Spelling and Capital Letters

Begin the names of streets, towns, and cities with capital letters.

Stone **R**oad **W**eston **A**tlanta

Proofread these directions. Use proofreading marks to fix four spelling mistakes and three missing capital letters.

Example: *We began our ~~tripe~~ trip in portland.*

Get a map at the hiking clob in jackson. Begin your hike at webster road. Follow the stone trail markers so you don't get lost. Watch your stap! The trail is not flatt, and you might slep.

Basic

1. trip
2. swim
3. step
4. nest
5. club
6. stone
7. next
8. brave
9. glad
10. lost

Review

11. flat
12. slip

Challenge

13. branches
14. storm

Proofreading Marks

- ∧ Add
- Delete
- ≡ Make a capital letter
- / Make a small letter

Write an Ad

Write an ad for a great summer camp. Remember to write the name of the camp and the address. Try to use spelling words. Share your ad with a friend.

Camp Green Wood

Check that you began the names of streets, towns, and cities with capital letters.

Vocabulary Enrichment

Spelling Word Link

brave

Using a Thesaurus Write a word you could use in place of the word in dark print. Use your Thesaurus. The first one is done for you.

Our camping trip was ~~**bad**~~ terrible!

Why? What happened?

It rained and we got **wet**.

Then a **big** bear sat by our tent.

What did you do?

Well, I tried hard to be **brave**.

I was **happy** to come home!

Show What You Know! On a separate sheet of paper, draw your own cartoon about a camping trip. Use words you wrote on this page.

Vocabulary Enrichment

Recreation

Camping and Hiking All the words in the box have something to do with camping and hiking. Write those words to finish this page from a diary. Use your Spelling Dictionary.

Spelling Word Link

trip

gear
cabin
clearing
camper

June 24

Today I was the only __(1)__ walking on the trail. My __(2)__ was in a backpack. I rested at a log __(3)__. It was in a __(4)__ in the woods.

1. ______
2. ______
3. ______
4. ______

Try This CHALLENGE

Yes or No? Is the word in the dark print used correctly? Write **yes** or **no**.

5. There are six apartments in our **cabin**.
6. The **camper** set up her tent.
7. I hid behind some trees in the **clearing**.
8. Sid keeps a bathtub in his camping **gear**.

5. ______
6. ______
7. ______
8. ______

Fact File

Do you want to take a long hike? Follow the Appalachian Trail. It is about 2,000 miles long and passes through 14 states from Maine to Georgia.

UNIT 10

Words Spelled with k or ck

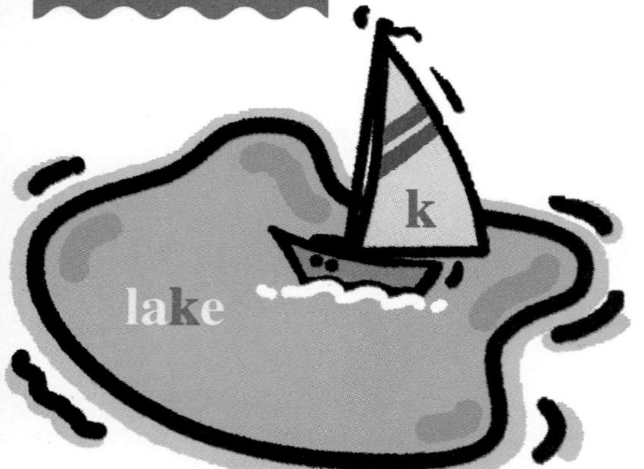

A.

B.

Read and Say

READ the sentences. **SAY** each word in dark print.

Basic Words

1. lake — They swim in the **lake**.
2. rock — Step over that **rock**.
3. ask — Did you **ask** him to go?
4. pick — I will **pick** out a toy.
5. truck — John drives a **truck**.
6. black — She has **black** mittens.
7. back — We sat in the **back** row.
8. bake — Eva had bread to **bake**.
9. clock — A **clock** tells the time.
10. kick — I can **kick** the ball!

Think and Write

Each word ends with the same sound. It is the first sound you hear in [picture]. This consonant sound is spelled two different ways.

k → la**k**e, as**k** **ck** → ro**ck**, pi**ck**

Is the vowel sound before **ck** short or long?

A. Write **three** Basic Words that have the last consonant spelled **k**.

B. Write **seven** Basic Words that have the last consonant sound spelled **ck**.

Review
11. kite **12.** take

Challenge
13. dock **14.** snake

Independent Practice

Spelling Strategy The words **lake** and **rock** end with the same consonant sound. This consonant sound may be spelled **k** or **ck**.

Phonics Write Basic Words to answer the questions.

1–2. Which two words are spelled with the vowel-consonant-**e** pattern?

3–5. Which three words begin with a consonant cluster?

Word Groups Think how the words in each group are alike. Write the missing Basic Words.

6. say, tell, _______

7. side, front, _______

8. catch, throw, _______

Word Meaning Write the Basic Word that means the same or almost the same as the word in dark print.

9. Can you skip a **stone** across the water?

10. Try to **choose** one that is smooth and flat.

Phonics

1. ________
2. ________
3. ________
4. ________
5. ________

Word Groups

6. ________
7. ________
8. ________

Word Meaning

9. ________
10. ________

Dictionary

Entry Words To find entry words in a dictionary, you use ABC order. When entry words begin with the same letter, you must look at the second letter. See how these entry words are put in ABC order.

l**a**ke   l**e**g   l**i**st

Practice Write the entry word in each group that would come first in the dictionary.

1.	ask	apple	any
2.	crown	cup	clock
3.	top	time	truck
4.	black	bake	bent
5.	tell	told	take
6.	key	know	kite

Review: Spelling Spree

Rhyme Time Finish the sentences. Write a Basic or Review Word to rhyme with the word in dark print.

7. Tick and **tock** are the sounds of a ____.
8. The wind will **shake** the homes by the ____.
9. The player is **quick**, but can he ____?
10. To cook a **cake**, you must know how to ____.
11. If the fish do not **bite**, go fly your ____.
12. The lump in my **sock** is a gray ____.

How Are You Doing?
Write each word in a sentence. Practice with a partner any words you spelled wrong.

Entry Words

1. ____
2. ____
3. ____
4. ____
5. ____
6. ____

Rhyme Time

7. ____
8. ____
9. ____
10. ____
11. ____
12. ____

Proofreading and Writing

Proofread for Spelling Proofread this post card. Use proofreading marks to fix six spelling mistakes.

Example: Did you swim and fly your ~~kit~~ kite?

May 26, 1998

Dear Rosa,

The truk ride around the lake was bumpy! Don't aks me how we ever got bak! We are going to tak a boat trip on Sunday. I can try to pik up a blak rock for your collection.

Your friend,

Megan

Basic

1. lake
2. rock
3. ask
4. pick
5. truck
6. black
7. back
8. bake
9. clock
10. kick

Review

11. kite
12. take

Challenge

13. dock
14. snake

Proofreading Marks

- ∧ Add
- Delete
- ≡ Make a capital letter
- / Make a small letter

Write a Post Card

Pretend you are on a trip with your family. Write a post card to a friend. What exciting things do you do? Try to use spelling words. Draw a picture on your post card. Share it with a friend.

Proofreading Tip **Check each word to make sure you have not switched the order of the letters.**

Phonics and Spelling

Words with k **and** ck Write **k** or **ck** to finish each word. Then write the word.

des______

so______

chal______

1. __________

2. __________

3. __________

lo______

par______

bri______

4. __________

5. __________

6. __________

Work Together Write three rhyming words that end with **ick** like the word **brick**. Work with a friend.

7. __________

8. __________

9. __________

Science

Rivers and Lakes All the words in the box have something to do with rivers and lakes. Write those words to finish this page from a report. Use your Spelling Dictionary.

wade
shore
brook
flow

This little **(1)** has cool water. It will **(2)** into a big river. Birds **(3)** in the water. They live on the rocky **(4)**.

1. ______
2. ______
3. ______
4. ______

Try This CHALLENGE

Yes or No? Is the word in dark print used correctly? Write **yes** or **no**.

5. Bob is **shore** we can swim in this lake.
6. I am going to **wade** into the river.
7. The huge ship sailed up to the **brook**.
8. This water will **flow** into the ocean.

5. ______
6. ______
7. ______
8. ______

Fact File

The longest river in the world is the Nile in Africa. It is more than 4,000 miles long. A trip down the Nile would be longer than a trip across the whole United States!

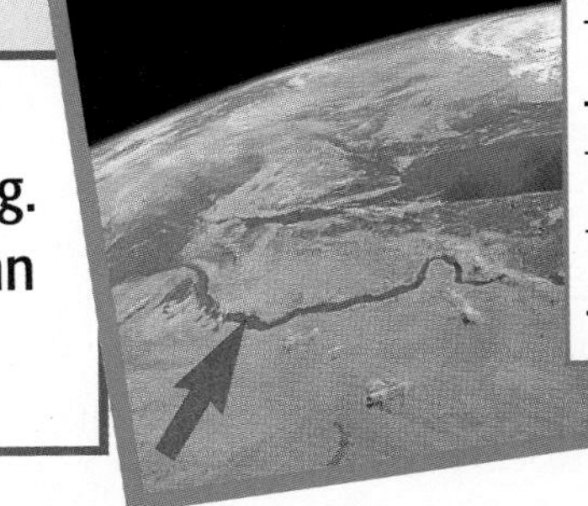

UNIT 11

Words with Double Consonants

Read and Say

READ the sentences. **SAY** each word in dark print.

Basic Words	
1. bell	Who will ring the **bell**?
2. off	Take that hat **off**.
3. dress	She likes this **dress**.
4. add	I will **add** those numbers.
5. hill	Jason ran up the **hill**.
6. well	Did you sleep **well**?
7. egg	The **egg** was cracked.
8. will	Maria **will** feed Duke.
9. grass	Please cut the **grass**.
10. tell	I cannot **tell** you to go.

egg

gg

Think and Write

Each word ends with a consonant sound. The last consonant sound is spelled with two letters that are the same.

be**ll**, o**ff**, dre**ss**, a**dd**, e**gg**

How many vowel sounds do you hear in each word? Do any of the words have a long vowel sound?

A. Write the Basic Words. Then draw a line under the letters that spell the last consonant sound in each word.

A. bell ✓
off ✓
dress ✓
add ✓
hill ✓
will ✓
well ✓
egg ✓
grass ✓
tell ✓

Review

11. at **12.** hot

Challenge

13. brass **14.** skill

Independent Practice

Spelling Strategy In words like **bell**, **off**, and **dress**, the final consonant sound is spelled with two letters that are the same.

Phonics Write Basic Words to answer the questions.

1. Which word begins with the same consonant cluster as ?
2. Which word begins with the same consonant cluster as ?

3–4. Which two words rhyme with **spill**?

Word Meaning Write the Basic Word that means the opposite of each word below.

5. sick **6.** ask **7.** on

Word Clues Write a Basic Word for each clue.

8. what you do to one and two to get three
9. what a mother or father bird keeps warm
10. what you ring at someone's door

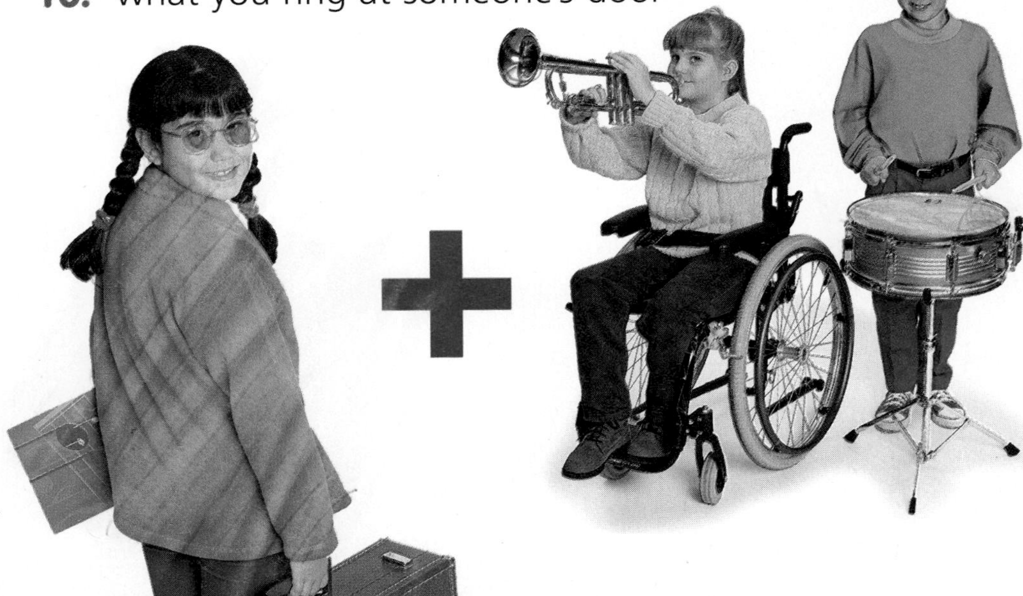

Phonics

1. dress
2. grass
3. will
4. well

Word Meaning

5. well
6. tell
7. off

Word Clues

8. add
9. egg
10. bell

Guide Words

1.

2.

3.

4.

Picture Clues

5.

6.

7.

8.

Jobs Match

9.

10.

11.

12.

Dictionary

Guide Words The two words at the top of a dictionary page are called **guide words**. They help you find entry words because they name the first and last entry word on the page.

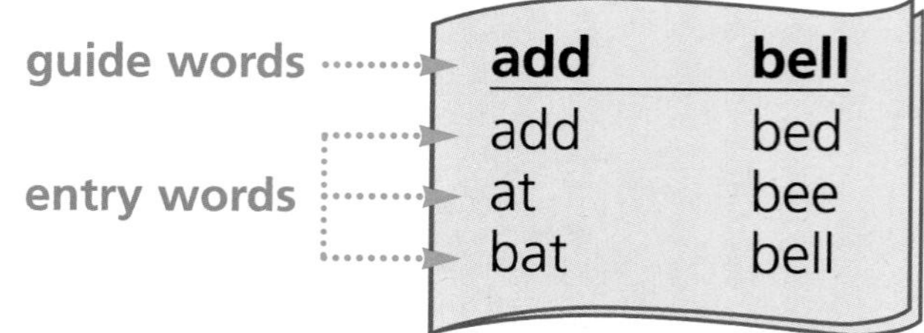

Practice 1–4. Write the four entry words from the box that you would find on the same page as the guide words **fun** and **ice**.

grass	hill	egg	dress	hot	give

Review: Spelling Spree

Picture Clues Write a Basic Word for each picture.

5. 

6. $\begin{array}{r} 4 \\ +5 \\ \hline 9 \end{array}$

7. 

8. 

Jobs Match Look at the list of workers. Write a Basic Word that names something each person makes, uses, or works with on the job.

9. gardener
10. tailor
11. chicken farmer
12. firefighter

How Are You Doing?
List the spelling words that are hard for you. Practice them with a partner.

Proofreading and Writing

Proofread for Spelling Proofread this ad. Use proofreading marks to fix five spelling mistakes.

Example: Start singing when you hear the ~~bel~~ bell.

Sing-Along Songs

You wil love these songs! They all tel a story. Sing them on a hill. Hum them on the grass. Whistle them att home. Play them on a hawt day when you go of to the beach. They can add to your fun!

Basic

1. bell
2. off
3. dress
4. add
5. hill
6. well
7. egg
8. will
9. grass
10. tell

Review

11. at
12. hot

Challenge

13. brass
14. skill

Proofreading Marks

- ∧ Add
- Delete
- ≡ Make a capital letter
- / Make a small letter

Write a List

Which instrument do you like to play or listen to? Make a list that tells why this instrument is your favorite. Give two or three reasons. Try to use spelling words. Discuss your list with a friend.

Proofreading Tip

If you use a computer when you write, use a spell checker.

Phonics and Spelling

Rhyming Words

Words with ill Help Don Drumble find the band. Draw a line through all of the letters you can use to build words that rhyme with the spelling word **hill**. Then write the words.

1. ______
2. ______
3. ______
4. ______
5. ______
6. ______

Show What You Know! On another sheet of paper, write two sentences. Tell how Don Drumble found the band. Use some of the words you made.

Vocabulary Enrichment

Music

Songs and Instruments All the words in the box have something to do with songs and instruments. Write those words to finish this bulletin board message. Use your Spelling Dictionary.

Spelling Word Link

bell

tune
harp
tuba
pit

Come hear us play a famous (1). We sit and practice in the (2) after school. Lin blows the big brass (3). I play the strings of a (4). We get better every day!

The Band

1. ______
2. ______
3. ______
4. ______

Try This CHALLENGE

Riddle Time! Write a word from the box to answer each riddle.

5. What is plucked but is not a chicken?
6. What needs air but does not breathe?
7. What can be played, sung, or whistled?
8. What is a hole that is filled with music?

5. ______
6. ______
7. ______
8. ______

Fact File

Mozart was a famous composer who lived in Austria during the 1700s. He started playing music at the age of four. He began writing music when he was only five years old!

12 Review: Units 7–11

1. line
2. same
3. made
4. five
5. ate
6. side
7. hope
8. these
9. cute
10. nose
11. home
12. bone

Unit 7 Vowel-Consonant-e pages 60-65

ī five

five	made	side
ate	same	line

Spelling Strategy The long **a** and the long **i** vowel sounds may be spelled by the vowel-consonant-**e** pattern.

Write the spelling word that rhymes with each word.

1. mine **2.** name **3.** trade **4.** hive

Write the missing spelling words.

5. We _______ all the food Dad cooked.

6. Then we played tag by the _______ of our house.

Unit 8 More Vowel-Consonant-e pages 66–71

ō bone

bone	nose	these
home	cute	hope

Spelling Strategy The long **o**, **u**, and **e** vowel sounds may be spelled by the vowel-consonant-**e** pattern.

Change the letter in dark print. Write a spelling word.

7. **r**ope **8.** th**o**se **9.** cu**b**e **10.** **r**ose

Write the missing spelling words.

11. Spot likes to eat dinner in his new _______.

12. We put his bowl and favorite _______ inside.

Unit 9 Consonant Clusters pages 72–77

trip	swim	club
stone	next	glad

sw
swim

Spelling Strategy A **consonant cluster** is two consonant letters whose sounds are blended together.

Write the spelling word that means the same.

13. happy **14.** after **15.** rock

Write the missing spelling words.

Six people are in our sports __(**16**)__. We will take a __(**17**)__ to the beach and __(**18**)__ all day.

13. glad
14. next
15. stone
16. club
17. trip
18. swim

Unit 10 Words Spelled with k or ck pages 78–83

lake	ask	truck
black	back	kick

k
lake

Spelling Strategy The final consonant sound in **lake** and **truck** may be spelled **k** or **ck**.

Write the spelling word that means the opposite.

19. tell **20.** front **21.** white

Write the missing spelling words.

We went to the __(**22**)__ in our new red __(**23**)__. Mom showed me how to __(**24**)__ my legs in the water.

19. ask
20. back
21. black
22. lake
23. truck
24. kick

25. egg ✓
26. hill ✓
27. grass ✓
28. well ✓
29. off ✓
30. add ✓
31. have ✓
32. one ✓
33. goes ✓
34. give ✓
35. goes ✓
36. have ✓

Unit 11 Double Consonants pages 84-89

gg
egg

off	add	hill
well	egg	grass

Spelling Strategy A final consonant sound may be spelled with two letters that are the same.

Write the spelling word that goes with each word.

25. hen **27.** cut
26. climb **28.** pail

Write the missing spelling words.

29. Take ________ your coats and sit down.
30. Today we will ________ more to our class story.

Elephant Words Units 7–11 pages 60–89

ONE

give	have
one	goes

Spelling Strategy Elephant Words have unusual spellings. Check them carefully when you write them.

Write the missing words. Use some words two times.

I __(**31**)__ six brothers. Each __(**32**)__ of us __(**33**)__ to school every day. Some days Mom will __(**34**)__ us a ride. When she __(**35**)__ to work on the train, we __(**36**)__ to take the bus.

Spelling-Meaning Strategy

Word Families

You know that words have families. Words in the same family are alike in spelling and meaning.

I like to **bake** cookies.

Dad says I am a good **baker**.

I **baked** a cake this morning.

Baking is fun on rainy days.

Think How are words in this family alike in meaning? How are they alike in spelling?

Apply and Extend

Write a word from the bake **family in each sentence.**

1. The _______ wears a white hat.
2. He _______ bread this morning.
3. We saw it _______ in the oven.
4. He can _______ good muffins too.

With a partner, think of words in these families. Make a list for each family.

Check the Word Families list that begins on page 272. Did you miss any words? Add them to your lists.

1. _______
2. _______
3. _______
4. _______

UNIT 12

A Story About Yourself

from

The New Girl at School

by Judy Delton

Marcia told what happened on her first day at a new school. How does Marcia feel about her new school?

When I walked into school, everyone stared. Everyone was with a friend but me.

I had on my new shirt with the grasshopper on it. (No one even looked at the grasshopper.)

The children called me Martha. (My name is Marcia.)

Everyone knew where the lunchroom was. (I had to ask.)

Everyone could do subtraction. (I was the only one who couldn't.)

"I don't like this school," I said to my mother that night.

"It will get better," she said.

Think and Discuss

1. How did Marcia feel on her first day at school? What things happened to make her feel that way?
2. What **one idea** does Marcia tell about, her first day at school or her new clothes?

The Writing Process

A Story About Yourself

Write a story about something that happened to you. Follow the guidelines. Use the Writing Process.

1 Prewriting

- List special things you have done.
- Choose one idea that would make the best story.

2 Draft

- Draw the beginning of your story. Then write about it.

3 Revise

- Make sure all your sentences tell about one idea.
- Remember to use your Thesaurus to find exact words.
- Read your story to a friend. Make changes.

4 Proofread

- Did you spell each word correctly?
- Did you begin the names of people, pets, and places with capital letters?

5 Publish

- Copy your story neatly. Add a good title. Act out your story.

Guidelines for Writing a Story About Yourself

✓ The story should tell about one idea.

✓ Use enough details to make your story interesting.

Composition Words

made
home
those
glad
ask
tell

UNIT 13

More Long a Spellings

A. way
play
pay
hay

B. train
mail
trail
sail
nail
rain

C. they
great

Read and Say

READ the sentences. **SAY** each word in dark print.

Basic Words

1.	train	He rode on the **train**.
2.	way	We found our **way** home.
3.	mail	Can you **mail** the letter?
4.	play	She can **play** with me.
5.	trail	They hiked the **trail**.
6.	pay	Let me **pay** for the toy.
7.	sail	I will **sail** on the lake.
8.	hay	Horses like to eat **hay**.
9.	nail	I need a longer **nail**.
10.	rain	Will it **rain** all day?
11.	they	Did **they** buy a car?
12.	great	The game was **great**!

Think and Write

Most of the words have the long **a** vowel sound spelled **ay** or **ai**.

the long **a** sound → w**ay**, tr**ai**n

How are the Elephant Words different?

A. Write **four** Basic Words with the long **a** sound spelled **ay**.

B. Write **six** Basic Words with the long **a** sound spelled **ai**.

C. Now write the **two** Elephant Words.

Review
13. stay **14.** day

Challenge
15. railroad **16.** subway

Independent Practice

Spelling Strategy The vowel sound in **way** and **train** is the long **a** sound. The long **a** sound may be spelled **ay** or **ai**.

Phonics Write Basic Words to answer the questions.

1. Which word begins and ends like **meal**?

2–5. Which four words rhyme with **stay** and end in **ay**?

Word Groups Think how the words in each group are alike. Write the missing Basic Words.

6. sidewalk, path, ______
7. hammer, saw, ______
8. drive, fly, ______
9. snow, sleet, ______
10. plane, boat, ______

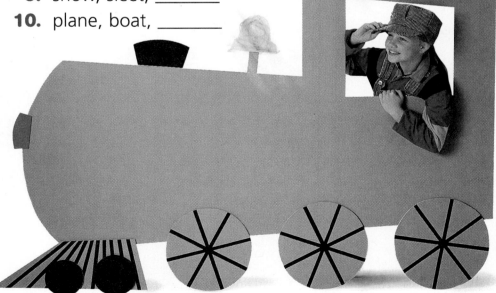

Elephant Words Write an Elephant Word to answer each question.

11. Which word has the long **a** sound spelled **ey**?
12. Which word has the long **a** sound spelled **ea**?

Phonics

1. mail
2. way
3. play
4. pay
5. hay

Word Groups

6. trail
7. nail
8. train
9. rain
10. mail

Elephant Words

11. they
12. great

UNIT
13

Review: Spelling Spree

Code Breaker Use the code to write Basic or Review Words.

▲ = a	∩ = g	+ = r	↑ = w
☆ = d	ꝏ = h	● = s	□ = y
☽ = e	⊥ = p	⊖ = t	

Example: ꝏ ▲ □ = **hay**

1. ↑▲□
2. ⊖ꝏ☽□
3. ☆▲□
4. ●⊖▲□
5. ∩+☽▲⊖
6. ⊥▲□

Word Match Write the Basic Word that goes with each place or thing.

7. post office
8. barn
9. toolbox
10. boat
11. cloud
12. mountain

How Are You Doing?
Write each word in a sentence. Practice with a partner any words you spelled wrong.

Code Breaker

1. way
2. they
3. day
4. stay
5. great
6. pay

Word Match

7. mail
8. hay
9. nail
10. sail
11. rain
12. railroad

Proofreading and Writing

Proofread: Spelling and Using I When you talk about another person and yourself, always name yourself last.

Ben and **I** will buy the tickets.

Proofread these sentences from a diary. Use proofreading marks to fix four spelling mistakes and two mistakes using **I**.

Example: ~~I and Ana~~ will ~~pai~~ for the trip. (Ana and I; pay)

March 3

I and my family had a grait day on the trane. I and Dad ate in the dining car. Mom and I tried to play checkers along the wey, but the pieces would not stae on the board.

Basic

1. train
2. way
3. mail
4. play
5. trail
6. pay
7. sail
8. hay
9. nail
10. rain
11. they
12. great

Review

13. stay
14. day

Challenge

15. railroad
16. subway

Proofreading Marks

- ∧ Add
- ℘ Delete
- ≡ Make a capital letter
- / Make a small letter

Write a Story

Write a story about something special you and a friend did together. What made it fun? Try to use spelling words. Have your friend draw pictures to go with the story.

Proofreading Tip **Check your writing. Make sure that you named yourself last.**

Vocabulary Enrichment

Word Builder

Spelling Word Link

great

Using a Thesaurus Write a word you could use in place of the word in dark print. Use your Thesaurus.

1. The children **look** out the window.
2. The white stars are **bright**.
3. The night sky is **pretty**.
4. They are having a **great** ride!

1. ______________________

2. ______________________

3. ______________________

4. ______________________

Show What You Know! On another sheet of paper, write a sentence about this picture. Use another word for **fast** found in your Thesaurus.

Vocabulary Enrichment

Social Studies

Trains All of the words in the box have something to do with trains. Write those words to finish this ad. Use your Spelling Dictionary.

Spelling Word Link

train

caboose
engine
crossing
coach

Come for a Ride on Tobo Train!

A steam (1) pulls Tobo Train into the station every day. Sit in the (2) and read. Watch the red lights flash when the train comes to a (3). Visit the workers in the (4) at the end of the train.

RAILROAD CROSSING

1. ______
2. ______
3. ______
4. ______

Try This CHALLENGE

Write an Ad How is a train trip better than a trip by bus, car, or plane? Write an ad for a railroad company. Tell why traveling by train is fun. Use words from the box on this page.

Fact File

Trains have changed over the years. One of the first trains used a horse as an engine! The horse ran on a belt and that made the wheels of the train turn.

UNIT 14

More Long e Spellings

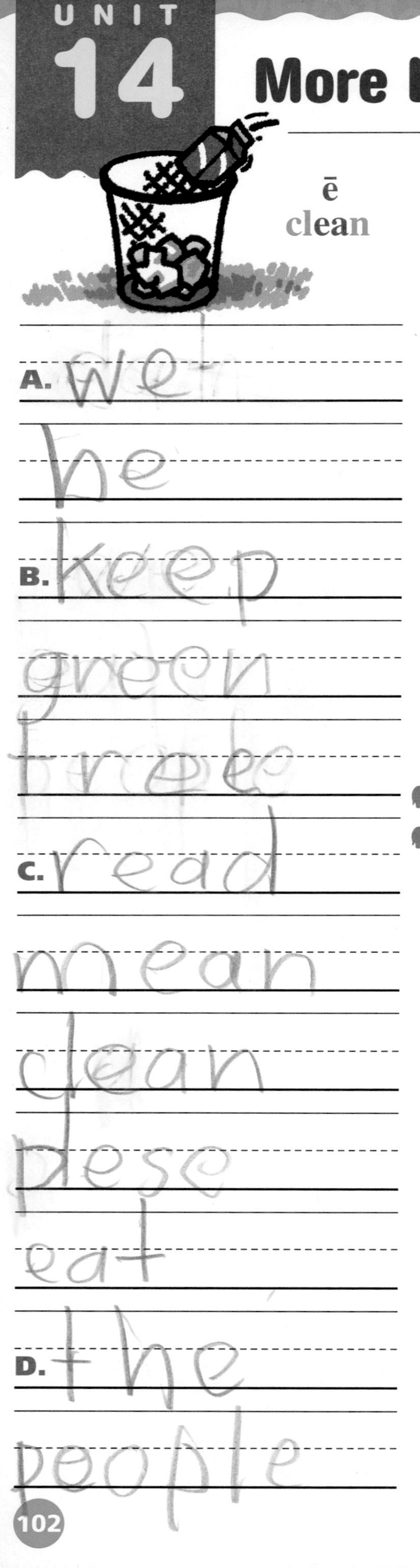

Read and Say

READ the sentences. **SAY** each word in dark print.

Basic Words

1. clean	His shop is **clean**.
2. keep	You can **keep** playing.
3. please	Will you **please** stay?
4. green	My truck is **green**.
5. we	Did **we** win?
6. be	Amanda will **be** late.
7. eat	I want to **eat** now.
8. tree	A nest is in that **tree**.
9. mean	She did not **mean** it.
10. read	I love to **read**!
11. the	Can Emil fix **the** sail?
12. people	Many **people** have pets.

Think and Write

Most of the words have the long **e** vowel sound spelled **e**, **ee**, or **ea**.

the long **e** sound → w**e**, k**ee**p, cl**ea**n

Which Elephant Word can you say two ways?
How is the other Elephant Word different?

A. Write **two** Basic Words with the long **e** sound spelled **e**.
B. Write **three** Basic Words with the long **e** sound spelled **ee**.
C. Write **five** Basic Words with the long **e** sound spelled **ea**.
D. Now write the **two** Elephant Words.

Review
13. he **14.** feet

Challenge
15. stream **16.** street

Independent Practice

Spelling Strategy The vowel sound in **we**, **keep**, and **clean** is the long **e** sound. The long **e** sound may be spelled **e**, **ee**, or **ea**.

Phonics Write Basic Words to answer the questions.

1. Which word rhymes with **sleep**?
2. Which word begins and ends like **moon**?
3. Which word begins with the same consonant cluster as **play**?

4–6. Which three words end with the long **e** sound?

Word Clues Write a Basic Word for each clue.

7. what you do when you are hungry
8. what you might do with a good book
9. how you feel after a bath
10. how a frog or leaf looks

Elephant Words Write the missing Elephant Words.

11. Many _______ helped clean up that dirty lake.
12. Now _______ fish have a clean home!

Phonics

1. keep
2. mean
3. please
4. we
5. be
6. tree

Word Clues

7. eat
8. read
9. clean
10. green

Elephant Words

11. people
12. the

UNIT
14

Dictionary

Guide Words Use guide words and ABC order to help you find words in a dictionary. If the guide words begin with the same letter as the word you are looking for, look at the second letter of each word.

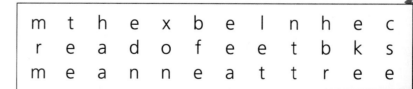

guide words → **lake** **man** | **mean** **my**

entry words →

lake	lock	mean	mud
leaf	lunch	milk	my
lid	man	moon	

Practice Write **yes** or **no** to tell if each entry word below would be on the same page as the guide words **feet** and **fry**.

1. flag **2.** funny **3.** green **4.** fox

Review: Spelling Spree

Hidden Words 5–12. Find the Basic and Review Words hidden in each row. Write the words.

m	t	h	e	x	b	e	l	n	h	e	c
r	e	a	d	o	f	e	e	t	b	k	s
m	e	a	n	n	e	a	t	t	r	e	e

How Are You Doing?
Write each word as a family member reads it aloud. Did you spell any words wrong?

Guide Words

1. fox
2. funny
3. flag
4. green

Hidden Words

5. fox
6.
7.
8.
9.
10.
11.
12.

Proofreading and Writing

Proofread for Spelling Proofread this sign. Use proofreading marks to fix six spelling mistakes.

Example: Who put a sign on this ~~tre~~ tree?

Campers, Please Read!

This grene forest is where wea animals live. All popul are welcome to visit, but pleaz be careful! Help keap our home kleen!

Basic

1. clean
2. keep
3. please
4. green
5. we
6. be
7. eat
8. tree
9. mean
10. read
11. the
12. people

Review

13. he
14. feet

Challenge

15. stream
16. street

Proofreading Marks

- ∧ Add
- Delete
- ≡ Make a capital letter
- / Make a small letter

Write a Speech

Write a speech. Tell why children should throw their trash away when they are on the playground. Try to use spelling words. Have some friends listen to your speech.

Proofreading Tip

Proofread your paper. Circle any words you are not sure of.

Phonics and Spelling

Rhyming Words

Long e Words Make rhyming words that have the long **e** vowel sound. Use the letters in the picture. Write each word under the correct bin.

1. ______	4. ______	7. ______
2. ______	5. ______	8. ______
3. ______	6. ______	9. ______

Show What You Know! On another sheet of paper, write a sign for the picture above. Use words that you wrote on this page.

Science

Protecting Our Earth All the words in the box have something to do with protecting our earth. Write those words to finish this story from a town newspaper. Use your Spelling Dictionary.

Spelling
Word Link
clean
trash
dump
collect
sewer

Section A

Smithtown Is in Trouble!

Where will all our __(1)__ go? Our town __(2)__ is getting full. Rain is even washing leaves and paper into the __(3)__. We need a new way to __(4)__ our papers, cans, and bottles. Let's come up with some answers!

1. ______
2. ______
3. ______
4. ______

Try This CHALLENGE

Yes or No? Write **yes** or **no** to answer each question.

5. Would you find a **dump** on a camel?
6. Is **trash** something you throw away?
7. Would you wash a car in a **sewer**?
8. Could you **collect** litter in a bag?

5. ______
6. ______
7. ______
8. ______

Fact File

Paper is made from trees. It can also be made from many kinds of used paper. You can save a tree! Take used paper to a place that will make it into new paper.

WE RECYCLE

UNIT 15

The Vowel Sound in ball

A. log ✓ dog ✓

B. saw ✓ paw ✓ draw ✓

C. all ✓ fall ✓ ball ✓ call ✓ small ✓

Read and Say

READ the sentences. **SAY** each word in dark print.

Basic Words	
1. dog	My **dog** likes bones.
2. paw	My cat hurt its **paw**.
3. call	I will **call** you at home.
4. saw	Marie **saw** a baby bird.
5. ball	That is my **ball**.
6. all	We are **all** sleepy.
7. draw	Can you **draw** a tree?
8. small	The kitten is **small**.
9. log	Pat cut the **log**.
10. fall	Did she **fall** down?

Think and Write

Each word has the same vowel sound. It is the vowel sound you hear in ball. This vowel sound is spelled **o**, **aw**, or **a** when **a** comes before **ll**.

the ball vowel sound → d**o**g, p**aw**, c**all**

A. Write **two** Basic Words with the vowel sound spelled **o**.

B. Write **three** Basic Words with the vowel sound spelled **aw**.

C. Write **five** Basic Words with the vowel sound spelled **a** before **ll**.

Review
11. best **12.** came

Challenge
13. stall **14.** claw

Independent Practice

Spelling Strategy The words **dog**, **paw**, and **call** have the same vowel sound. This vowel sound may be spelled **o**, **aw**, or **a** before **ll**.

Phonics Write Basic Words to answer the questions.

1–2. Which two words rhyme with **fog**?

3–4. Which two words begin with a consonant cluster?

Word Pairs Write a Basic Word to finish the second sentence in each pair.

5. **Summer** comes after **spring**.
Winter comes after _______.

6. You use a **hammer** to hit a **nail**.
You use a **bat** to hit a _______.

7. You cut **paper** with **scissors**.
You cut **wood** with a _______.

8. A **horse** has a **hoof**.
A **cat** has a _______.

Word Meaning Write the Basic Word that means the same or almost the same as each word below.

9. shout **10.** every

Phonics

1. log
2. dog
3. draw
4. small

Word Pairs

5. fall
6. ball
7. saw
8. paw

Word Meaning

9. call
10. all

UNIT
15

Hink Pinks

5. blest
6. small
7. log
8. dog
9. claw
10. stall

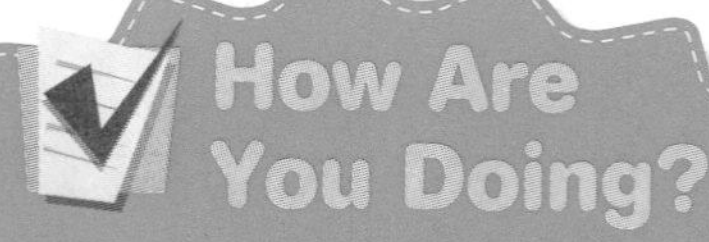

How Are You Doing?

Write your words in ABC order. Practice with a family member any words you spelled wrong.

Dictionary

Word Meanings A dictionary gives the **meaning** of an entry word you look up. It may also give a **sample sentence** to help make the meaning clear.

entry word — meaning

paw The foot of a four-footed animal that has claws: *My dog stuck her **paw** in the mud.*

sample sentence

Practice Follow the directions below. Use your Spelling Dictionary. Write your answers on another sheet of paper.

1. Look up **draw**. Write the meaning.
2. Look up **log**. Write the sample sentence.
3. Look up **small**. Write the meaning.
4. Look up **best**. Write the sample sentence.

Review: Spelling Spree

Hink Pinks Write a Basic or Review Word that answers the question and rhymes with the word in dark print.

5. What is the most wonderful nap? the ______ **rest**
6. What is a tiny room? a ______ **hall**
7. What is a tree trunk for a pig? a **hog** ______
8. What is a run with a puppy? a ______ **jog**
9. What is a tool for a kitten? a **paw** ______
10. What is a yell in October? a **fall** ______

Proofreading and Writing

Proofread for Spelling Proofread this letter. Use proofreading marks to fix six spelling mistakes.

Example: Rufus ~~sor~~ saw the doctor on Monday.

July 31, 1998

Dear Doctor Walsh,

We are al glad you kame to fix our dog Pal's pau after his fawl. Today he chased a boll! I will drow a picture of him for you.

Best wishes,

Kate Rizzo

Basic

1. dog
2. paw
3. call
4. saw
5. ball
6. all
7. draw
8. small
9. log
10. fall

Review

11. best
12. came

Challenge

13. stall
14. claw

Proofreading Marks

- ∧ Add
- Delete
- ≡ Make a capital letter
- / Make a small letter

Write Instructions

Pal

Pretend you are going on vacation, and you have to leave your pet at home. Write sentences that tell a pet sitter what to do to take care of your pet. Try to use spelling words. Have a friend read your instructions. Are they clear?

Proofreading Tip **Make sure you have written your a's and o's the right way.**

Phonics and Spelling

Rhyming Words

More ball **Words** Make rhyming words that have the **ball** vowel sound. Use the letters in the picture.

1. ____________
2. ____________
3. ____________
4. ____________
5. ____________
6. ____________
7. ____________

Show What You Know! Finish these sentences about the picture. Use words that you wrote on this page.

8. A kitten is jumping on the _______.
9. A horse is eating some _______.

8. ____________
9. ____________

Vocabulary Enrichment

Careers

Animal Doctors All the words in the box have something to do with animal doctors. Write those words to finish this diary. Use your Spelling Dictionary.

Spelling Word Link

dog

clip
healthy
ill
cure

September 9

Rusty is still very __(1)__ with a cold. The doctor will __(2)__ him. She will even __(3)__ his nails. My dog will be __(4)__ again.

1. ______
2. ______
3. ______
4. ______

Try This CHALLENGE

Yes or No? Is the word in the dark print used correctly? Write **yes** or **no**.

5. Rex is **ill** with a terrible haircut.
6. Walking a dog will keep it **healthy**.
7. I will use a hose to **clip** Koko's claws.
8. Dr. Ming has a **cure** for the leash.

5. ______
6. ______
7. ______
8. ______

Fact File

Long ago, many towns did not have an animal doctor nearby. In those towns, the blacksmith, who made horseshoes, also worked as the horse doctor!

UNIT 16

Words Spelled with sh or ch

sh

A. dish

wish

ship

wash

sheep

B. chase

each

chop

much

such

C. catch

sure

Read and Say

READ the sentences. **SAY** each word in dark print.

Basic Words	
1. sheep	The farmer has **sheep**.
2. chase	Did he **chase** the cat?
3. wish	Make a **wish**.
4. much	We stayed **much** longer.
5. chop	Anna will **chop** the log.
6. each	They like **each** puppy.
7. dish	Marco broke a **dish**.
8. such	I am **such** a good cook.
9. wash	Will you **wash** the cup?
10. ship	We saw the **ship** sail.
11. catch	Did Sing **catch** a fish?
12. sure	Are you **sure** you saw her?

Think and Write

Each word begins or ends with the first sound you hear in  or .

the **sh** sound → **sh**eep, wi**sh**

the **ch** sound → **ch**ase, mu**ch**

How are the Elephant Words different?

A. Write **five** Basic Words spelled with **sh**.

B. Write **five** Basic Words spelled with **ch**.

C. Now write the **two** Elephant Words.

Review

13. she **14.** chin

Challenge

15. shout **16.** lunch

Independent Practice

Spelling Strategy The sound that begins **sheep** and ends **wish** may be spelled **sh**. The sound that begins **chase** and ends **much** may be spelled **ch**.

Phonics Write Basic Words to answer the questions.

1–2. Which two words have the short **u** sound?

3–4. Which two words have the long **e** sound?

Word Meaning Write the Basic Word that means the same or almost the same as each word below.

5. plate
6. boat
7. hope
8. follow
9. cut
10. clean

Elephant Words Write the missing Elephant Words.

11. Watch Tex ________ the bundles of hay.

12. I am ________ he works very hard.

Phonics

1. such
2. much
3. sheep
4. each

Word Meaning

5. dish
6. ship
7. wish
8. chase
9. chop
10. wash

Elephant Words

11. catch
12. sure

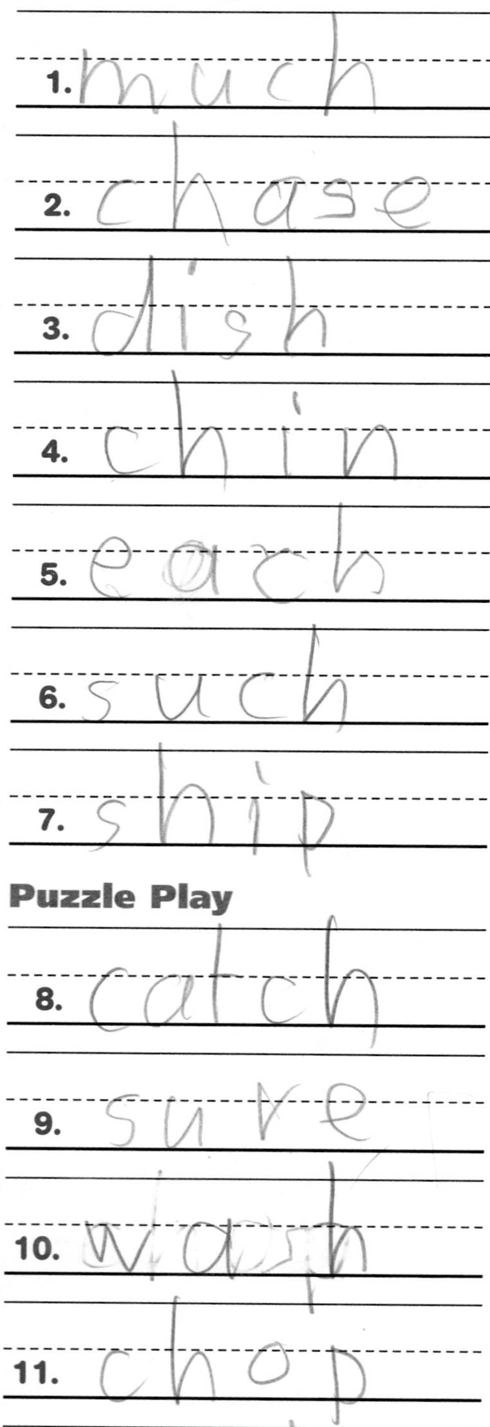

Letter Swap

1.
2.
3.
4.
5.
6.
7.

Puzzle Play

8.
9.
10.
11.
12.

Review: Spelling Spree

Letter Swap Make Basic or Review Words by using **sh** or **ch** in place of each letter in dark print. Write the words.

1. mu**g**
2. **c**ase
3. di**g**
4. **w**in
5. ea**t**
6. su**n**
7. **l**ip

Puzzle Play Write the missing Basic Words. Use the letters that would be in the boxes to spell what someone does in a classroom.

8. I _ _ ☐ _ _ the rope Mom throws to me.
9. I am not _ _ _ ☐ when the rodeo is coming.
10. We _ ☐ _ _ the sheep's dirty wool.
11. Can you ☐ _ _ _ down this tree?
12. I _ _ _ ☐ I could ride the new pony!

Secret Word: _ _ _ _ _

How Are You Doing?

List the spelling words that are hard for you. Practice them with a partner.

Proofreading and Writing

Proofread: Spelling and Using er **and** est

Add **er** to adjectives to compare two people or things. Add **est** to compare more than two.

The small**est** pony chased the other four.

Proofread this tall tale. Use proofreading marks to fix four spelling mistakes and two mistakes using **er** or **est**.

Example: Shirley is ~~mush quickest~~ much quicker than Roy is.

Long ago, Roy Ram raced with a sheap named Shirley. He was shure he could cach up to her, but Shirley was fastest. She ran with such speed that shee blew down each tree along her path. That is why their ranch has the fewer trees of all!

Basic

1. sheep
2. chase
3. wish
4. much
5. chop
6. each
7. dish
8. such
9. wash
10. ship
11. catch
12. sure

Review

13. she
14. chin

Challenge

15. shout
16. lunch

Proofreading Marks

- ∧ Add
- Delete
- ≡ Make a capital letter
- / Make a small letter

Write a Description

Draw some pictures of ranch animals. Then write about them. Tell how they are alike and different. Try to use spelling words.

Example: The sheep is shorter than the horse.

Proofreading Tip

Check that you added er **or** est **to adjectives when comparing two or more people or things.**

Phonics and Spelling

Word Builder

Words with ch Write **ch** to finish each word. Then write each word under the correct label.

Animals	Things to Eat	Places to Sit
1.	3.	5.
2.	4.	6.

Work Together Write four more words that begin or end with **ch**. Work with a friend.

7.	9.
8.	10.

Vocabulary Enrichment

Social Studies

Ranching All the words in the box have something to do with ranching. Write those words to finish the beginning of this story. Use your Spelling Dictionary.

Spelling Word Link

sheep

graze
cattle
herd
stray

Life on a Ranch

A rancher leads a __(1)__ of cows. Her dog runs after a __(2)__ calf. The __(3)__ are going to a field. They will __(4)__ there all day.

1. ____________
2. ____________
3. ____________
4. ____________

Yes or No? Write **yes** or **no** to answer each question.

5. Would sheep **graze** in a barn?
6. Does a **stray** stay close to a group?
7. Is there more than one cow in a **herd**?
8. Would you call a group of pigs **cattle**?

5. ____________
6. ____________
7. ____________
8. ____________

Fact File

Many songs and stories are about ranching. Agnes De Mille, a famous dancer, even made a dance about a cowgirl on a ranch. The dance is called **Rodeo**.

UNIT 17

Words Spelled with th or wh

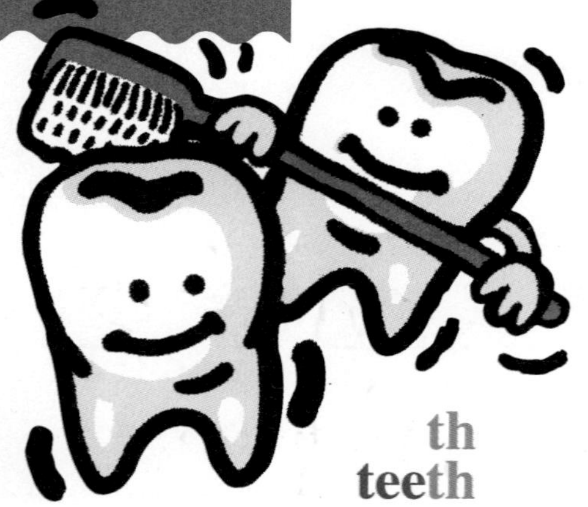

Read and Say

READ the sentences. **SAY** each word in dark print.

Basic Words	
1. teeth	I must brush my **teeth**.
2. when	You know **when** to clap.
3. then	Jess will leave by **then**.
4. wheel	Turn the **wheel** fast!
5. with	Can you play **with** me?
6. what	I will get **what** I want.
7. than	He is older **than** I am.
8. while	Can I read for a **while**?
9. them	Hit the ball to **them**.
10. which	Pick **which** toy you want.

Think and Write

Each word is spelled with **th** or **wh**. The letters **th** spell two different sounds in these words. The letters **wh** spell one sound.

the **th** sounds → **th**en, tee**th**

the **wh** sound → **wh**en

A. Write **five** Basic Words spelled with **th**.
B. Write **five** Basic Words spelled with **wh**.

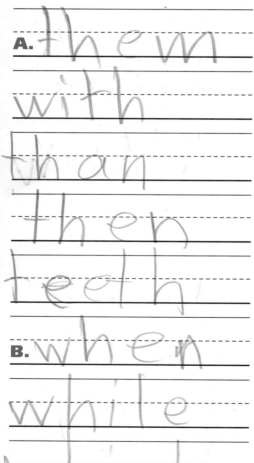

A. them
with
than
then
teeth

B. when
while
which
what
wheel

Review
11. white 12. bath

Challenge
13. mouth 14. whistle

Independent Practice

Spelling Strategy The sounds that begin **then** and end **teeth** may be spelled **th.** The sound that begins **when** may be spelled **wh**.

Phonics Write Basic Words to answer the questions.

1. Which word has the short **a** sound?
2. Which word rhymes with **smile**?

3–4. Which two words have the short **i** sound?

5–6. Which two **th** words have the short **e** sound?

Word Clues Write a Basic Word for each clue.

7. This question word has a **hat** in it.
8. This question word has a **hen** in it.

Word Pairs Write a Basic Word to finish the second sentence in each pair.

9. Some things are **square** like a **box**.
   Some things are **round** like a _______.
10. More than one **foot** is **feet**.
    More than one **tooth** is _______.

Phonics

1. than
2. while
3. with
4. which
5. witht
6. which

Word Clues

7. what
8. then

Word Pairs

9. wheel
10. teeth

UNIT
17

Dictionary

Entry Words You know you use ABC order to find words in a dictionary. When entry words begin with the same two letters, you must look at the third letter of each word. See how these words are put in ABC order.

te**a**m te**e**th te**n**t

Practice Write the word in each group that would come first in the dictionary. Use ABC order.

1.	why	white	whose	**4.**	wheel	who	while
2.	them	thin	than	**5.**	bath	baby	ball
3.	play	plug	plow	**6.**	sink	silly	side

Entry Words

1. white
2. than
3. play
4. wheel
5. baby
6. side

Review: Spelling Spree

Rhyme Time Finish the sentences. Write a Basic or Review Word to rhyme with the word in dark print.

7. I left a muddy **path** all the way to the ______.
8. I see bugs on a **stem**, and I don't like ______.
9. How would it **feel** to be round like a ______?
10. The tail of my **kite** is red, green, and ______.
11. This is the last **mile** I will run for a ______!
12. Now and ______ I count to **ten**.

Rhyme Time

7. bath
8. them
9. wheel
10. white
11. while
12. then

Write each spelling word in a sentence. Practice with a family member any words you spelled wrong.

Proofreading and Writing

Proofread for Spelling Proofread these jokes. Use proofreading marks to fix six spelling mistakes.

while
Example: Tell me a joke ~~wile~~ we eat.

Marta: Do you know wich teeth cry more thann the others?

Nick: I know! Baby teeth do!

Carrie: Do you know wat to do wen your teth fall out?

Jon: Of course! Stick them back in whith white toothpaste!

Basic

1. teeth
2. when
3. then
4. wheel
5. with
6. what
7. than
8. while
9. them
10. which

Review

11. white
12. bath

Challenge

13. mouth
14. whistle

Proofreading Marks

- ∧ Add
- Delete
- ≡ Make a capital letter
- / Make a small letter

Write a Label

Pretend you invented a new toothpaste. Draw a picture of your toothpaste tube and write a label for it. Tell how to use your toothpaste and why it is special. Try to use spelling words.

Proofreading Tip **Read your paper aloud to a friend.**

Phonics and Spelling

Word Builder

Words with th **and** wh Write **th** or **wh** to finish each word. Then write the word.

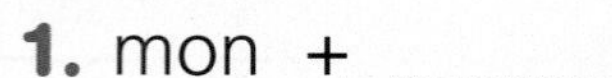

1. mon + _______ **4.** _______ + orn

2. pa + _______ **5.** _______ + ale

3. _______ + irty **6.** _______ + isker

1. ____________

2. ____________

3. ____________

4. ____________

5. ____________

6. ____________

Work Together Write three more words that begin or end with **th**. Work with a friend.

7. ____________ **8.** ____________ **9.** ____________

Vocabulary Enrichment

Careers

Dentist All the words in the box have something to do with dentists. Write those words to finish this list. Use your Spelling Dictionary.

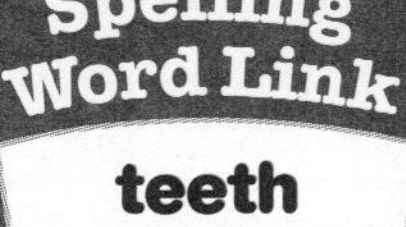

toothbrush
rinse
roots
braces

Dr. Dan's Checklist

- Have Cara __(1)__ her mouth with water.
- Look at the __(2)__ of her teeth on an x-ray.
- Put __(3)__ on her teeth.
- Give her a __(4)__ when I am done.

1. ____________
2. ____________
3. ____________
4. ____________

Try This CHALLENGE

Riddle Time! Write a word from the box to answer each riddle.

5. What makes crooked things straight?
6. What do both trees and teeth have?
7. What kind of brush is not used for hair?
8. How do you get rid of soap or toothpaste?

5. ____________
6. ____________
7. ____________
8. ____________

Fact File

Did you know that President George Washington had to wear false teeth? In fact, he had four pairs! They were made of many things, such as gold and ivory.

18 Review: Units 13–17

1. train
2. mail
3. play
4. rain
5. hay
6. pay
7. green
8. clean
9. tree
10. read
11. please
12. be

Unit 13 More Long a Spellings pages 96–101

ā
train

train	mail	play
pay	hay	rain

Spelling Strategy The long **a** sound may be spelled **ay** or **ai**.

Change the letters in dark print. Write spelling words.

1. trai**l** **2.** mai**d** **3.** **gr**ay **4.** **r**ail

Write the missing spelling words.

5. The _______ in our field is high.

6. We will _______ someone to cut it.

Unit 14 More Long e Spellings pages 102–107

ē
clean

clean	please	green
be	tree	read

Spelling Strategy The long **e** sound may be spelled **e, ee,** or **ea.**

Write the spelling word that goes with each word.

7. color **8.** wash **9.** branch **10.** story

Write the missing spelling words.

11. Will you _______ help me wash the dishes?

12. Then we will _______ done with our work.

Unit 15 The Vowel Sound in ball pages 108–113

dog	call	saw
all	draw	log

Spelling Strategy The vowel sound in **dog** may be spelled **o, aw,** or **a** before **ll.**

Write the missing spelling words.

Gram and Papa ___(**13**)___ us in for lunch. We ___(**14**)___ wash quickly. I bring in a ___(**15**)___ for the fire.

Write the spelling word that goes with each place.

16. tool shed **17.** art class **18.** pet shop

Unit 16 Words with sh or ch pages 114–119

sheep	chase	chop
each	dish	ship

Spelling Strategy the **sh** sound → **sheep, dish**
the **ch** sound → **chop, each**

Write the spelling word that rhymes with each word.

19. peach **21.** trip
20. stop **22.** deep

Write the missing spelling words.

23. One day the cat ate from the dog's _______.
24. Then the dog began to _______ the cat!

13. call
14. all
15. log
16. saw
17. draw
18. dog
19. each
20. chop
21. ship
22. sheep
23. dish
24. chase

UNIT
18

25. than
26. them
27. teeth
28. then
29. wheel
30. while
31. great
32. the
33. people
34. catch
35. they
36. sure

Unit 17 Words with th or wh pages 120–125

th
teeth

teeth	then	wheel
than	while	them

Spelling Strategy the **th** sounds → **teeth, then**
the **wh** sound → **wheel**

Change the letters in dark print. Write spelling words.

25. **pl**an **26.** **st**em

Write the missing spelling words.

27. brush your _______ **29.** steering _______

28. now and _______ **30.** once in a _______

Elephant Words Units 13–17 pages 96–125

SURE

they	great	the
people	catch	sure

Spelling Strategy Elephant Words have unusual spellings. Check them carefully when you write them.

Write the missing spelling words.

We had a **(31)** time at **(32)** ball game. Many **(33)** came to see Mike Magoo **(34)** balls. One player hit the balls so hard, **(35)** almost knocked Mike down! I am **(36)** Mike is the best player.

Spelling-Meaning Strategy

Word Families

Look at this word family. Remember that words in the same family are alike in spelling and meaning.

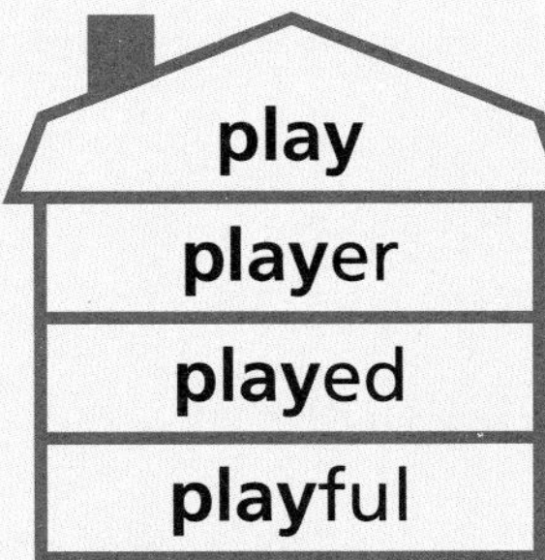

Kim loves to **play** tennis.
She is a good **player**.
She **played** a game on Monday.
Her **playful** dog chased the balls.

Think How are the words in this family alike in meaning? How are they alike in spelling?

Apply and Extend

Write a word from the play **family in each sentence.**

1. We watched the seals _______.
2. One _______ seal had a ball.
3. He _______ with it in the water.
4. He looked like a soccer _______!

1. ________
2. ________
3. ________
4. ________

With a partner, think of words in these families. Make a list for each family.

Check the Word Families list that begins on page 272. Did you miss any words? Add them to your lists.

Literature and Writing

from

A Thousand Pails of Water

by Ronald Roy

The story is about a little boy who lived in Japan. Who is this boy in this story, and what is the story about?

Yukio lived in a village where people fished to make their living.

One day Yukio walked down to the sea. As he walked by the edge of the water, he saw a whale. The whale was stuck between some rocks.

Yukio knew that the whale would not live long out of the sea.

"I will help you," he said to the whale. But how? The whale was huge.

Think and Discuss

1. Who is this story about? What does he find by the water?
2. What problem must Yukio solve?
3. Do you think this is the **beginning**, the **middle**, or the **end** of the story? Why?
4. What do you think will happen in the rest of this story?

The Writing Process

Story

What kinds of stories do you like? Write a story you would like to read. Follow the guidelines. Use the Writing Process.

1 Prewriting

- Make a story map. Draw or write about what happens in the beginning, the middle, and the end of your story.

2 Draft

- Write two beginnings. Which one do you like better?

3 Revise

- Add details that tell what your characters say and do.
- Remember to use your Thesaurus to find exact words.
- Read your story to a friend. Make changes.

4 Proofread

- Did you spell each word correctly?
- Did you use words that compare correctly?

5 Publish

- Copy your story neatly.
- Add a title.
- Read your story aloud to classmates.

Guidelines for Writing a Story

✓ Use details that will make your characters interesting.

✓ The story should have a beginning, a middle, and an end.

✓ Write a title that will make the reader want to find out more.

Composition Words

they
people
saw
wish
when
which

UNIT 19

Words That End with nd, ng, or nk

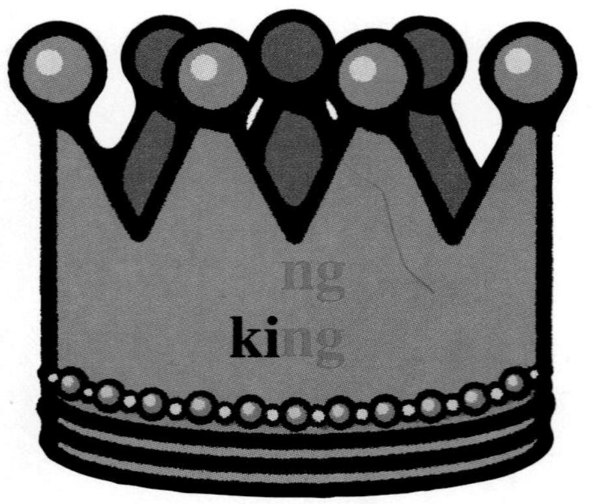

Read and Say

READ the sentences. **SAY** each word in dark print.

Basic Words

1.	king	*king*	A **king** rules a country.
2.	thank	*thank*	Will you **thank** her today?
3.	hand	*hand*	Hold my **hand**.
4.	sing	*sing*	I like to hear you **sing**.
5.	and	*and*	He has a dog **and** a cat.
6.	think	*think*	I **think** you are nice.
7.	bring	*bring*	Did you **bring** the ball?
8.	long	*long*	Swans have **long** necks.
9.	end	*end*	It is the **end** of the day.
10.	thing	*thing*	What is that **thing**?

Think and Write

Each word ends with the consonants **nd**, **ng**, or **nk**. In words that end with the consonant cluster **nd**, you hear the sounds of **n** and **d**. In words that end with **ng** or **nk**, you may not hear the **n** sound.

nd → ha**nd**
ng → ki**ng**
nk → tha**nk**

A. Write **three** Basic Words that end with **nd**.
B. Write **five** Basic Words that end with **ng**.
C. Write **two** Basic Words that end with **nk**.

Review
11. an **12.** men

Challenge
13. grand **14.** young

Independent Practice

Spelling Strategy You hear the sounds of **n** and **d** in words that end with the consonant cluster **nd**. You may not hear the sounds of **n** in words that end with the consonants **ng** or **nk**.

Phonics Write Basic Words to answer the questions.

1. Which word begins with a vowel sound and rhymes with **stand**?

2–4. Which three words begin with the same sound?

Word Groups Think how the words in each group are alike. Write the missing Basic Words.

5. shoulder, arm, _______
6. take, carry, _______
7. prince, queen, _______
8. hum, whistle, _______

Word Meaning Write the Basic Word that means the opposite of each word in dark print.

9. We want to hear the **beginning** of the story.
10. It is a **short** fairy tale about a wise princess.

Phonics

1. end
2. thang
3. thing
4. think

Word Groups

5. hand
6. bring
7. king
8. sing

Word Meaning

9. end
10. long

Fill-In Fun

1. ______
2. ______
3. ______
4. ______
5. ______
6. ______

Word Search

7. ______
8. ______
9. ______
10. ______
11. ______
12. ______

Review: Spelling Spree

Fill-In Fun Write the missing Basic or Review Words.

1. ______ and women
2. short and ______
3. ______ and queen
4. beginning and ______
5. ______ and foot
6. ______ and dance

Once upon a time...

Word Search Write the Basic or Review Word that is hidden in each sentence. Each hidden word is made with letters from the end of one word and the beginning of the next.

Example: You must co(me n)ow! **men**

7. We rub rings to make them shine.
8. Where are the three thin knights?
9. They built a new stone tower.
10. Do the queen's birds fly higher than kites?
11. The dragon began dreaming of caves.
12. Prince Hal has thin green gloves.

How Are You Doing?

Write your spelling words in ABC order. Practice with a partner any words you spelled wrong.

Proofreading and Writing

Proofread: Spelling and Capital Letters

Always begin the names of the days of the week with capital letters.

Monday **W**ednesday **S**unday

Proofread this sign. Use proofreading marks to fix four spelling mistakes and two missing capital letters.

Example: On friday the queen will ~~thenk~~ thank us.

The king returns on wednesday night. All min an women will meet him on thursday morning. Come to the ind of the great hall to sing a song for him. If you play an instrument, birng it with you.

Basic

1. king
2. thank
3. hand
4. sing
5. and
6. think
7. bring
8. long
9. end
10. thing

Review

11. an
12. men

Challenge

13. grand
14. young

Proofreading Marks

- ∧ Add
- Delete
- ≡ Make a capital letter
- / Make a small letter

Write a Weekly Plan

Pretend you are a king or a queen. Make a plan for the week. Tell one or two things you would do on each day. Try to use spelling words.

Queen's Plan

Proofreading Tip

Check that you began the names of the days of the week with capital letters.

Phonics and Spelling

Rhyming Words

Words with nd **or** ng Make rhyming words that end with the consonants **nd** or **ng**. Use the letters in the picture.

b
w
s
sw
and
ing
st
sl

1. ______
2. ______
3. ______
4. ______
5. ______
6. ______

Show What You Know! Finish this poem about the picture. Use words that you wrote on this page.

The king fell off his _______.
Now his arm is in a _______!

7. ______
8. ______

Vocabulary Enrichment

Social Studies

Castles and Kings All the words in the box have something to do with castles and kings. Write the words to finish this invitation. Use your Spelling Dictionary.

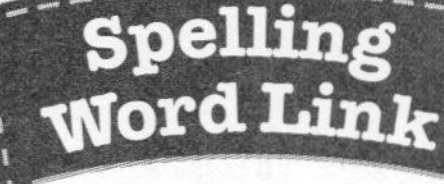

king

- throne
- castle
- page
- feast

July 2, 1998

Dear People of the Kingdom,

Please come to the King's birthday party on Sunday, July 11. The doors to the __(1)__ will open at one o'clock. The King will sit on his __(2)__ and greet everyone. The cooks are making a big __(3)__! When lunch is ready, a young __(4)__ will tell you where to sit.

Your friend,
The Queen

1. ____________
2. ____________
3. ____________
4. ____________

Try This CHALLENGE

Clue Match Write a word from the box for each clue.

5. This can be made of sand or stone.
6. This can be found in a book or in a castle.
7. This is a chair for a very special person.
8. Many people can enjoy this together.

5. ____________
6. ____________
7. ____________
8. ____________

Fact File

Castles were damp and chilly! To help keep the cold out, heavy pieces of cloth were hung on the walls. Colorful pictures or designs were woven into them.

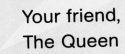

UNIT 20

Words That End with s or es

es
bikes

Read and Say

READ the sentences. **SAY** each word in dark print.

Basic Words

1. dishes	*dishes*	I will wash the **dishes**.
2. dresses	*dresses*	Try on these **dresses**.
3. bells	*bells*	Did you ring the **bells**?
4. boxes	*boxes*	Jacob packed the **boxes**.
5. beaches	*beaches*	The **beaches** are sandy.
6. days	*days*	I was away for two **days**.
7. bikes	*bikes*	Ride your **bikes** home.
8. wishes	*wishes*	Liza made six **wishes**.
9. things	*things*	He has ten **things** to do.
10. names	*names*	They told us their **names**.
11. children	*children*	Are the **children** home?

Think and Write

Each word names more than one of something. The **s** and **es** endings make these words mean more than one.

s → bell**s**, bike**s**

es → dress**es**, box**es**, dish**es**, beach**es**

How is the Elephant Word different?

A. Write **five** Basic Words that have the **s** ending.

B. Write **five** Basic Words that have the **es** ending.

C. Now write the Elephant Word.

A.

B.

C.

Review

12. cups **13.** frogs

Challenge

14. coins **15.** classes

Independent Practice

Spelling Strategy Add **s** to most words to name more than one. Add **es** to words that end with **s**, **x**, **sh**, or **ch** to name more than one.

Phonics Write Basic Words to answer the questions.

1. Which word begins like 30 ?
2. Which word begins with the same consonant cluster as [drum] ?
3. Which word has the long **i** sound?
4. Which word rhymes with **tells**?

Word Clues Write a Basic Word for each clue.

5. People make them at birthday parties.
6. Sand castles may be found there.
7. People are known by them.
8. Gifts may come in them.
9. Nights come after them.
10. Food is put on them.

Elephant Word Think of the missing letters in the Elephant Word. Write the word.

11. The **child** ren sold juice to earn money.

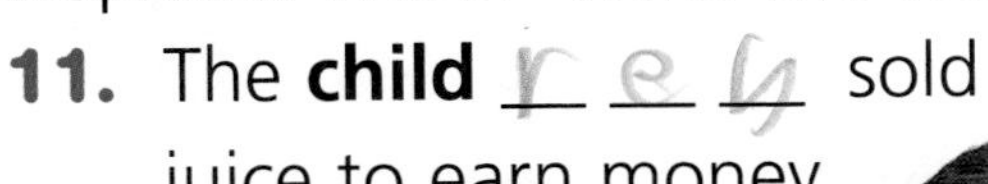

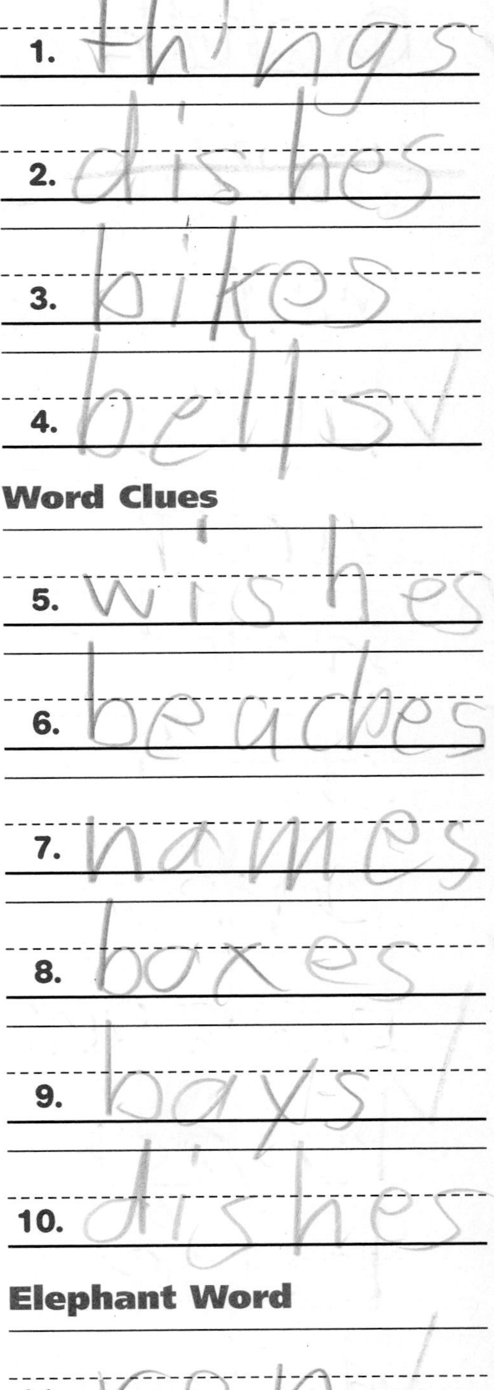

Phonics

1. things
2. dishes
3. bikes
4. bells

Word Clues

5. wishes
6. beaches
7. names
8. boxes
9. days
10. dishes

Elephant Word

11. ren

Code Breaker

1.
2.
3.
4.

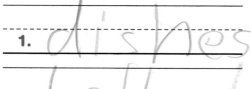

Letter Math

5.
6.
7.

Letter Swap

8.
9.
10.
11.
12.

Review: Spelling Spree

Code Breaker Use the code to write Basic Words.

⊖ = w	⊥ = d	☆ = s	☽ = g
∗ = n	● = i	◇ = h	□ = t
∩ = e	↑ = b	▲ = l	

Example: ☆ ∩ □ ☆ = **sets**

1. ⊥ ● ☆ ◇ ∩ ☆ **3.** □ ◇ ● ∗ ☽ ☆

2. ↑ ∩ ▲ ▲ ☆ **4.** ⊖ ● ☆ ◇ ∩ ☆

Letter Math Add and take away letters to make Basic or Review Words. Write the words.

5. d r + l e s s − l + e s = ______

6. c h + w i l d − w + r e n = ______

7. f r + l o g − l + s = ______

Letter Swap Change the first letter in each word to make a Basic or Review Word. Write the words.

8. **p**ups **10.** **r**ays **12.** **g**ames

9. **p**eaches **11.** **h**ikes

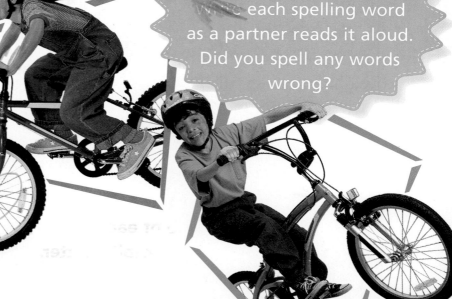

How Are You Doing?

Write each spelling word as a partner reads it aloud. Did you spell any words wrong?

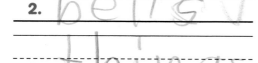

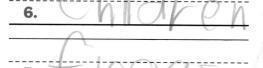

Independent Practice

Spelling Strategy The vowel sound in **go**, **boat**, and **slow** is the long **o** sound. The long **o** sound may be spelled **o**, **oa**, or **ow**.

Phonics Write Basic Words to answer the questions.

1. Which word begins with a vowel sound?
2. Which word begins with the first sound you hear in  ?

3–4. Which two words rhyme with **float**?

5–6. Which two words begin with the same consonant clusters as **slide** and **green**?

Word Meaning Write the Basic Word that means the opposite of each word below.

7. come **8.** asked **9.** yes **10.** hot

Elephant Words Write an Elephant Word to answer each question.

11. Which word ends with the letter **o** but does not have the long **o** sound?
12. Which word has the long **o** sound spelled **oe**?

Phonics

1. old
2. show
3. boat
4. coat
5. slow
6. grow

Word Meaning

7. go
8. told
9. no
10. cold

Elephant Words

11. do
12. toe

UNIT

21

Dictionary

Finding the Right Meaning Some words have more than one meaning. A dictionary lists all the meanings of a word. Each meaning is numbered.

> **coat** **1.** A type of outer clothing with sleeves: *I wore a warm* ***coat****.* **2.** An outer covering of fur or hair on an animal: *I brushed the horse's* ***coat****.*

Practice Write **1** or **2** to tell which meaning of **coat** is used in each sentence.

1. The fisherman wore a wool **coat**.
2. Rags licked his sandy **coat** clean.
3. A seal's thick **coat** helps keep it warm.
4. I bought a heavy **coat** to wear sailing.

Review: Spelling Spree

Word Hunt Write the Basic or Review Word you see in each longer word.

5. sayings
6. tugboat
7. nosy
8. goat
9. folder
10. tiptoe
11. hairdo
12. also

How Are You Doing?
Write each word in a sentence. Practice with a family member any words you spelled wrong.

Dictionary

1. 1.
2. 2.
3. 2.
4. 1.

Word Hunt

5. say
6. boat
7. so
8. go
9. old
10. toe
11. do
12. so

Proofreading and Writing

Proofread for Spelling Proofread these tips for whale watching. Use proofreading marks to fix six spelling mistakes.

Example: **How long doe whales live?**

Tips for Whale Watching

- **Take a warm koat. The boat is sloe. You will be out in the coald wind for a long time.**
- **Listen to the captain. You will be toweld how the whales live and how they gro to be so big.**
- **Don't forget to sho me your pictures!**

Basic

1. boat
2. cold
3. go
4. slow
5. no
6. old
7. coat
8. grow
9. told
10. show
11. toe
12. do

Review

13. so
14. say

Challenge

15. coast
16. rainbow

Proofreading Marks

- ∧ Add
- Delete
- ≡ Make a capital letter
- / Make a small letter

Write a Program

The animals in the ocean are having a talent show! Write a program for the show. List all the animals and tell what they might do. Try to use spelling words.

TALENT SHOW

Proofreading Tip

Proofread for one kind of error at a time.

Vocabulary Enrichment

Word Builder

Spelling Word Link
boat

Using a Thesaurus Write a word you could use in place of the underlined word. Use your Thesaurus. The first one is done for you.

We were ready to ~~go~~ leave. An old sailor gave us directions. Our boat went out to sea. It was quiet on the water. I shivered in the cold air.

Show What You Know! On another sheet of paper, write a sentence about each picture. Use a different word for **say** each time. Use your Thesaurus.

Science

The Seashore All the words in the box have something to do with the seashore. Write those words to finish this poster. Use your Spelling Dictionary.

Spelling Word Link

boat

ocean
jellyfish
shrimp
crab

SEA ANIMALS

Many animals live in the __(1)__. A __(2)__ has a fan-shaped tail. A __(3)__ is hard and has claws. A __(4)__ has a very soft body.

1. ____________
2. ____________
3. ____________
4. ____________

Try This CHALLENGE

Riddle Time! Write a word from the box to answer each riddle.

5. I am not angry, but I might pinch you.
6. My waves do not mean "good-bye."
7. You might make fun of me for being small.
8. Part of my name tastes good with peanut butter.

5. ____________
6. ____________
7. ____________
8. ____________

Fact File

There are many different kinds of whales. The blue whale is the largest animal in the world. It can weigh more than 200,000 pounds.

UNIT 22

The Vowel Sounds in moon and book

Read and Say

READ the sentences. **SAY** each word in dark print.

Basic Words

1. zoo	*zoo*	We saw bears at the **zoo**.
2. food	*food*	He will eat his **food**.
3. look	*look*	I like to **look** at the fish.
4. moon	*moon*	The **moon** is in the sky.
5. book	*book*	Read this **book**.
6. soon	*soon*	They will come **soon**.
7. took	*took*	Rafi **took** my hat.
8. good	*good*	She had a **good** time.
9. room	*room*	Kim has a big **room**.
10. foot	*foot*	I have a cut on my **foot**.
11. you	*you*	Did **you** feed the goats?
12. who	*who*	Seth knows **who** called.

Think and Write

Most of the words are spelled with the letters **oo**. These letters make two different vowel sounds.

the vowel sound → z**oo**, f**oo**d

the vowel sound → l**oo**k, t**oo**k

How are the Elephant Words different?

A. Write **seven** Basic Words with the vowel sound. Remember the Elephant Words.

B. Write **five** Basic Words with the vowel sound.

A. moon
room
zoo
food
you
who
soon

B. book
took
look
foot
good

Review
13. clap **14.** like

Challenge
15. hoof **16.** moose

Independent Practice

Spelling Strategy The vowel sounds in **moon** and **book** may be spelled **oo**.

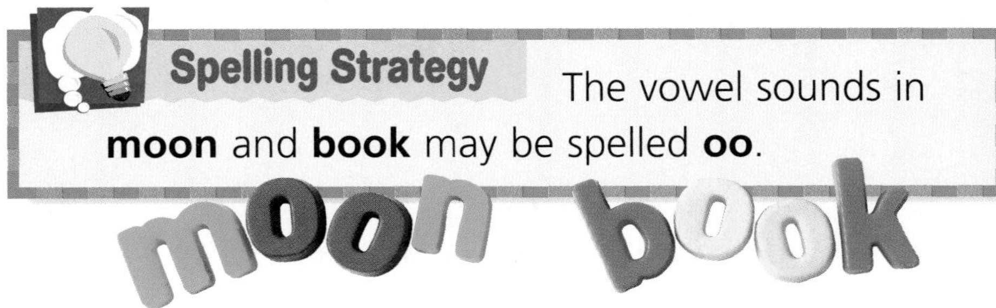

Phonics Write Basic Words to answer the questions.

1. Which word rhymes with **wood**?

2–3. Which two words rhyme with **noon**?

4–6. Which three words rhyme with **cook**?

Word Pairs Write the missing Basic Words.

7. You see **paintings** at a **museum**.
You see **animals** at a _______.

8. A **jet** is one kind of **plane**.
A **kitchen** is one kind of _______.

9. You **drink** your **milk**.
You **eat** your _______.

10. You **catch** with your **hand**.
You **kick** with your _______.

Elephant Words Write an Elephant Word to answer each question.

11. Which word has the ☾ sound spelled **o**?

12. Which word has the ☾ sound spelled **ou**?

Phonics

1. good
2. moon
3. soon
4. book
5. took
6. look

Word Pairs

7. zoo
8. room
9. food
10. foot

Elephant Words

11. who
12. you

UNIT
22

Review: Spelling Spree

Puzzle Play Write a Basic or Review Word for each clue. Use the letters that would be in the boxes to spell an animal in the zoo.

1. a place with four walls r o o [m]
2. the opposite of **bad** g [o] o d
3. a short time from now s o o [n]
4. to see with your eyes l o o [k]
5. to think someone or something is nice l i k [e]
6. a person who is not me, him, or her [y] o u

Secret Word: m o n k e y

Hidden Words Find the hidden Basic or Review Word in each box. Write the word.

7. wethwholle 8. stuttookom 9. kasclappat

Jobs Match Write the Basic Word that tells where the person works or what the person makes or works with on the job.

10. astronaut
11. animal trainer
12. author

How Are You Doing?

List the spelling words that are hard for you. Practice them with a family member.

Puzzle Play

1. room
2. good
3. soon
4. look
5. like
6. you

Hidden Words

7. who
8. took
9. clap

Jobs Match

10. moon
11. zoo
12. book

Proofreading and Writing

Proofread: Spelling and Capital Letters
Always begin the names of the months of the year with capital letters.

January **A**pril **N**ovember

Proofread this page from a travel book. Use proofreading marks to fix four spelling mistakes and two missing capital letters.

Example: Is december a ~~goud~~ good time to go?

You will ~~lik~~ like Betty's Wild Animal Park in june or july. There is ~~rume~~ room for animals to run there and plenty of ~~fode~~ food for them to eat. The best way to explore the zoo is on ~~fot~~ foot.

Basic

1. zoo
2. food
3. look
4. moon
5. book
6. soon
7. took
8. good
9. room
10. foot
11. you
12. who

Review

13. clap
14. like

Challenge

15. hoof
16. moose

Proofreading Marks

- ^ Add
- Delete
- ≡ Make a capital letter
- / Make a small letter

Write Some Riddles

I am orange. You can pick me in October. What am I? Write riddles. Try to use spelling words and months of the year in your clues. Have a friend guess the answers.

Check that you began the name of each month with a capital letter.

Phonics and Spelling

Rhyming Words

More moon **and** book **Words** Make rhyming words that have the **moon** and **book** vowel sounds. Use the letters in the picture.

oom	ook	ool
1.	4.	7.
2.	5.	8.
3.	6.	9.

Work Together On another sheet of paper, write two silly sentences. Use words that you wrote on this page. Work with a friend.

Science

Zoos All the words in the box have something to do with zoos. Write those words to finish this sign. Use your Spelling Dictionary.

Spelling Word Link

zoo

tame
diet
groom
perch

Parrots like to __(1)__ on branches. They __(2)__ their own feathers. Fruit is part of their __(3)__. A __(4)__ parrot makes a good pet.

1. ______
2. ______
3. ______
4. ______

Try This CHALLENGE

Yes or No? Write **yes** or **no** to answer each question.

5. Would a **tame** monkey live in a jungle?
6. Do some animals **groom** themselves?
7. Could an elephant **perch** on a branch?
8. Could a bear live on a **diet** of rocks?

5. ______
6. ______
7. ______
8. ______

Fact File

The biggest parrots are called **macaws**. They can be as big as three feet long from head to tail! Macaws live in Mexico and in Central and South America.

UNIT 23

Homophones

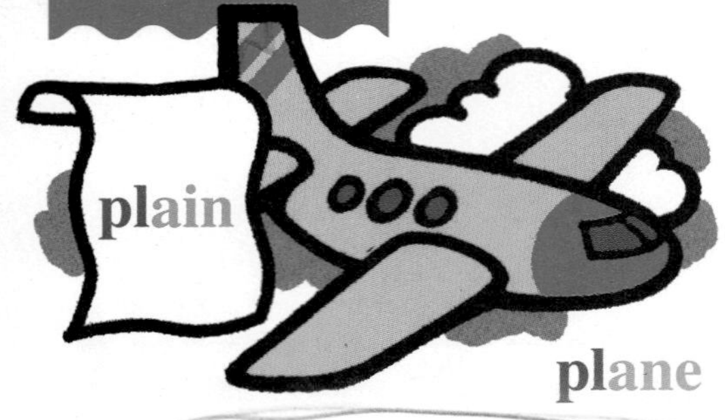

Read and Say

READ the sentences. **SAY** each word in dark print.

Basic Words

1. plane	*plane*	Zack can fly a **plane**.
2. plain	*plain*	She likes **plain** food.
3. tail	*tail*	My dog Pal wags his **tail**.
4. tale	*tale*	Mom told us a **tale**.
5. rode	*rode*	Mia **rode** on the bus.
6. road	*road*	Stay on this **road**.
7. hole	*hole*	How deep is that **hole**?
8. whole	*whole*	I ate the **whole** cake!
9. to	*to*	We will go **to** the club.
10. too	*too*	Can they play **too**?
11. two	*two*	Eric has **two** bikes.

Think and Write

Each word is a homophone. **Homophones** are words that sound alike but do not have the same spelling or the same meaning.

HOMOPHONE	MEANING
pl**ane**	an airplane
pl**ain**	not fancy

How are the Elephant Words different?

A. Write the first **eight** Basic Words in order. Then draw a circle around each pair of homophones.

B. Now write the **three** Elephant Words.

A.

B.

Review
12. see **13.** by

Challenge
14. threw **15.** through

Independent Practice

Spelling Strategy **Homophones** are words that sound alike but do not have the same spelling or the same meaning.

Phonics Write Basic Words to answer the question.

1–3. Which three words have the long **o** sound spelled with the **o**-consonant-**e** pattern?

Word Meaning Write the Basic Word that means the same or almost the same as each word below.

4. street **5.** simple **6.** story

Word Pairs Write a Basic Word to finish the second sentence in each pair.

7. A bird **flaps** its **wings**.
A dog **wags** its _______.

8. You **drive** a car.
You **fly** a _______.

Elephant Words Write the missing Elephant Words.

9. Sam and I have _______ kites.

10. Do you have a kite _______?

11. We can all go _______ the park and fly them!

Phonics

1. rode
2. road
3. hole

Word Meaning

4. road
5. plane
6. tale

Word Pairs

7. tail
8. plain

Elephant Words

9. two
10. too
11. to

UNIT
23

Dictionary

Using Homophones When you do not know which homophone to write, look up the words in a dictionary. The meanings will help you decide.

> **hole** An opening into or through something:
> *I found a **hole** in my shoe.*
> ♦ *These sound alike* **hole, whole**.

Practice Write the correct word in dark print to finish each sentence. Use your Spelling Dictionary.

1. Grandma lives ______ the airport. **(buy, by)**
2. Dad read me a ______ about jets. **(tale, tail)**
3. Do all jets have only ______ wings? **(two, to)**

Review: Spelling Spree

Hink Pinks Write two Basic Words to answer each question. The two words must rhyme.

4–5. What is a jet that is not fancy? a ____ ____

6–7. What is all of something you dig? a ____ ____

Letter Swap Make Basic Words by changing the letters in dark print. Write the words.

8. r**i**de
9. **s**ale
10. **p**ail
11. **l**oad

How Are You Doing?

Write your words in ABC order. Practice with a family member any words you spelled wrong.

Using Homophones

1. ______
2. ______
3. ______

Hink Pinks

4. ______
5. ______
6. ______
7. ______

Letter Swap

8. ______
9. ______
10. ______
11. ______

Proofreading and Writing

Proofread for Spelling Proofread this ad. Use proofreading marks to fix five spelling mistakes.

Example: We ~~road~~ rode high in the sky.

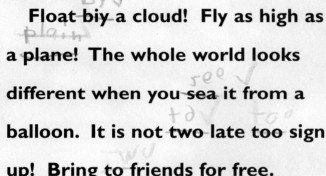

BALLOON RIDES

Float biy a cloud! Fly as high as a plane! The whole world looks different when you sea it from a balloon. It is not two late too sign up! Bring to friends for free.

Basic

1. plane
2. plain
3. tail
4. tale
5. rode
6. road
7. hole
8. whole
9. to
10. too
11. two

Review

12. see
13. by

Challenge

14. threw
15. through

Proofreading Marks

- ∧ Add
- Delete
- ≡ Make a capital letter
- / Make a small letter

Write a Description

Pretend you invented a new flying machine. Tell about the machine and how it works. Try to use spelling words. Read your description to a friend. Have your friend draw a picture of the machine from your description.

A computer spell checker cannot tell you if you have used the correct homophone.

Vocabulary Enrichment

Word Builder

Spelling Word Link

see

seeing
seashell
seen
sea horse
sightseeing
seashore

Building Word Families Some homophones belong to word families, just as other words do. Words in the same word family are alike in spelling and meaning.

Help build these houses. Write each word from the box in the correct house. The first one is done for you.

see "to look"	sea "the ocean"
seeing	

Show What You Know! Write a word from one of the houses to finish each sentence. Use your Spelling Dictionary.

1. We went _____ on the bus.
2. I found a _____ on the beach.
3. The _____ curled its tail.
4. I have _____ the new movie.
5. Miguel is _____ his father after school.
6. Liane made a sandcastle at the _____.

1. ____ 3. ____ 5. ____

2. ____ 4. ____ 6. ____

Social Studies

Things That Fly All the words in the box have something to do with things that fly. Use those words to finish this timetable. Use your Spelling Dictionary.

Spelling Word Link

plane

pilot
glide
land
crew

12:30	The __(1)__ turns on the engines and flies the plane.
1:00	Some __(2)__ members serve you lunch.
2:00	The plane will __(3)__ over Swan Lake.
2:30	You should __(4)__ in Swanville.

1. ____________
2. ____________
3. ____________
4. ____________

Write a Message Pretend you are a skywriter. Write one or two messages. Try to use some words from the box on this page.

Fact File

In 1903, Orville Wright made the first flight in an airplane. His famous ride lasted only 12 seconds. He flew just 120 feet, which is about as long as three school buses!

24 Review: Units 19–23

1. end
2. thank
3. think
4. and
5. sing
6. bring
7. dresses
8. boxes
9. beaches
10. bikes
11. days
12. wishes

Unit 19 Words with nd, ng, or nk pages 132–137

ng
king

thank	sing	and
think	bring	end

Spelling Strategy

Some words end with the consonants **nd, ng,** or **nk.**

Write the spelling word that rhymes with each word.

1. send **2.** bank **3.** pink **4.** land

Write the missing spelling words.

5. We will _______ songs at home tonight.

6. Grandpa will _______ his banjo and play for us.

Unit 20 Words with s or es pages 138–143

es
bikes

dresses	boxes	beaches
days	bikes	wishes

Spelling Strategy

s → days, bikes

es → dresses, boxes, wishes, beaches

Write the spelling word that goes with each word.

7. skirts **8.** cardboard **9.** sand **10.** tires

Write the missing words.

11. How many _______ are there until my birthday?

12. I will make _______ as I blow out the candles.

Unit 21 More Long o Spellings pages 144–149

boat	go	slow
old	coat	told

Spelling Strategy The long **o** sound may be spelled **o, oa,** or **ow.**

Write the spelling word that means the opposite.

13. fast **14.** new **15.** stop

Write the missing spelling words.

Dad __(**16**)__ me I could go for a ride in the __(**17**)__. I put on my __(**18**)__ and ran to the dock.

Unit 22 Sounds in moon and book pages 150–155

food	look	moon
took	good	room

Spelling Strategy The vowel sounds in **moon** and **look** may be spelled **oo.**

Write the spelling word that is hidden in each box.

19. uslookim **20.** pagoodye **21.** otookacg

Write the missing spelling words.

We had a snack in our __(**22**)__ late last night. We ate our __(**23**)__ by the light of the __(**24**)__.

13. slow
14. old
15. go
16. told
17. boat
18. coat
19. look
20. good
21. took
22. room
23. food
24. moon

25. rode
26. hole
27. road
28. tale
29. tail
30. whole
31. children
32. who
33. to
34. two
35. too
36. do

Unit 23 Homophones pages 156–161

plain
plane

tail	tale	rode
road	hole	whole

Spelling Strategy **Homophones** sound alike but do not have the same spelling or the same meaning.

Change the letter in dark print. Write a spelling word.

25. ro**l**e **26.** ho**m**e **27.** **t**oad

Write the missing spelling words.

I read a __(**28**)__ about how the squirrel got a bushy __(**29**)__. I read the __(**30**)__ story in one night!

Elephant Words Units 19–23 pages 132–161

who

children	do	who
to	too	two

Spelling Strategy Elephant Words have unusual spellings. Check them carefully when you write them.

Write the missing spelling words.

There are six __(**31**)__ from school __(**32**)__ are coming __(**33**)__ my house today. We will play in my tree house. We will ride on my swing. Can you bring __(**34**)__ friends and come __(**35**)__? Please __(**36**)__!

Spelling-Meaning Strategy

Word Families

Look at this word family. Remember that words in the same family are alike in spelling and meaning.

thank	It is important to **thank** people.
thankful	I am **thankful** for many things.
thanks	I give **thanks** for a good home.
thanked	I **thanked** my Mom for helping me.

Think How are the words in this family alike in meaning? How are they alike in spelling?

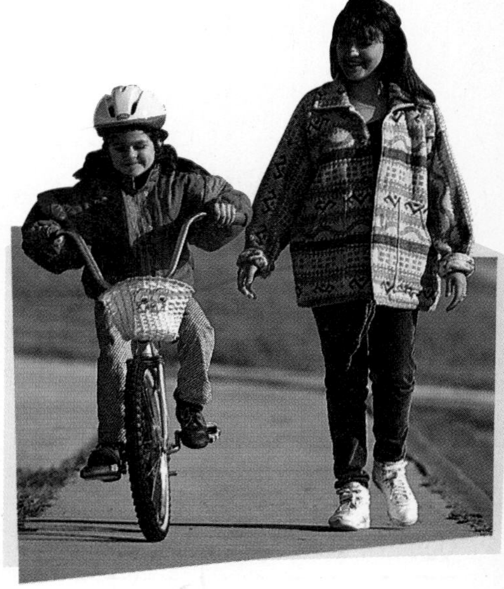

Apply and Extend

Write a word from the thank **family in each sentence.**

1. The Pilgrims were very _______.
2. How could they _______ the Indians?
3. They _______ them by making a meal.
4. Everyone gave _______ for their food.

1. thankful
2. thank
3. thanked
4. thanks

With a partner, think of words in these families. Make a list for each family.

Check the Word Families list that begins on page 272. Did you miss any words? Add them to your lists.

based on

The Case of the Stolen Code Book

by Barbara Rinkoff

Alex finds a secret message. He tells his friends how to write a message like the one he found. Alex might have written these instructions. What are the steps for writing a secret message?

It is easy to write a secret message. First, take a piece of white paper. Next, get a paintbrush and a bowl of milk. Then write your message with the brush and milk. Finally, let the message dry. It will look like there is nothing on the paper. When you want to see the message, hold the paper next to a light. The writing will come out in brown letters!

Think and Discuss

1. What **steps** are given for writing a secret message?
2. In what order are the steps written?
3. What **order words**, like **first** and **next**, are used to make the steps clear?
4. Which sentence tells the **main idea**, the one idea the paragraph is about?

The Writing Process

Instructions

Think of some things you know how to do well. Write instructions for one of your ideas. Follow the guidelines. Use the Writing Process.

1 Prewriting

- Write a few words about each step on a sheet of paper.
- Draw a picture to go with each step.

2 Draft

- Write the steps in an order that makes sense.

3 Revise

- Cross out steps that do not belong.
- Remember to use your Thesaurus to find exact words.
- Read your instructions to a friend. Make changes.

4 Proofread

- Did you spell each word correctly?
- Did you begin the names of holidays and months with capital letters?

5 Publish

- Copy your instructions neatly. Then tape-record your instructions. Have a friend follow your instructions.

Guidelines for Writing Instructions

✓ Begin with a sentence that tells the main idea.

✓ List the steps in order.

✓ Use order words to make the steps clear.

Composition Words

bring
things
show
soon
you
whole

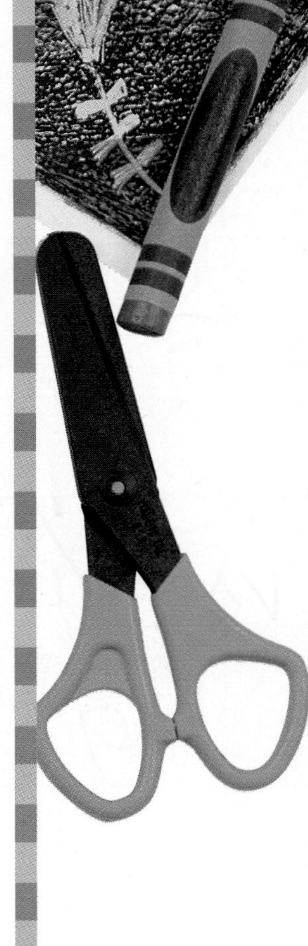

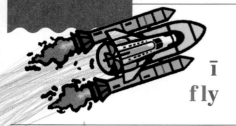

UNIT 25

More Long i Spellings

ī
fly

A.

B.

C.

D.

Read and Say

READ the sentences. **SAY** each word in dark print.

Basic Words

1.	sky	*sky*	I see a star in the **sky**.
2.	find	*find*	Help me **find** my book.
3.	night	*night*	Mom works at **night**.
4.	high	*high*	How **high** can you jump?
5.	fly	*fly*	Can you **fly** a plane?
6.	try	*try*	I will **try** to draw a pig.
7.	light	*light*	It is **light** outside.
8.	dry	*dry*	The brown grass is **dry**.
9.	right	*right*	Show me the **right** way.
10.	kind	*kind*	Jon is **kind** to animals.
11.	eye	*eye*	He can close one **eye**.
12.	buy	*buy*	They will **buy** a car.

Think and Write

Most of the words have the long **i** vowel sound spelled **y**, **i**, or **igh**.

the long **i** sound → sk**y**, f**i**nd, n**igh**t

How are the Elephant Words different?

A. Write **four** Basic Words with the long **i** sound spelled **y**.

B. Write **two** Basic Words with the long **i** sound spelled **i**.

C. Write **four** Basic Words with the long **i** sound spelled **igh**.

D. Now write the **two** Elephant Words.

Review
13. why **14.** cry

Challenge
15. flight **16.** behind

Independent Practice

Spelling Strategy The vowel sound in **sky**, **find**, and **night** is the long **i** sound. The long **i** sound may be spelled **y**, **i**, or **igh**.

Phonics Write Basic Words to answer the questions.

1. Which word begins with the same consonant cluster as [flag]?
2. Which word begins with the same consonant cluster as [skate]?
3. Which word begins with the same consonant cluster as [truck]?

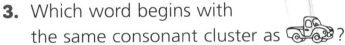

4–5. Which two words rhyme with **mind**?

Word Meaning Write the Basic Word that means the opposite of each word below.

6. wet
7. low
8. dark
9. wrong
10. day

Elephant Words Write an Elephant Word to answer each riddle.

11. I sound like **I**, but I am what you use to look at the stars.
12. I sound like **by**, but I am something you do with money.

Phonics

1. fly
2. sky
3. fry
4. kind
5. find

Word Meaning

6. dry
7. high
8. light
9. right
10. night

Elephant Words

11. eye
12. buy

UNIT
25

Dictionary

1.

2.

3.

4.

ABC Words

5.

6.

7.

8.

9.

Word Hunt

10.

11.

12.

Dictionary

Finding the Right Meaning Some entry words may have three different meanings. Each meaning is numbered.

> **fly** **1.** To move through the air using wings: *The birds **fly** to their nests.* **2.** To operate a plane or a spacecraft: *Captain Roy will **fly** the plane.* **3.** To move quickly: *I have to **fly**, or I will be late for school.*

Practice Write **1**, **2**, or **3** to tell which meaning of **fly** is used in each sentence below.

1. Did you see that robin **fly** by?
2. I had to **fly** to catch the school bus.
3. My uncle knows how to **fly** jets.
4. Bees **fly** from flower to flower.

Review: Spelling Spree

ABC Words Use ABC order to write the missing letter in each group. Make Basic or Review Words.

Example: r_s_t j_k_l x_y_z = **sky**

5. a__c t__v x__z
6. e__g k__m x__z
7. b__d q__s x__z
8. v__x g__i x__z
9. d__f x__z d__f

Word Hunt Write the Basic Word you see in each longer word.

10. slightly
11. brightest
12. kindness

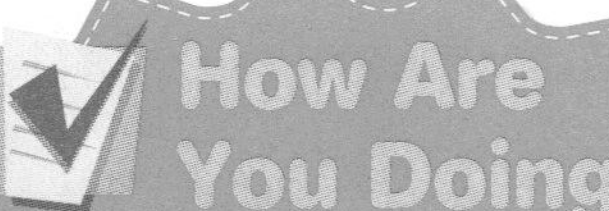

How Are You Doing?

Write each word in a sentence. Practice with a partner any words you spelled wrong.

Proofreading and Writing

Proofread for Spelling Proofread this page from a book about stars. Use proofreading marks to fix six spelling mistakes.

Example: Do you know ~~wiy~~ why stars shine?

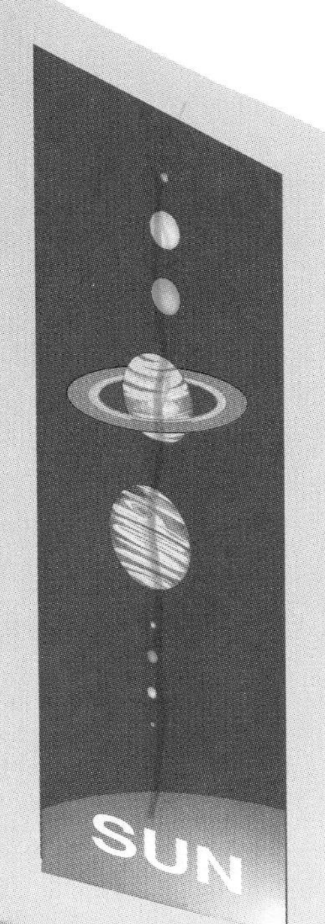

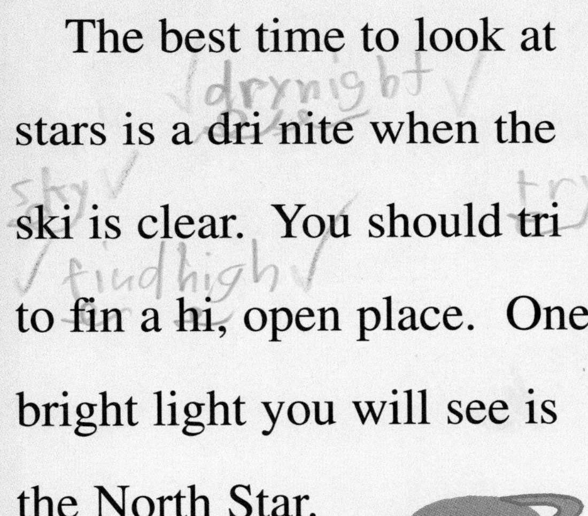

The best time to look at stars is a dri nite when the ski is clear. You should tri to fin a hi, open place. One bright light you will see is the North Star.

Basic

1. sky
2. find
3. night
4. high
5. fly
6. try
7. light
8. dry
9. right
10. kind
11. eye
12. buy

Review

13. why
14. cry

Challenge

15. flight
16. behind

Proofreading Marks

- ∧ Add
- Delete
- ≡ Make a capital letter
- / Make a small letter

Write Some Captions

Pretend you were the first child to go to the moon. Draw some pictures that show what you did on your trip. Then write a caption for each picture. Try to use spelling words.

Proofreading Tip

Check to make sure that your n's **don't look like your** r's.

Vocabulary Enrichment

Word Builder

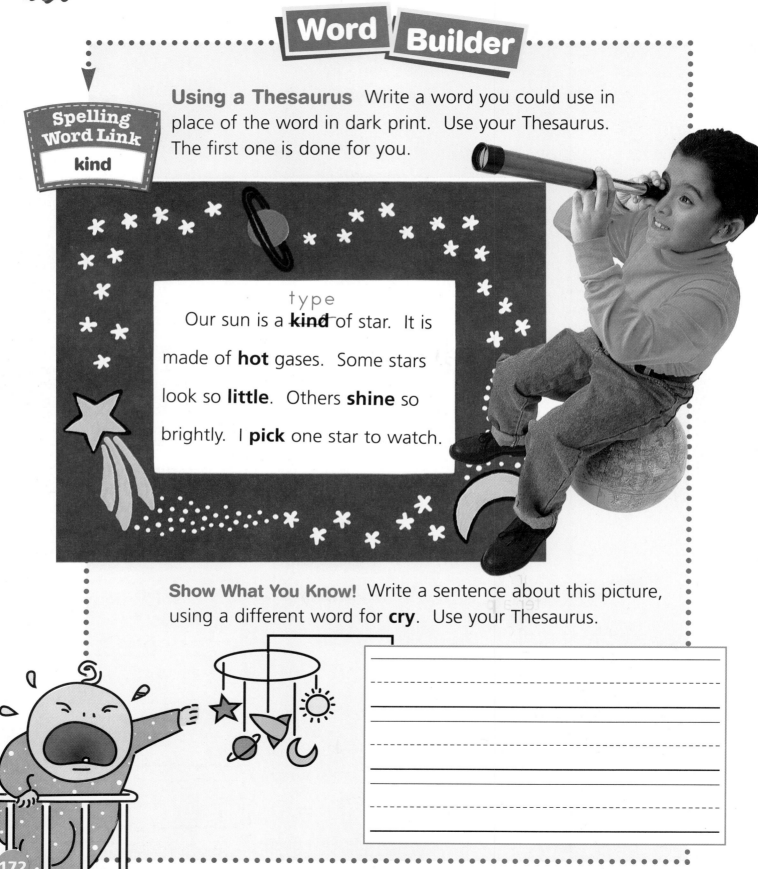

Spelling Word Link
kind

Using a Thesaurus Write a word you could use in place of the word in dark print. Use your Thesaurus. The first one is done for you.

Our sun is a ~~**kind**~~ type of star. It is made of **hot** gases. Some stars look so **little**. Others **shine** so brightly. I **pick** one star to watch.

Show What You Know! Write a sentence about this picture, using a different word for **cry**. Use your Thesaurus.

Science

Stars and Planets All the words in the box have something to do with the stars and the planets. Write those words to finish this speech. Use your Spelling Dictionary.

Spelling
Word Link
sky
Mars
space
planet
Pluto

We live on the (1) Earth. One day we will be able to fly through (2) and land on (3), which is next to Earth. Who knows, we may even travel all the way to tiny, cold (4)!

1. ________
2. ________
3. ________
4. ________

Try This CHALLENGE

Yes or No? Write **yes** or **no** to answer each question.

5. Is **Mars** a star?
6. Do you water a **planet** to make it grow?
7. Could you take a train ride to **Pluto**?
8. Is **space** bigger than an ocean?

5. ________
6. ________
7. ________
8. ________

Fact File

Have you ever looked up in the sky and seen the Big Dipper? It is a group of seven stars in the shape of a cup with a long handle. Two of the stars point to the North Star.

UNIT 26

The Final Sound in puppy

puppy

Read and Say

READ the sentences. **SAY** each word in dark print.

Basic Words

1. puppy	*puppy*	My **puppy** has big feet.
2. baby	*baby*	A kitten is a **baby** cat.
3. lucky	*lucky*	I have a **lucky** penny.
4. happy	*happy*	The **happy** boy sang.
5. very	*very*	That nest is **very** big.
6. lady	*lady*	The **lady** made us lunch.
7. funny	*funny*	Your joke was **funny**.
8. silly	*silly*	They are acting **silly**.
9. many	*many*	He has **many** games.
10. only	*only*	I have **only** one dress.
11. cookie	*cookie*	Suki ate a big **cookie**.

A.

B.

Think and Write

Each word has two parts called **syllables**. Each syllable has one vowel sound. You hear the long **e** vowel sound in the second syllable of each word. In most of the words, the long **e** sound is spelled **y**.

puppy → pup p**y**   baby → ba b**y**

How is the Elephant Word different?

A. Write the first **ten** Basic Words. Then draw a line under the letter that spells the final long **e** sound in each word.

B. Now write the Elephant Word.

Review

12. me **13.** bee

Challenge

14. furry **15.** noisy

Independent Practice

Spelling Strategy The words **puppy** and **baby** have two syllables. The long **e** sound at the end of a two-syllable word may be spelled **y**.

Phonics Write Basic Words to answer the questions.

1. Which word has the short **e** sound spelled **e**?
2. Which word has the long **o** sound in the first syllable?

3–4. Which two words have the long **a** sound in the first syllable?

Word Meaning Write a Basic Word for each meaning. Use your Spelling Dictionary.

5. feeling joy
6. having good luck
7. a young dog
8. not showing good sense
9. the opposite of **few**
10. causing laughter

Elephant Word Think of the missing letters in the Elephant Word. Write the word.

11. I baked a **cook**__ __ shaped like a little lamb.

Phonics

1.

2.

3.

4.

Word Meaning

5.

6.

7.

8.

9.

10.

Elephant Word

11.

Review: Spelling Spree

Letter Math Add and take away letters to make Basic or Review Words. Write each word.

1. m a n e − e + y = _______
2. m + s e e − s − e = _______
3. v e r b − b + y = _______
4. b + t r e e − t r = _______
5. o n e − e + l y = _______

Puzzle Play Write a Basic Word for each clue. Use the letters that would be in the boxes to spell what baby animals like to do.

6. glad __ __ ☐ __ __
7. foolish __ __ __ ☐ __
8. a woman __ ☐ __ __
9. a very young child __ __ __ ☐

Secret Word: __ __ __ __

Short Cuts Write the Basic Words that have these shorter words in them.

10. cook 11. pup 12. luck

How Are You Doing?
Write each spelling word as a family member reads it aloud. Did you spell any words wrong?

Letter Math

1. ______
2. ______
3. ______
4. ______
5. ______

Puzzle Play

6. ______
7. ______
8. ______
9. ______

Short Cuts

10. ______
11. ______
12. ______

Proofreading and Writing

Proofread: Spelling and Titles for People

Always begin a person's title with a capital letter. Put a period after **Mrs.**, **Mr.**, **Dr.**, and **Ms.**, but not after **Miss**.

Mrs. Kitt Dr. Doe Miss Bryd

Proofread Josh's letter. Use proofreading marks to fix four spelling mistakes and three titles that are wrong.

Example: How ~~maney~~ many cats does ms. Woo have?

February 14, 1998

Dear Miss. Smith,

I got Puff from mrs. Barnes! I am very ~~luky~~ lucky. I asked dr. Vetto why Puff acts so ~~funnie~~ funny. He told ~~mee~~ me that being ~~sily~~ silly is how kittens have fun!

Your friend,

Josh

Basic

1. puppy
2. baby
3. lucky
4. happy
5. very
6. lady
7. funny
8. silly
9. many
10. only
11. cookie

Review

12. me
13. bee

Challenge

14. furry
15. noisy

Proofreading Marks

- ∧ Add
- Delete
- ≡ Make a capital letter
- / Make a small letter

Write a Letter

Pretend you have a new pet. Write a letter to a vet, asking for information on how to take care of your pet. Try to use spelling words.

Check that you began and ended each person's title correctly.

Phonics and Spelling

Rhyming Words

Words That End Like puppy Which picture names rhyme with the words below? Write each picture name next to the word it rhymes with.

Example: guppy **puppy**

Zoe's room

20

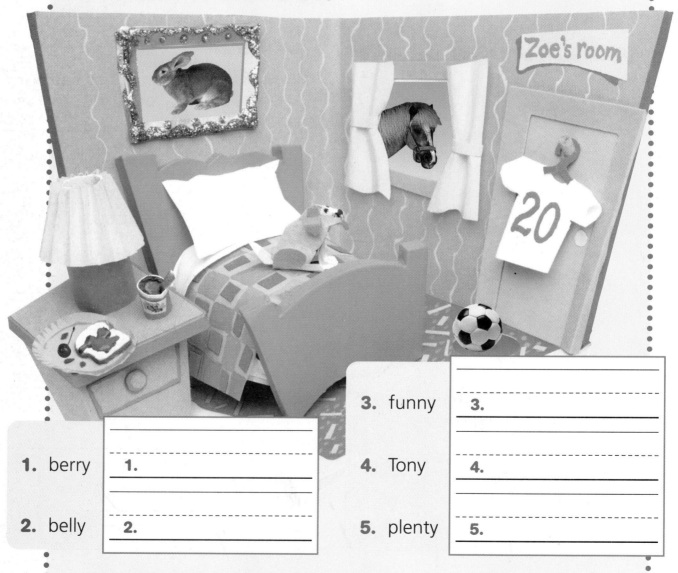

1. berry 1. ____________
2. belly 2. ____________
3. funny 3. ____________
4. Tony 4. ____________
5. plenty 5. ____________

Work Together On another sheet of paper, write three more words that have the long **e** sound spelled **y** like **baby**. Work with a friend.

Science

Baby Animals All the words in the box have something to do with baby animals. Write those words to finish this page from a diary. Use your Spelling Dictionary.

Spelling Word Link

puppy

piglet
kid
tadpole
hatch

October 9

Dad and I went to a farm today. We saw a goat and her **(1)**. A pink **(2)** played in a nearby pen. A tiny **(3)** swam in the pond. We even saw some chicks **(4)**!

1. ____________
2. ____________
3. ____________
4. ____________

Questions and Answers Write a word from the box to answer each question.

5. Which animal lives in water?
6. Which animal may have little horns?
7. What do baby birds do?
8. Which animal may have a curly tail?

Fact File

At first a tadpole looks like a little fish. Slowly it grows legs. Then it loses its tail and becomes a frog!

5. ____________
6. ____________
7. ____________
8. ____________

UNIT 27 The Vowel Sound in cow

ow
cow

A. now
cow
town
how
brown
down

B. should
could
found
house

C. could
should

Read and Say

READ the sentences. **SAY** each word in dark print.

Basic Words

1. town	town	I live in a small **town**.
2. house	house	My **house** is by the pond.
3. out	out	Mom went **out** for a walk.
4. down	down	He ran **down** the hill.
5. cow	cow	Our **cow** gives us milk.
6. now	now	Will we eat **now**?
7. found	found	You **found** my kite!
8. how	how	Teach me **how** to cook.
9. mouse	mouse	Boots chased the **mouse**.
10. brown	brown	Can I have a **brown** bag?
11. could	could	We **could** go with you.
12. should	should	I ate more than I **should**.

Think and Write

Most of the words have the same vowel sound. It is the vowel sound you hear in .

the vowel sound → t**ow**n, h**ou**se

How are the Elephant Words different?

A. Write **six** Basic Words with the vowel sound spelled **ow**.

B. Write **four** Basic Words with the vowel sound spelled **ou**.

C. Now write the **two** Elephant Words.

Review
13. name **14.** cat

Challenge
15. couch **16.** crowded

Independent Practice

Spelling Strategy The words **town** and **house** have the same vowel sound. This vowel sound may be spelled **ow** or **ou**.

Phonics Write Basic Words to answer the questions.

1. Which word begins with a consonant cluster?
2. Which word begins and ends like **den**?
3. Which word begins and ends like **tin**?

4–6. Which three words rhyme with **plow**?

Word Pairs Write a Basic Word to finish the second sentence in each pair.

7. **People** means more than one **person**.
   Mice means more than one _______.
8. If you **lose** something, it is **lost**.
   If you **find** something, it is _______.
9. The opposite of **left** is **right**.
   The opposite of **in** is _______.
10. A **bear** lives in a **cave**.
    A **person** lives in a _______.

Elephant Words Think of the missing letters in each Elephant Word. Write each word.

11. sh o u ld
12. c o u ld

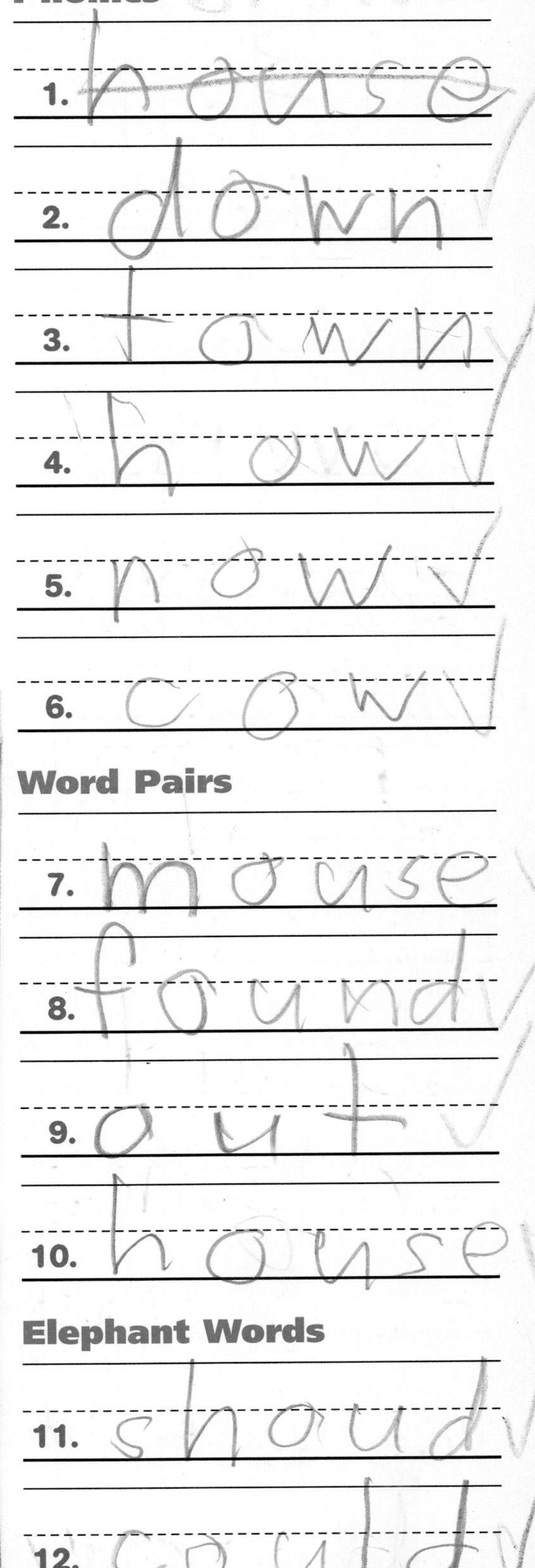

Phonics

1. house
2. down
3. town
4. how
5. now
6. cow

Word Pairs

7. mouse
8. found
9. out
10. house

Elephant Words

11. shoud
12. could

Dictionary

1.
2.
3.
4.

Hidden Words

5.
6.
7.

Letter Swap

8.
9.
10.
11.
12.

Dictionary

Finding the Right Meaning You know that words may have more than one meaning. Use a dictionary to find all the different meanings of a word.

> **brown** **1.** The color of chocolate: *Zia has long **brown** hair.* **2.** To cook until brown on the outside: *I can **brown** the rolls in the oven.*

Practice Look up the word **out** in your Spelling Dictionary. Write **1**, **2**, **3**, or **4** to tell which meaning of the word is used in each sentence.

1. The lights were **out** in my house all day.
2. The stars come **out** at night.
3. We went **out** to see the play.
4. My teacher was **out** this morning.

Review: Spelling Spree

Hidden Words Find the hidden Basic Word in each box. Write the word.

5. cithowwer **6.** fostownick **7.** maunnowus

Letter Swap Change each letter in dark print. Write a Basic or Review Word.

8. ca**p**
9. **s**ame
10. **r**ound
11. ou**r**
12. **f**rown

How Are You Doing?

Write your words in ABC order. Practice with a family member any words you spelled wrong.

Proofreading and Writing

Proofread for Spelling Proofread these directions. Use proofreading marks to fix six spelling mistakes.

Example: I painted the walls ~~broun~~. brown

Do you know how to plan a hous for a pet? First, decide how big it shoud be. A kow needs more room than a mous! Next, find out what else your pet needs. Most pets cood use a bed to lie doun on, food, and water. Last, draw your plan on paper.

Basic

1. town
2. house
3. out
4. down
5. cow
6. now
7. found
8. how
9. mouse
10. brown
11. could
12. should

Review

13. name
14. cat

Challenge

15. couch
16. crowded

Proofreading Marks

- ^ Add
- Delete
- ≡ Make a capital letter
- / Make a small letter

Write a Story

Think of friends you visited in their house or apartment. Write a story about your visit. Tell why it was fun or exciting. Try to use spelling words. Then share your story with a friend.

Read your paper again slowly to see if any words have been left out.

Unit 27 BONUS

Phonics and Spelling

Rhyming Words

More cow **Words** Make rhyming words that have the **cow** vowel sound. Use the letters in the pictures.

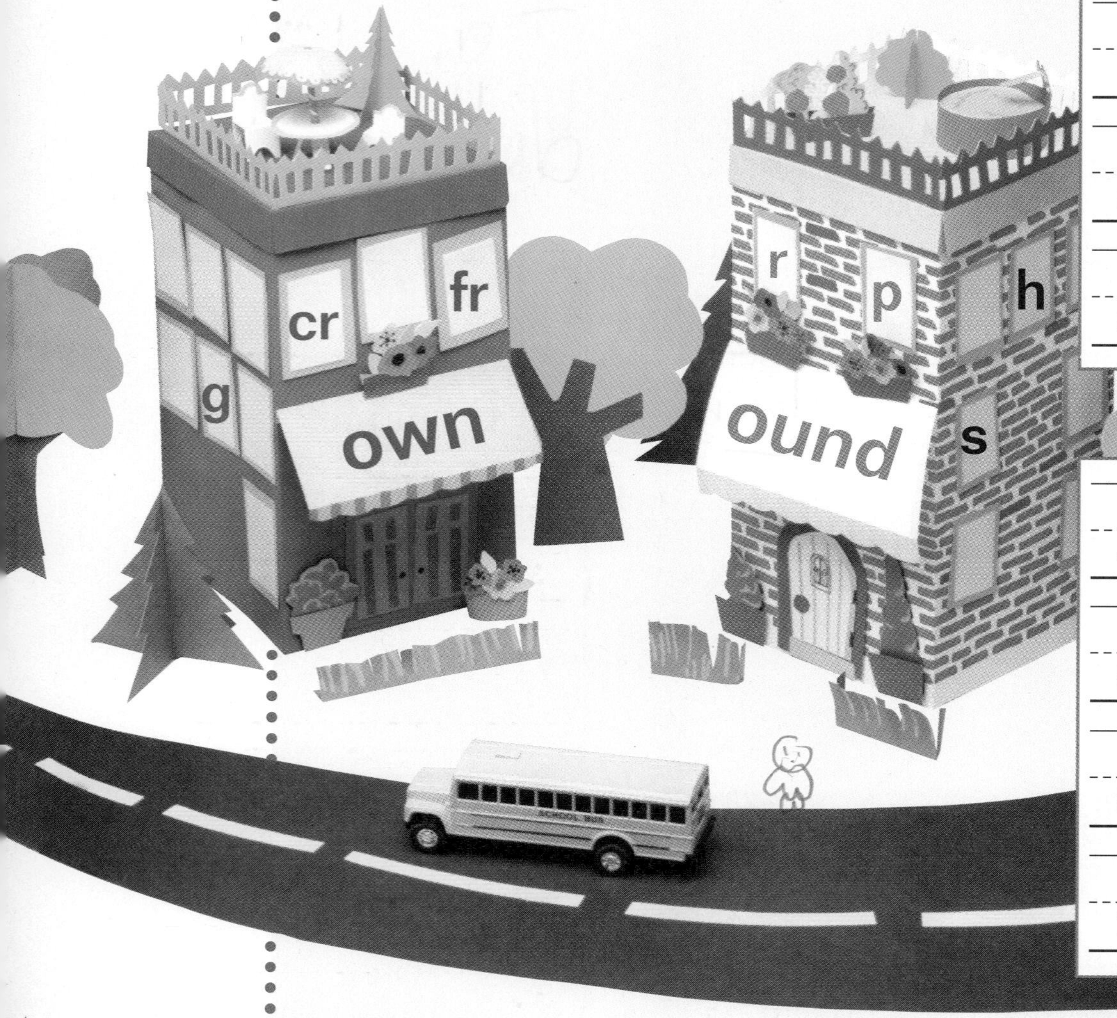

cr fr g own

r p h s ound

own

1. ____________________

2. ____________________

3. ____________________

ound

4. ____________________

5. ____________________

6. ____________________

7. ____________________

Work Together On another sheet of paper, write three rhyming words that end with **out**. Work with a friend.

Social Studies

Places to Live All the words in the box have something to do with places to live. Use those words to write labels for these pictures. Use your Spelling Dictionary.

Spelling Word Link
house
cottage
igloo
trailer
palace

1. ____________
2. ____________
3 ____________
4. ____________

Try This CHALLENGE

Riddle Time! Write a word from the box to answer each riddle.

5. What home might have huge, fancy rooms?
6. What has wheels but often does not move?
7. What can be a home or a kind of cheese?
8. What is frozen but can keep people warm?

5. ____________
6. ____________
7. ____________
8. ____________

Fact File

People have lived in apartment houses for hundreds of years! Long ago, American Indians built homes in the sides of cliffs. Some were four stories high!

UNIT 28

Compound Words

A. bath|tub
bed|time
my|self
some|one
may|be
in|to
up|on
any|one
with|out
can|not

Read and Say

READ the sentences. **SAY** each word in dark print.

Basic Words

1.	bathtub	*bathtub*	I wash in the **bathtub**.
2.	bedtime	*bedtime*	When is your **bedtime**?
3.	myself	*myself*	I played by **myself**.
4.	someone	*someone*	Did **someone** call me?
5.	maybe	*maybe*	I think **maybe** I can do it.
6.	into	*into*	We walked **into** the store.
7.	upon	*upon*	The frog sat **upon** a rock.
8.	anyone	*anyone*	Pia did not see **anyone**.
9.	without	*without*	He cooks **without** help.
10.	cannot	*cannot*	They **cannot** stay.

Think and Write

Each word is a **compound word**. A compound word is made up of two shorter words.

bath + tub → bathtub

bed + time → bedtime

my + self → myself

A. Write the **ten** Basic Words. Then draw a line between the two words that make up each compound word.

Review
11. stop **12.** flag

Challenge
13. playground **14.** nobody

Independent Practice

Spelling Strategy A **compound word** is a word that is made up of two shorter words.

BEDTIME

Phonics Write Basic Words to answer the questions.

1. Which word has three syllables?
2. Which word has the long **i** sound spelled **y**?

3–4. Which two words have the short **i** sound in the first syllable?

5–6. Which two words have the short **o** sound in the second syllable?

Word Meaning Write the Basic Word that means the same or almost the same as each word below.

7. somebody 8. perhaps

Word Clues Write the Basic Word for each clue.

9. This is sometimes filled with bubbles.
10. This is when you go to sleep.

Phonics

1. anyone
2. maybe
3. intoont
4. without
5. upon
6. someone

Word Meaning

7. someone
8. maybe

Word Clues

9. bathtup
10. bedtime

UNIT
28

Word Puzzles

1. myself
2. someone
3. cannot
4. withoat

Hidden Compounds

5. bedtime
6. maybe
7. bathtub
8. anyone

Fill-In Fun

9. falg
10. upon
11. stop
12. into

Review: Spelling Spree

Word Puzzles Make Basic Words by matching the puzzle pieces. Write the words.

1.	can	self
2.	some	out
3.	my	not
4.	with	one

any one

Hidden Compounds Put together two words in each sentence to make a Basic Word. Write the word.

5. Do you go to bed at the same time each night?
6. You may slip, so please be careful.
7. Did you take a bath in that old tub?
8. He said any child could be the one who wins.

Fill-In Fun Write the missing Basic or Review Words.

9. raise the _______
10. once _______ a time
11. _______ and go
12. get _______ shape

How Are You Doing?
List the spelling words that are hard for you. Practice them with a family member.

Proofreading and Writing

Proofread: Spelling and Book Titles Begin the first, the last, and each important word in a book title with a capital letter. Draw a line under the title.

Herman the Loser   Amos and Boris

Proofread Ariana's book report. Use proofreading marks to fix four spelling mistakes and two mistakes in book titles.

Example: Can you read swimmy wifout help? (without)

The book Gregory the Terrible eater is about a goat who canot stap eating healthy food. I think enyone would like this funny book! It is funnier than Clyde Monster, a book about a monster who is afraid at bedtime. Maybe you know somone like that too!

Basic

1. bathtub
2. bedtime
3. myself
4. someone
5. maybe
6. into
7. upon
8. anyone
9. without
10. cannot

Review

11. stop
12. flag

Challenge

13. playground
14. nobody

Proofreading Marks

- ^ Add
- Delete
- ≡ Make a capital letter
- / Make a small letter

Write Book Titles

Write three titles for some books about exercising. Try to use spelling words. Share your titles with a friend.

Example: Anyone Can Exercise

Proofreading Tip **Check that you wrote each book title correctly.**

Unit 28 BONUS

Vocabulary Enrichment

Word Builder

Spelling Word Link
bedtime

Building Compound Words with bed Jamal is thirsty! Help him find some water. Draw a path by making new words with **bed**. Then write the words you made.

1. ______
2. ______
3. ______
4. ______

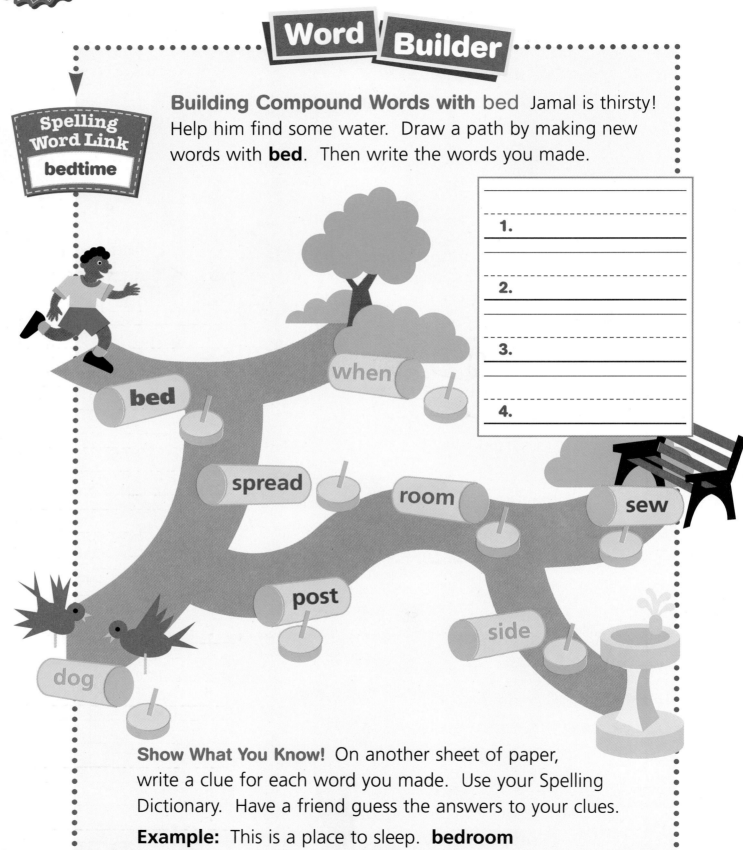

bed
when
spread
room
sew
post
side
dog

Show What You Know! On another sheet of paper, write a clue for each word you made. Use your Spelling Dictionary. Have a friend guess the answers to your clues.

Example: This is a place to sleep. **bedroom**

Vocabulary Enrichment

Health

Taking Care of Yourself All the words in the box have something to do with taking care of yourself. Write those words to finish these health club posters. Use your Spelling Dictionary.

Spelling Word Link

playground

jog
fit
muscles
shape

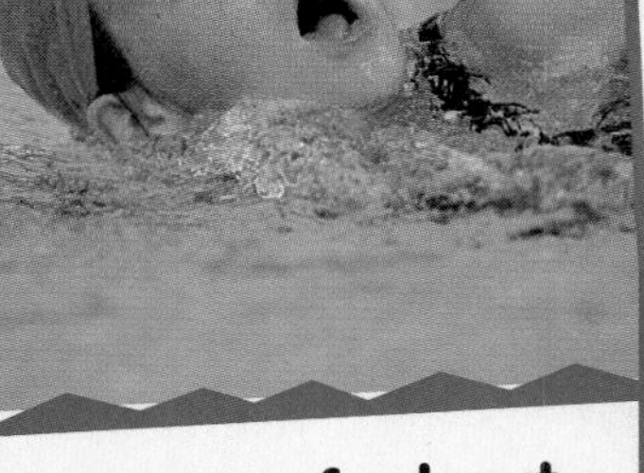

Do you feel out of __(1)__? Swim some laps!

Keep your leg __(2)__ strong! Try to __(3)__ two miles each day.

How can you stay __(4)__? Exercise!

1. ____________________
2. ____________________
3. ____________________
4. ____________________

Yes or No? Write **yes** or **no** to answer each question.

5. Should a football player stay **fit**?
6. Will swimming make your **muscles** strong?
7. Could a runner **jog** in a park?
8. Will combing your hair keep you in **shape**?

5. ____________________
6. ____________________
7. ____________________
8. ____________________

Fact File

You have more than 600 muscles in your body! Your muscles help you move. You can take care of them by exercising and eating healthy foods.

UNIT 29

Contractions

A.

Read and Say

READ the sentences. **SAY** each word in dark print.

Basic Words

1.	I'll	I'll	I said that **I'll** be there.
2.	we've	we've	I know **we've** had fun!
3.	don't	don't	Why **don't** you rest?
4.	you're	you're	We think **you're** great!
5.	isn't	isn't	It **isn't** time to play.
6.	didn't	didn't	Mom **didn't** eat dinner.
7.	you'll	you'll	I hope **you'll** stay.
8.	I've	I've	I think **I've** lost my pen.
9.	hasn't	hasn't	She **hasn't** called yet.
10.	we'll	we'll	Next time **we'll** sing.
11.	can't	can't	I **can't** go to the park.

Think and Write

Each word is a **contraction.** A contraction is a short way of writing two words. One or more letters are left out, and a mark called an **apostrophe** is put in their place.

I + will → **I'll** we + have → **we've**

What two words were used to make each contraction? Were two words used to make the Elephant Word?

A. Write the **eleven** Basic Words. Beside each word, write the letter or letters that the apostrophe takes the place of. Remember the Elephant Word.

Review
12. it **13.** us

Challenge
14. they're **15.** wouldn't

Independent Practice

Spelling Strategy A **contraction** is a short way of writing two words. An **apostrophe** takes the place of the letter or letters that are left out.

Phonics Write Basic Words to answer the questions.

1. Which word has the long **o** sound?
2. Which word begins like **happy**?

3–4. Which two words have the long **e** sound?

Word Meaning Write the Basic Word that means the same as the pair of words in dark print.

5. I think **I will** get an ant farm.
6. An ant farm **is not** hard to care for.
7. Perhaps **you will** be surprised to learn that ants work together in groups.
8. **I have** heard that each ant has its own job.
9. Maybe you **did not** know that a queen ant's only job is to lay eggs.
10. If **you are** interested in ants, you can buy an ant farm to set up at home.

Elephant Word Write the Elephant Word that means the same as the word in dark print.

11. An ant **cannot** tap-dance.

Phonics

1.

2.

3.

4.

Word Meaning

5.

6.

7.

8.

9.

10.

Elephant Word

11.

UNIT
29

Review: Spelling Spree

Letter Math Add and take away to make Basic or Review Words. Write the words.

1. bugs − b − g = ______
2. cannot − no + ’ = ______
3. you are − a + ’ = ______
4. knits − kn − s = ______
5. we have − ha + ’ = ______

Word Wheels 6–12. Make contractions that are Basic Words. Join the word in the center of each wheel with another word on the same wheel. Write the contractions.

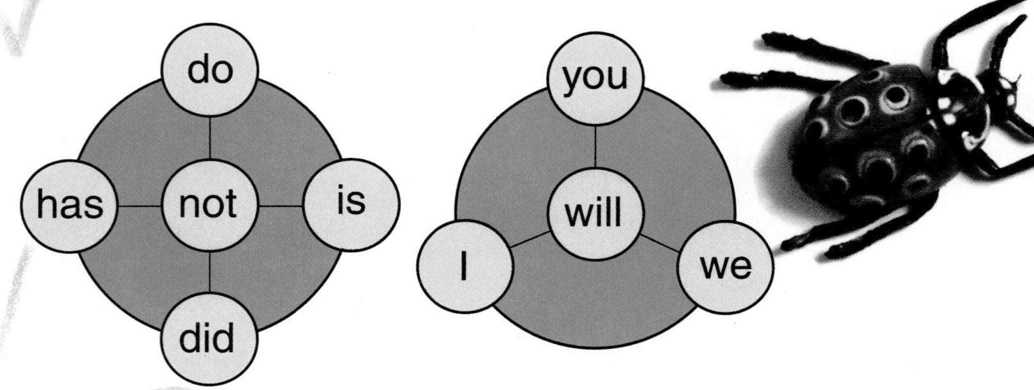

How Are You Doing?
Write each spelling word as a partner reads it aloud. Did you spell any words wrong?

Letter Math

1. ______
2. ______
3. ______
4. ______
5. ______

Word Wheels

6. ______
7. ______
8. ______
9. ______
10. ______
11. ______
12. ______

Proofreading and Writing

Proofread: Spelling and Commas Always put a **comma** between the day and the year in a **date**.

Will the picnic be on June 22, 1998?

Proofread the ant's message. Use proofreading marks to fix four spelling mistakes and two missing commas.

Example: Be sure ~~youre~~ you're there on May 20, 1998!

Ive set a date for our picnic. We cant have et on July 4 1998. People don't want ants at picnics, and there isn't ever enough food for all of us. Instead, you'ill be coming on January 1 1999. In winter, people will not bug us!

Basic

1. I'll
2. we've
3. don't
4. you're
5. isn't
6. didn't
7. you'll
8. I've
9. hasn't
10. we'll
11. can't

Review

12. it
13. us

Challenge

14. they're
15. wouldn't

Proofreading Marks

- ∧ Add
- Delete
- ≡ Make a capital letter
- / Make a small letter

Write Some Diary Entries

Pretend you are a bee. Pick three days of the week and write a diary entry for each day. Include the date and two or three sentences about what you saw and did. Try to use spelling words.

Proofreading Tip

Check that you wrote each date correctly.

Vocabulary Enrichment

Word Builder

Spelling Word Link

we'll

toe
tow
sail
sale

Homophones The word **we'll** is a contraction for **we will**. It is also a homophone for **wheel**.

We'll get a new **wheel** for your bike.

Each pair of pictures below shows a pair of homophones. Write the correct homophone for each picture, using one of the words in the box. Use your Spelling Dictionary.

1. ______________________

2. ______________________

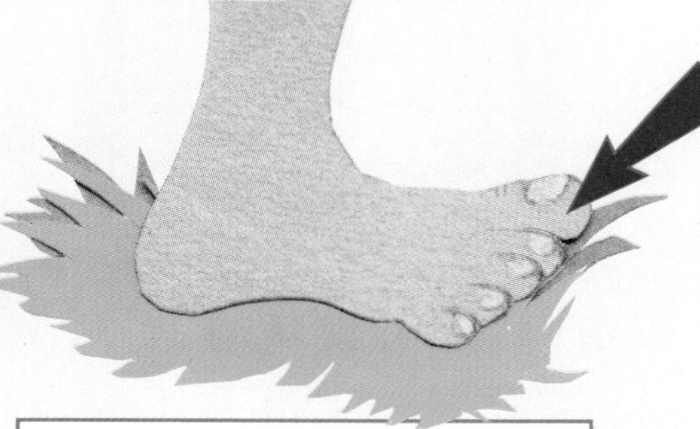

3. ______________________

4. ______________________

Show What You Know! On another sheet of paper, draw your own pictures for the homophones **sun** and **son**. Then label each picture with the correct homophone. Use your Spelling Dictionary.

Science

Insects All the words in the box have something to do with insects. Write those words to finish this science log. Use your Spelling Dictionary.

Spelling Word Link
they're

flea
moth
beetle
crawl

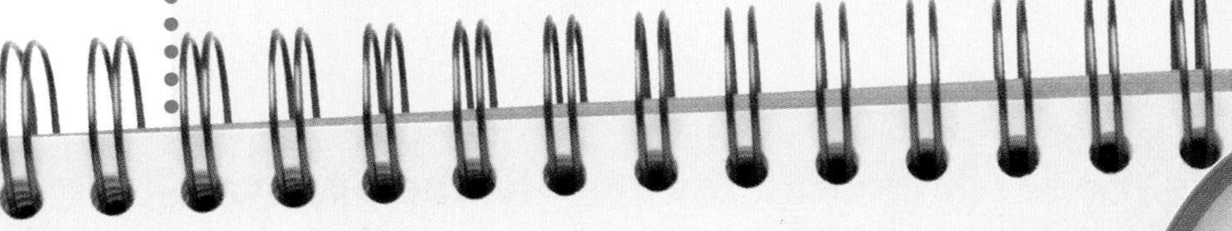

July 15

Today I saw a bug **(1)** up a tree. Was it a tiny jumping **(2)**? Was it a **(3)** with soft wings? No, it was a big black **(4)**. I love looking for insects, but sometimes they're hard to find!

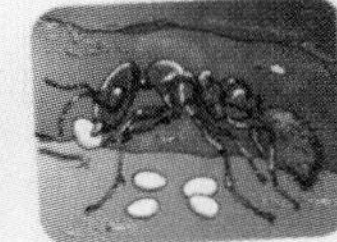

1. ______
2. ______
3. ______
4. ______

Try This CHALLENGE

Write Some Riddles What insect can jump, but cannot fly? A flea! Write more insect riddles. Try to use some words from the box on this page. Have a friend guess the answers to your riddles.

Fact File

Did you know that there are more than 1,000,000 different kinds of insects? Insects live almost everywhere. They even live near the North Pole!

30 Review: Units 25–29

1.
2.
3.
4.
5.
6.
7.
8.
9.
10.
11.
12.

Unit 25 More Long i Spellings pages 168–173

ī
fly

find	high	fly
light	dry	kind

Spelling Strategy The long **i** sound may be spelled **y**, **i**, or **igh**.

Write the spelling word that means the opposite.

1. lose **2.** mean

Write the missing spelling words.

Dad and I hang clothes to ___(**3**)___ in the bright ___(**4**)___. Birds ___(**5**)___ by ___(**6**)___ over the trees.

Unit 26 Final Sound in puppy pages 174–179

ē
puppy

puppy	baby	very
lady	silly	only

Spelling Strategy The long **e** sound at the end of a two-syllable word may be spelled **y**.

Write the spelling word that goes with each word.

7. crib **9.** dress
8. clown **10.** bone

Write the missing spelling words.

11. We had a ______ good time at the circus.
12. A man rode a bike that had ______ one wheel!

Unit 27 The Vowel Sound in cow pages 180–185

house	out	down
now	found	brown

ow
cow

Spelling Strategy The vowel sound in **down** and **house** may be spelled **ow** or **ou**.

Write the spelling word that rhymes with each word.

13. round **14.** shout **15.** cow

Write the missing spelling words.

Joy is painting our __(**16**)__ white and __(**17**)__. She moves her brush up and __(**18**)__ on the door.

Unit 28 Compound Words pages 186–191

bathtub	myself	someone
into	upon	cannot

bathtub

Spelling Strategy A **compound word** is a word that is made up of two shorter words.

Change the word in dark print. Write a spelling word.

19. some**time** **21.** up**set**

20. in**side** **22.** **him**self

Write the missing spelling words.

23. Mom is filling the _______ with warm water.

24. I _______ wait to play with my toy boat!

13.

14.

15.

16.

17.

18.

19.

20.

21.

22.

23.

24.

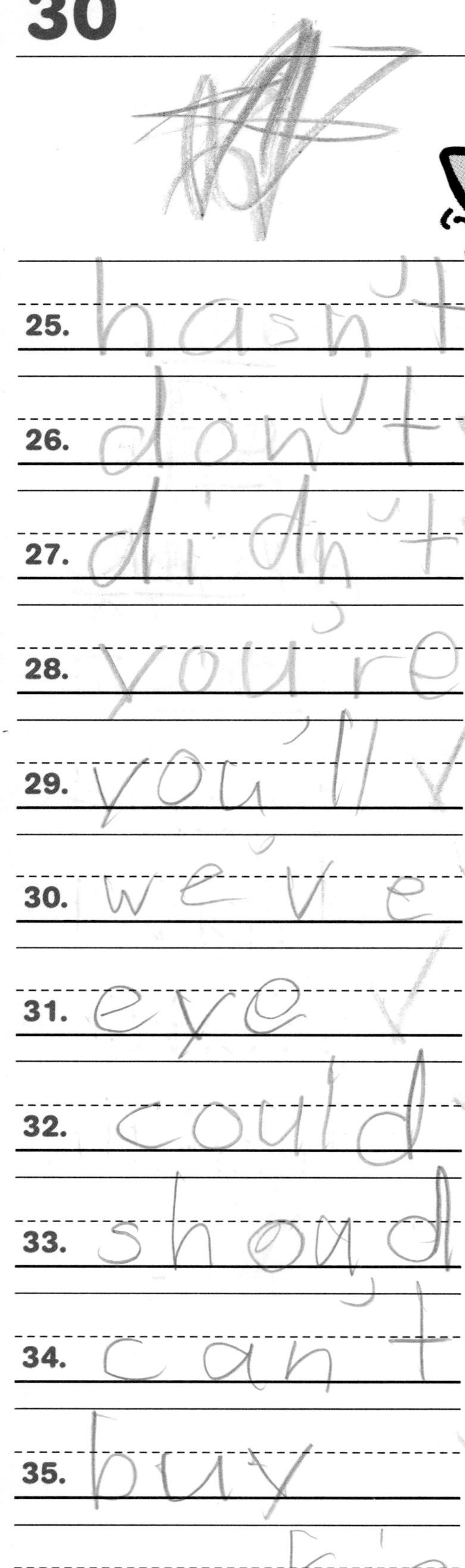

25.
26.
27.
28.
29.
30.
31.
32.
33.
34.
35.
36.

Unit 29 Contractions pages 192–197

we've	don't	you're
didn't	you'll	hasn't

Spelling Strategy

we + have → **we've**
do + not → **don't**

Write the spelling word that means the opposite.

25. has **26.** do **27.** did

Write the missing spelling words.

I know __(**28**)__ a good camper. If __(**29**)__ help, we can camp here. It feels as if __(**30**)__ been hiking all day long!

Elephant Words Units 25–29 pages 168–197

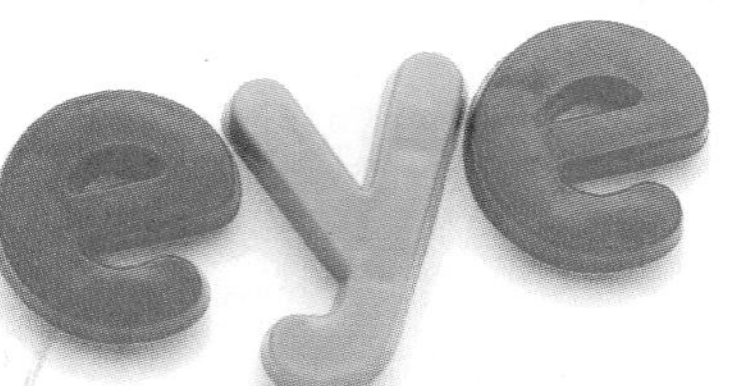

eye	buy	cookie
could	should	can't

Spelling Strategy Elephant words have unusual spellings. Check them carefully when you write them.

Write the missing spelling words.

Mom and I went to the __(**31**)__ doctor together. I tried, but I __(**32**)__ not read the chart. The doctor said I __(**33**)__ get glasses. Then if I __(**34**)__ see well, I can put them on. Mom let me __(**35**)__ a __(**36**)__ on the way home.

Spelling-Meaning Strategy

Word Families

Look at this word family. Remember that words in the same family are alike in spelling and meaning.

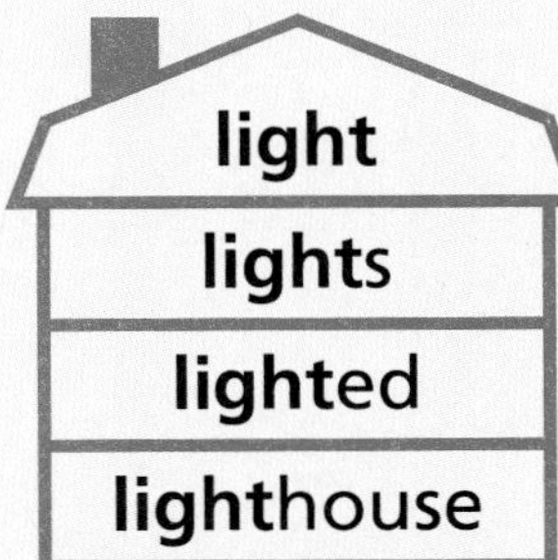

The **light** of the moon was bright.
The stars were twinkling **lights**.
Fireworks **lighted** the sky.
I watched from the **lighthouse**.

Think How are the words in this family alike in meaning? How are they alike in spelling?

Apply and Extend

Write a word from the light **family in each sentence.**

1. What is one of the brightest _______?
2. This _______ helps sailors at sea.
3. It has _______ the way for lost ships.
4. It is found on top of a tall _______.

1. lights
2. light
3. lighted
4. lighthouse

With a partner, think of words in these families. Make a list for each family.

Check the Word Families list that begins on page 272. Did you miss any words? Add them to your lists.

UNIT 30

Description

Literature and Writing

from

The Book of Giant Stories

by David L. Harrison

One day, a little boy went walking and met a giant who had tantrums. What words tell how the giant walked and talked during a tantrum?

Before long a huge giant came stamping down the path. He looked upset.

"Tanglebangled—ringlepox!" the giant yelled. Then he began hitting his head against a tree until the leaves shook off like snowflakes.

"Fanglewhangled—whippersnack!" the giant roared. Pulling up the tree, he whirled it around his head and knocked down another twenty-one other trees. Talking to himself, he stormed up the path toward the top of Mount Thistle.

Think and Discuss

1. What two **exact words** tell how the giant walked?
2. What two **exact words** tell how the giant sounded when he talked?
3. What **details** describe what the giant did to some of the trees in the woods?
4. How do you think the little boy felt when he met the giant?

The Writing Process

Description

Think of your favorite people, things, or places. Write a description of one of them. Follow the guidelines. Use the Writing Process.

1 Prewriting

- Draw a picture of what you are going to describe. Show it to a friend. Add more details if you need to.

2 Draft

- Write sentences that describe your topic. Put them in an order that makes sense.

3 Revise

- Add exact words and details.
- Remember to use your Thesaurus to find exact words.
- Read your description to a friend.
- Make changes.

4 Proofread

- Did you spell each word correctly?
- Did you begin the titles of people with capital letters?

5 Publish

- Copy your description neatly. Read it to a friend.

Guidelines for Writing a Description

✓ Use exact words and details to tell how things look, sound, smell, taste, and feel.

✓ Put the details in an order that is clear.

Composition Words

kind
happy
very
funny
brown
without

UNIT 31

The Vowel + r Sound in car

Read and Say

READ the sentences. **SAY** each word in dark print.

Basic Words

1. car	*car*	Our **car** had a flat tire.
2. start	*start*	Dad will **start** the truck.
3. arm	*arm*	I broke my **arm**.
4. far	*far*	My home is not **far**.
5. yard	*yard*	Trees grow in my **yard**.
6. part	*part*	A leaf is **part** of a tree.
7. barn	*barn*	The cow is in the **barn**.
8. hard	*hard*	That old bun is **hard**.
9. party	*party*	Taj came to my **party**.
10. farm	*farm*	Sheep live on a **farm**.
11. are	*are*	They **are** sleeping.
12. warm	*warm*	The sun is **warm**.

Think and Write

Each word has a vowel sound that is not short or long. The vowel sound is different because the vowel is followed by **r**.

the vowel + **r** sound → c**ar**, st**ar**t

How are the Elephant Words different?

A. Write the first **ten** Basic Words. Then draw a line under the letters that spell the vowel + **r** sound in each word.

B. Now write the **two** Elephant Words.

A. car, start, arm, far, yard, part, barn, hard, party, farm

B. are, warm

Review
13. cut 14. fast

Challenge
15. large 16. carpet

Independent Practice

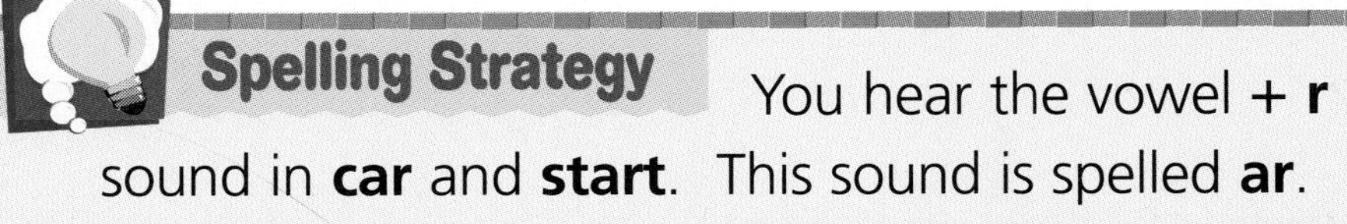

Spelling Strategy You hear the vowel + **r** sound in **car** and **start**. This sound is spelled **ar**.

Phonics Write Basic Words to answer the questions.

1. Which word ends with the long **e** sound?
2. Which word begins and ends like **head**?
3. Which word begins and ends like **form**?
4. Which word rhymes with **yarn**?

Word Groups Think how the words in each group are alike. Write the missing Basic Words.

5. finger, hand, _______
6. inch, foot, _______
7. bus, truck, _______
8. close, nearby, _______

Word Meaning Write the Basic Word that means the same or almost the same as each word below.

9. piece
10. begin

Elephant Words Write an Elephant Word to answer each question.

11. Which word has the vowel + **r** spelling but not the vowel + **r** sound?
12. Which word has the vowel + **r** sound but is spelled **a**-consonant-**e**?

Phonics

1. party
2. hard
3. farm
4. barn

Word Groups

5. arm
6. yard
7. car
8. far

Word Meaning

9. part
10. start

Elephant Words

11. warm
12. are

UNIT
31

Dictionary

Finding the Right Meaning Use a dictionary to find all the different meanings of a word.

> **hard** **1.** The opposite of **soft**: *The glass broke when it hit the **hard** floor.* **2.** The opposite of **easy**; difficult: *That problem is too **hard** for first graders.*

Practice Write **1**, **2**, or **3** to tell which meaning of **part** or **start** is used in each sentence. Use your Spelling Dictionary.

1. Did you get a **part** in the play?
2. The engine needs a new **part**.
3. We want to **start** a softball club.

Review: Spelling Spree

Hink Pinks Write the Basic or Review Word that answers the question and rhymes with the word in dark print.

4. Where do animals like to knit? a **yarn** _______
5. What is a clever beginning? a **smart** _______
6. What is a wagon piece? a **cart** _______
7. What is a warning on a ranch? a _______ **alarm**
8. What is a quick takeoff? a _______ **blast**

Word Match Write the Basic Word that goes with each word.

9. heat
10. sleeve
11. birthday

How Are You Doing?

List the spelling words that are hard for you. Practice them with a partner.

Dictionary

1. 3
2. 2
3. 1

Hink Pinks

4. barn
5. start
6. part
7. farm
8. fast

Word Match

9. warm
10. arm
11. party

Proofreading and Writing

Proofread for Spelling Proofread these directions. Use proofreading marks to fix six spelling mistakes.

Example: How ~~fas~~ fast can you go?

Start the toy kar in a part of the yord where the grass is kut short. Stay farr away from trees. Have a friend give you a hrad push. When you ar ready to stop, pull the red bar.

Basic

1. car
2. start
3. arm
4. far
5. yard
6. part
7. barn
8. hard
9. party
10. farm
11. are
12. warm

Review

13. cut
14. fast

Challenge

15. large
16. carpet

Proofreading Marks

- ∧ Add
- Delete
- ≡ Make a capital letter
- / Make a small letter

Write Some Bumper Stickers

A bumper sticker can tell people what you think of something. Write messages for bumper stickers on colored paper. Try to use spelling words. Add some pictures.

Proofreading Tip **Check that you used correct end marks.**

Word Builder

Words with Vowel + r Make words that have the same vowel sound you hear in **car**. Write an **ar** word for each clue. The letters on the tires will help you.

1. the sound a dog makes
2. what jam comes in
3. a birthday ______
4. sun, moon, and ______
5. a kind of string
6. On your ______, get set, go!

1. ______
2. ______
3. ______

4. ______
5. ______
6. ______

Show What You Know! On another sheet of paper, write your own clue for an **ar** word. Have a friend try and guess the answer to your clue.

Vocabulary Enrichment

Social Studies

Automobiles All the words in the box have something to do with automobiles. Write those words from the box to finish this diagram. Use your Spelling Dictionary.

car

hood
motor
trunk
traffic

What a __(4)__ jam!

1. ____________
2. ____________
3. ____________
4. ____________

Try This CHALLENGE

Riddle Time! Write a word from the box to answer each riddle.

5. What kind of jam does not go on toast?
6. What do both a car and an elephant have?
7. What might be part of a car and a coat?
8. What runs but has no legs?

5. ____________
6. ____________
7. ____________
8. ____________

Fact File

Do all cars need gas? Long ago, the motors in some cars ran on steam from boiling water. Today, some special cars run on power from the sun!

UNIT 32

The Vowel + r Sound in store

Read and Say

READ the sentences. **SAY** each word in dark print.

Basic Words

Basic Words		
1. store	store	I got eggs at the **store**.
2. corn	corn	The pig ate the **corn**.
3. for	for	I looked **for** my book.
4. more	more	Nate wants **more** food.
5. or	or	I will go by car **or** bus.
6. morning	morning	I jog every **morning**.
7. short	short	We took a **short** trip.
8. born	born	When were you **born**?
9. story	story	Will you tell me a **story**?
10. horn	horn	The car **horn** beeped.
11. four	four	Anna has **four** boxes.
12. your	your	Is that **your** house?

Think and Write

Each word has the vowel + **r** sound.

the vowel + **r** sound → c**or**n, st**ore**

How are the Elephant Words different?

A. Write the first **ten** Basic Words. Then draw a line under the letters that spell the vowel + **r** sound in each word.

B. Now write the **two** Elephant Words.

A.

B.

Review
13. fish **14.** game

Challenge
15. afford **16.** before

Independent Practice

Spelling Strategy You hear a vowel + **r** sound in **corn** and **store**. This sound is spelled **or** or **ore**.

Phonics Write Basic Words to answer the questions.

1. Which word begins like and sounds like **four**?
2. Which word begins with a vowel?

3–5. Which three words rhyme with **torn**?

Word Meaning Write a Basic Word for each meaning. Use your Spelling Dictionary.

6. a place where things are sold
7. the early part of the day
8. greater in number
9. the opposite of **tall**
10. a tale you may read or hear

Elephant Words Write an Elephant Word to answer each question.

11. Which word is a homophone for **for**?
12. Which word is a homophone for **you're**?

Phonics

1. for
2. or
3. born
4. corn
5. horn

Word Meaning

6. store
7. morning
8. more
9. short
10. story

Elephant Words

11. four
12. your

UNIT
32

Review: Spelling Spree

Word Tricks

1. corn
2. morning
3. horn
4. store
5. game
6. story

Fill-In Fun

7. or
8. born
9. for
10. your
11. four
12. short

Word Tricks Take away one word from the letters in each box. Write the Basic or Review Word that is left.

1. Take away **apple**. Find a vegetable. coapplern
2. Take away **night**. Find early day. mornnighting
3. Take away **song**. Find an instrument. hosongrn
4. Take away **farm**. Find a shop. stofarmre
5. Take away **work**. Find what you play. gaworkme
6. Take away **poem**. Find a tale. stopoemry

Fill-In Fun Write the missing Basic Words.

7. laugh _______ cry
8. a newly _______ baby
9. house _______ sale
10. on _______ mark
11. _______ or less
12. tall or _______

How Are You Doing?

Write each word in a sentence. Practice with a partner any words you spelled wrong.

Proofreading and Writing

Proofread: Spelling and Commas Use a comma between the name of a city and the name of a state.

The supermarket is in Atlanta, Georgia.

Proofread this sign. Use proofreading marks to fix four spelling mistakes and two missing commas.

Example: We buy ~~carn~~ corn at a farm in Ames, Iowa.

Get ~~Mor~~ more for Yer Money!

Come to Mick's Market in Portland Oregon.

Taste our fresh ~~fich~~ fish and vegetables.

We open every morning at eight and close at ~~for~~ four.

Our new store will open soon in Salem Oregon!

Basic

1. store
2. corn
3. for
4. more
5. or
6. morning
7. short
8. born
9. story
10. horn
11. four
12. your

Review

13. fish
14. game

Challenge

15. afford
16. before

Write a List

Pretend you have won the Super Shopper contest at your supermarket. The prize is a trip to any three cities you choose! List the cities you would like to visit. Tell why you would like to go there. Try to use spelling words.

Proofreading Tip **Make sure you put a comma between the name of a city and the name of a state.**

Proofreading Marks

- ∧ Add
- Delete
- ≡ Make a capital letter
- / Make a small letter

Phonics and Spelling

Rhyming Words

Words with Vowel + r Use the letter or letters that make the beginning sound of each picture name to make words that rhyme with **store**.

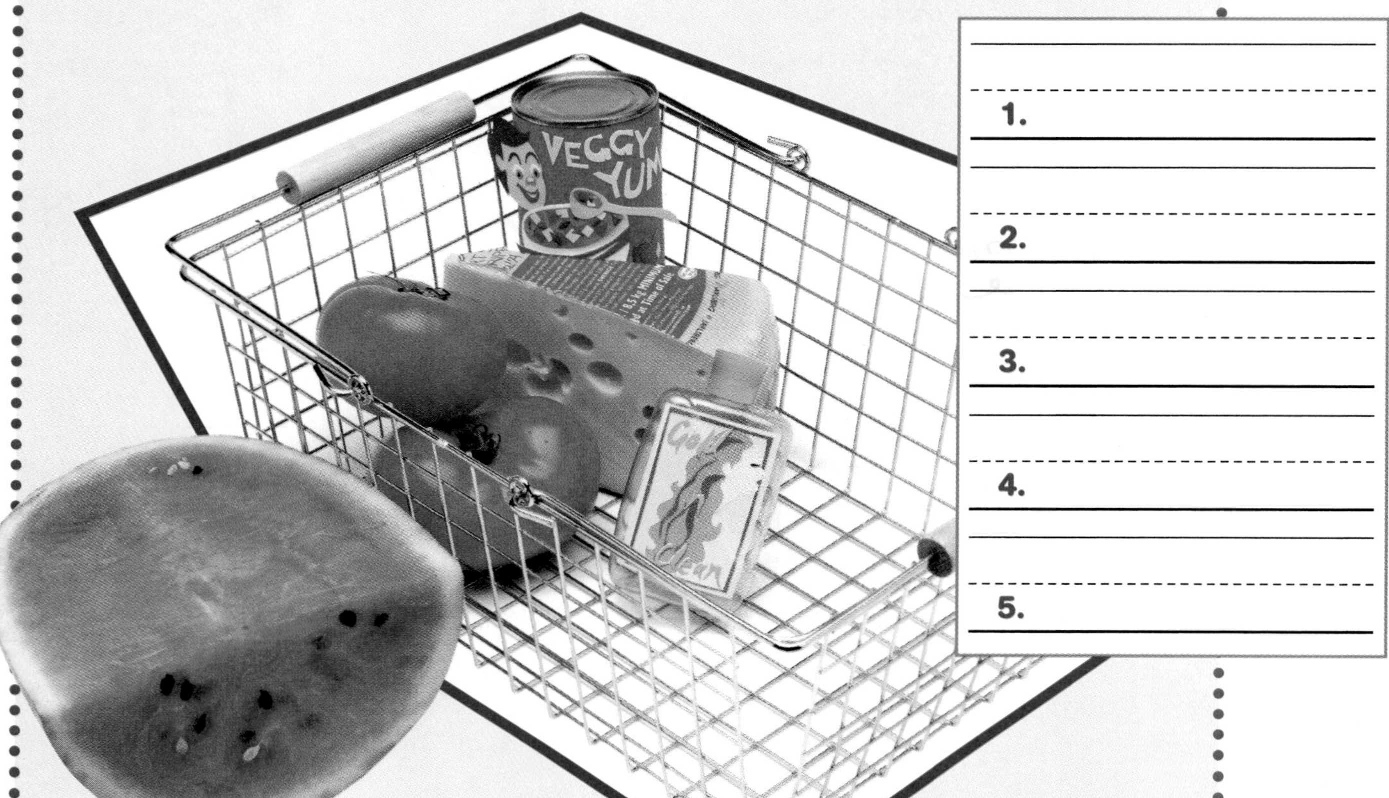

1.
2.
3.
4.
5.

Show What You Know! Pork chops are on sale at Wilson's Store. Write an ad for the sale. Use **or** and **ore** words.

Vocabulary Enrichment

Social Studies

Supermarkets All the words in the box have something to do with supermarkets. Write those words to finish these sentences. Use your Spelling Dictionary.

Spelling Word Link

store

dairy
counter
price
cart

The milk just arrived from the __(1)__. The __(2)__ of a carton is $1.89. Evan put two cartons in his __(3)__. He paid for them at the __(4)__.

1. ____________
2. ____________
3. ____________
4. ____________

Try This CHALLENGE

Yes or No? Is the word in dark print used correctly? Write **yes** or **no**.

5. Kristen writes in her **dairy** every day.
6. Manuel placed the cans on the **counter**.
7. The winner's **price** was a new bike.
8. Put the food in the shopping **cart**.

5. ____________
6. ____________
7. ____________
8. ____________

Fact File

If a dozen is twelve, what is a "baker's dozen"? Bakers sometimes add one extra for every twelve things they sell. That is why a baker's dozen is thirteen, not twelve!

UNIT 33

Words That End with er

Read and Say

READ the sentences. **SAY** each word in dark print.

Basic Words

1.	flower	*flower*	Can I smell the **flower**?
2.	water	*water*	The plants need **water**.
3.	under	*under*	My doll is **under** the bed.
4.	over	*over*	Our car went **over** a bump.
5.	better	*better*	I can swim **better** than you.
6.	sister	*sister*	My baby **sister** is crying.
7.	brother	*brother*	Is that your **brother**?
8.	mother	*mother*	I will call my **mother**.
9.	father	*father*	My **father** is at home.
10.	after	*after*	Champ ran **after** me.

Think and Write

Each word ends with the vowel + **r** sound you hear at the end of 🌼.

the vowel + **r** sound → flow**er**, wat**er**

Does each word on the list have more than one syllable?
How many syllables are there in each word?
In which syllable do you hear the vowel + **r** sound?

A. Write the **ten** Basic Words. Then draw a line under the letters that spell the vowel + **r** sound in each word.

A.

Review
11. that **12.** shop

Challenge
13. gather **14.** center

Independent Practice

Spelling Strategy The sound at the end of **flower** and **water** is a vowel + **r** sound. This sound is spelled **er**.

Phonics Write Basic Words to answer the questions.

1. Which word has the short **i** sound in the first syllable?
2. Which word has the short **e** sound in the first syllable?

3–4. Which two words have **other** in them?

Word Pairs Write a Basic Word to finish the second sentence in each pair.

5. A **plane** travels in the **air**.
   A **boat** travels in the _____.
6. A **woman** may be a **mother**.
   A **man** may be a _____.
7. You go **down** to go **under**.
   You go **up** to go _____.
8. A **trunk** is part of a **tree**.
   A **stem** is part of a _______.

petal

stem

Word Meaning Write the Basic Word that means the opposite of each word below.

9. before
10. above

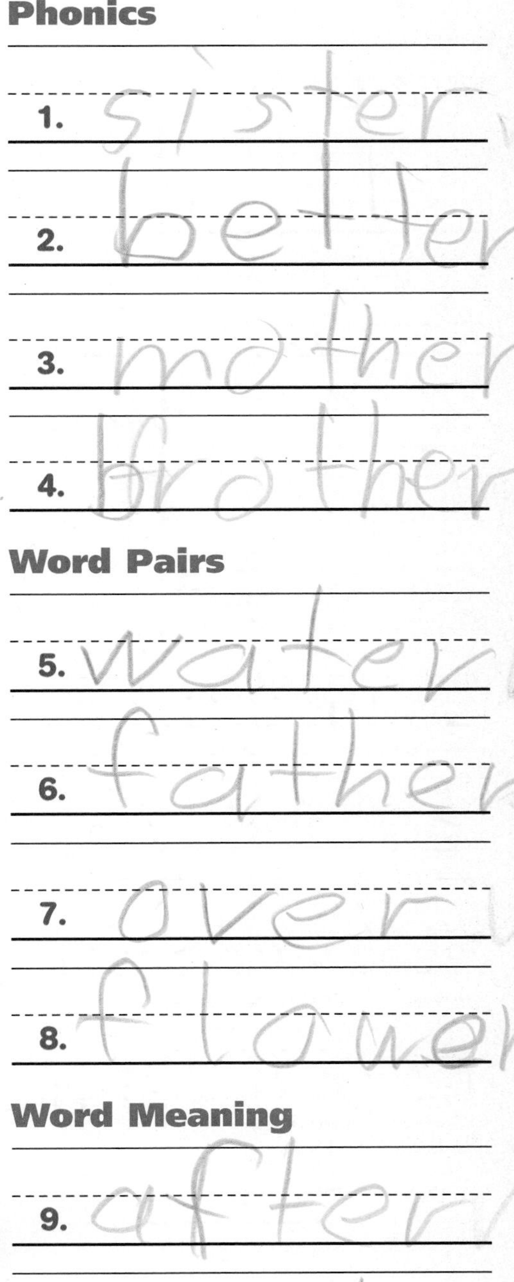

Phonics
1. sister
2. better
3. mother
4. brother
Word Pairs
5. water
6. father
7. over
8. flower
Word Meaning
9. after
10. under

UNIT
33

Review: Spelling Spree

Puzzle Play

1. ______
2. ______
3. ______
4. ______
5. ______
6. ______

Rhyme Time

7. ______
8. ______
9. ______
10. ______
11. ______
12. ______

Puzzle Play Write a Basic Word for each clue. Use the letters that would be in the boxes to spell something you use to cut grass.

1. a man in a family __ ☐ __ __ __ __
2. a woman in a family ☐ __ __ __ __ __
3. on top of ☐ __ __ __
4. melted ice ☐ __ __ __ __
5. a girl in a family __ __ __ __ ☐ __
6. behind __ __ __ __ ☐

Secret Words: __ __ __ __ __ __

Rhyme Time Finish the sentences. Write a Basic or Review Word to rhyme with the word in dark print.

7. Your **letter** is so much _______ than mine.
8. Did you buy your **mop** at that little _______ ?
9. My **other** _______ loves to work in his garden.
10. When I hear **thunder**, I hide _______ my quilt!
11. A rain **shower** may help your _______ grow.
12. The **hat** _______ you sat on is mine!

How Are You Doing?

Write your words in ABC order. Practice with a family member any words you spelled wrong.

Proofreading and Writing

Proofread: Spelling and Commas Use a comma after the **greeting** and after the **closing** in a letter.

Dear Tashia, Your friend,

Proofread this letter. Use proofreading marks to fix five spelling mistakes and two missing commas.

Example: Dear ~~Muther~~ Mother,

May 24, 1998

Dear Terrance

My fathar has a new garden thet is better than the old one. My sistur and I put in the plants. My bruther tried to help, but he sprayed watter all over us!

Your cousin

Nicole

Basic

1. flower
2. water
3. under
4. over
5. better
6. sister
7. brother
8. mother
9. father
10. after

Review

11. that
12. shop

Challenge

13. gather
14. center

Proofreading Marks

- ∧ Add
- Delete
- ≡ Make a capital letter
- / Make a small letter

Write a Letter

Pretend you are a rabbit and have just found a great vegetable garden. Write a letter to your family. Tell them about your adventure. Try to use spelling words.

Proofreading Tip **Check your letter to make sure that you put a comma after the greeting and closing.**

Vocabulary Enrichment

Word Builder

Spelling Word Link
under
over

down
in
big
tall

Opposites Some words have opposite meanings.

The ant crawled **under** a leaf and **over** a hill.

The pictures below show pairs of opposites. Write a word from the box that means the opposite of each word below.

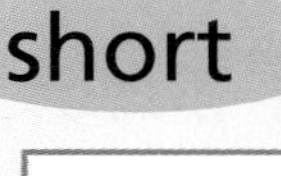

little ?

1. ____________

short ?

3. ____________

up ?

2. ____________

out ?

4. ____________

Work Together On another sheet of paper, draw pictures for two words that are opposites. Have a friend write a sentence for each of your opposites.

Science

Gardening All the words in the box have something to do with gardening. Write those words to finish these directions. Use your Spelling Dictionary.

Spelling Word Link

flower

soil
petals
shoot
hoe

How to Grow a Flower Garden

First, get a (1) from the tool shed. Next, dig into the (2) with it. Then plant the seeds and water them. In a few days, you will see the first long green (3). Before you know it, your flowers will have pretty (4)!

1. ____________
2. ____________
3. ____________
4. ____________

Try This CHALLENGE

Clue Match Write a word from the box for each clue.

5. A rose might have red ones.
6. Digging in it can make you dirty.
7. You hold it by a handle.
8. It is a plant that has just begun to grow.

5. ____________
6. ____________
7. ____________
8. ____________

Fact File

Some people think that plants grow only on land. Actually, most of the world's plants live in ocean water or grow on the ocean floor!

UNIT 34

Words That End with ed or ing

Read and Say

READ the sentences. **SAY** each word in dark print.

Basic Words

1. batted	*batted*	The girl **batted** the ball.
2. running	*running*	He is **running** in a race.
3. clapped	*clapped*	I **clapped** my hands.
4. stopped	*stopped*	She **stopped** the car.
5. getting	*getting*	My dog is **getting** big.
6. shopping	*shopping*	Will you go **shopping**?
7. stepped	*stepped*	You **stepped** on a bee!
8. hugging	*hugging*	He is **hugging** my cat.
9. pinned	*pinned*	Mom **pinned** my dress.
10. sitting	*sitting*	I am **sitting** next to you.
11. missed	*missed*	They **missed** the train.
12. telling	*telling*	Matt is **telling** a story.

Think and Write

Each word is made up of a base word and the ending **ed** or **ing**. The base word has a short vowel sound followed by a consonant.

bat + t + ed → bat**ted**
run + n + ing → run**ning**

What happens to the last letter in each base word before the ending **ed** or **ing** is added?
How are the Elephant Words different?

A. Write **six** Basic Words with the **ed** ending.
B. Write **six** Basic Words with the **ing** ending.

A. batted, clapped, stopped, steped, pinned, missed

B. running, getting, shopping, hugging, sitting, telling

Review
13. this 14. must

Challenge
15. jogging 16. flipped

Independent Practice

Spelling Strategy Some words end with a short vowel sound followed by one consonant. The final consonant in these words is usually doubled before **ed** or **ing** is added.

Phonics Write Basic Words to answer the questions.

1. Which word rhymes with **grinned**?
2. Which word rhymes with **tugging**?

3–4. Which two words have the short **e** sound in the base word and begin like **go** or **stay**?

Word Clues Write a Basic Word for each clue.

5. what the car did at the red light
6. what the children did at the end of the show
7. what you feel like doing when you are tired
8. what you would be doing at a store
9. what the baseball player did to hit the ball
10. what the racer was doing around the track

Elephant Words Write the missing Elephant Words.

11. Roberto _______ the first part of practice.
12. The coach was _______ the team what to do.

Phonics

1. pinned
2. hugging
3. getting
4. stepped

Word Clues

5. stopped
6. clapped
7. sitting
8. shopping
9. batted
10.

Elephant Words

11.
12.

Dictionary

Finding Words with Endings Words with endings like **ed** and **ing** are usually listed in the dictionary with their base word. To find **clapped**, you would look up the entry word **clap**.

entry word

clap To slap hands together: *Do not **clap** until the end of the song.* **clapped**, **clapping**

words with endings

Practice Write the entry word you would look up to find each of these words in the dictionary.

1. telling **2.** shopping **3.** pinned **4.** missed

Review: Spelling Spree

Picture Clues Write a Basic Word for each picture.

5.

6.

7.

Letter Swap Change the letters in dark print to make Basic Words. Write the words.

8. **sn**apped
9. **dr**opped
10. **s**elling
11. **dr**opping
12. **p**atted

How Are You Doing?
Write each word as a partner reads it aloud. Did you spell any words wrong?

Dictionary

1.

2.

3.

4.

Picture Clues

5.

6.

7.

Letter Swap

8.

9.

10.

11.

12.

Proofreading and Writing

Proofread for Spelling Proofread this newspaper story. Use proofreading marks to fix six spelling mistakes.

Example: The girls are ~~runing~~ running fast!

- City News Today -

A Great Race

The crowd stopped talking as Lisa steped ahead of Amy on the track. Was Amy gettin tired? Amy knew she mast win thes race. Could she do it? Later, people clapped as the judge penned a ribbon on Amy's shirt. If you weren't there, you missd a great race!

Basic

1. batted
2. running
3. clapped
4. stopped
5. getting
6. shopping
7. stepped
8. hugging
9. pinned
10. sitting
11. missed
12. telling

Review

13. this
14. must

Challenge

15. jogging
16. flipped

Proofreading Marks

- ∧ Add
- Delete
- ≡ Make a capital letter
- / Make a small letter

Write a Speech

Pretend you are a famous sports star. Write a thank-you speech for a prize you have won. Tell about yourself and your sport. Try to use spelling words. Give your speech in front of a small group.

Proofreading Tip **Use your mouse to highlight each line so that you can proofread one line at a time.**

Vocabulary Enrichment

Spelling Word Link
batted

Words That Look the Same Some words are spelled the same but have different meanings. These words are listed separately in a dictionary.

1. bat a wooden stick used for hitting the ball.

2. bat a small, furry animal with big wings.

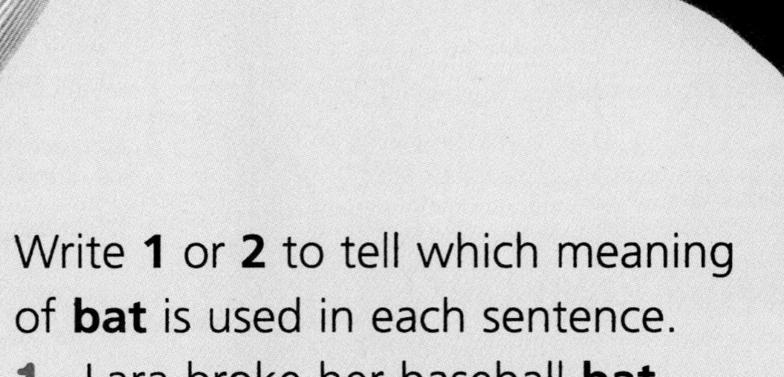

Write **1** or **2** to tell which meaning of **bat** is used in each sentence.

1. Lara broke her baseball **bat**.
2. The **bat** flew around the cave.
3. Did you see that **bat** eat a bug?
4. Ki hit the ball with his favorite **bat**.

1. ______ 2. ______ 3. ______ 4. ______

Show What You Know! On another sheet of paper, draw a picture for each meaning of the word **pen**. Then write a sentence for each picture. Use your Spelling Dictionary.

Physical Education

Sports All the words in the box have something to do with sports. Write those words to finish this sports report. Use your Spelling Dictionary.

Spelling Word Link
running

score
tie
goal
match

The Tigers and the Bears see the __(1)__ on the board. Will it be a __(2)__ game? The __(3)__ is almost over. Which team will make the next __(4)__?

1. ____________
2. ____________
3. ____________
4. ____________

Try This CHALLENGE

Yes or No? Write **yes** or **no** to answer each question.

5. Does a **tie** game mean one team wins?
6. Does making a **goal** help you win a game?
7. Can a **match** be played with only one team?
8. Do you use numbers when you keep **score**?

5. ____________
6. ____________
7. ____________
8. ____________

Fact File

Every four years, people from more than 170 countries play in the Olympic Games. The first games were held in Greece about 2,500 years ago!

UNIT 35

More Words with ed or ing

A. named
baked
liked
closed
named

B. hiding
riding
making
using
hoping

Read and Say

READ the sentences. **SAY** each word in dark print.

Basic Words

1.	liked	*liked*	I **liked** the show.
2.	hoping	*hoping*	We are **hoping** for rain.
3.	baked	*baked*	Rose **baked** a cake.
4.	using	*using*	Are you **using** the mop?
5.	chased	*chased*	The fox **chased** the sheep.
6.	making	*making*	They are **making** a kite.
7.	closed	*closed*	The store is **closed**.
8.	hiding	*hiding*	The dog is **hiding** a bone.
9.	named	*named*	Have you **named** the cat?
10.	riding	*riding*	Dad is **riding** his bike.

Think and Write

Each word is made up of a base word and the ending **ed** or **ing**. The base word has the vowel-consonant-**e** pattern.

like – e + ed → lik**ed**

hope – e + ing → hop**ing**

What is the base word for each word?
What happens to the last letter in each base word before the ending **ed** or **ing** is added?

A. Write **five** Basic Words that have the **ed** ending.

B. Write **five** Basic Words that have the **ing** ending.

Review
11. time **12.** sleep

Challenge
13. teasing **14.** decided

Independent Practice

Spelling Strategy Some words end with the vowel-consonant-**e** pattern. The final **e** in these words is dropped before **ed** or **ing** is added.

ed ing

Phonics Write Basic Words to answer the questions.

1. Which word has two syllables and has the long **a** sound?
2. Which word begins with a vowel?

3–4. Which two words have two syllables and have the long **i** sound?

Word Meaning Write the Basic Word that means the same or almost the same as each word below.

5. followed
6. enjoyed
7. shut
8. called

Word Groups Think how the words in each group are alike. Write the missing Basic Words.

9. wanting, wishing, _______
10. fried, boiled, _______

Phonics

1. making
2. using
3. hiding
4. liked

Word Meaning

5. chased
6. closed
7. liked
8. named

Word Groups

9. hoping
10. baked

UNIT
35

Dictionary

Finding Words with Endings Remember that words with endings like **ed** and **ing** are usually listed in the dictionary with their base word. To find **hoping**, you would look up the entry word **hope**.

entry word

hope To wish for something: *I **hope** that I will win this race.* **hoped, hoping**

words with endings

Practice Write the entry word you would look up to find each of these words in the dictionary.

1. making	**3.** chased	**5.** using
2. named	**4.** riding	**6.** closed

Dictionary

1. ____
2. ____
3. ____
4. ____
5. ____
6. ____

Review: Spelling Spree

ABC Words Use ABC order to write the missing letter in each group. Make Basic or Review Words.

7.	t _ v	r _ t	h _ j	m _ o	f _ h	
8.	r _ t	k _ m	d _ f	d _ f	o _ q	
9.	k _ m	h _ j	j _ l	d _ f	c _ e	
10.	g _ i	n _ p	o _ q	h _ j	m _ o	f _ h
11.	b _ d	k _ m	n _ p	r _ t	d _ f	c _ e
12.	g _ i	h _ j	c _ e	h _ j	m _ o	f _ h

ABC Words

7. ____
8. ____
9. ____
10. ____
11. ____
12. ____

How Are You Doing?

Write each spelling word in a sentence. Practice with a family member any words you spelled wrong.

Proofreading and Writing

Proofread for Spelling Proofread this page from a television guide. Use proofreading marks to fix six spelling mistakes.

Example: Wag loves to ~~slep~~ sleep on Pete's bed.

For Pete's Sake is about a boy naemd Pete and his dog, Wag. Last week, they chazed each other, played hiding games, and went rideing in a car. Pete liked makeing Wag happy. He bakked him a dog cookie. This tim, Wag will help Pete. Watch and find out how!

Basic

1. liked
2. hoping
3. baked
4. using
5. chased
6. making
7. closed
8. hiding
9. named
10. riding

Review

11. time
12. sleep

Challenge

13. teasing
14. decided

Proofreading Marks

- ∧ Add
- ⌒ Delete
- ≡ Make a capital letter
- / Make a small letter

Write a Story

Write a story about a time when you had a problem and a friend helped you. Try to use spelling words. Draw pictures to go with your story. Share your story with a friend.

Proofreading Tip **Read your paper again. Put a check mark on each word to show that you have looked at it.**

Vocabulary Enrichment

Word Builder

Building Words with ful When you add **ful** to a word, it changes the meaning of the word.

hope + ful = hope**ful**

The word **hopeful** means "full of hope."

Finish the chart below.

1. help + ful =
2. thank + ful =
3. play + ful =
4. pain + ful =

Work Together Make these sentences easier to read. Write a word that means the same as each group of words in dark print. Use the words you made in the chart. Work with a friend.

5. Rina's new kitten is **full of play**.
6. David is **full of help** around the house.
7. Dad was **full of thanks** when the car started.
8. My broken foot is **full of pain** when I stand on it.

5.	7.
6.	8.

Vocabulary Enrichment

Social Studies

Friendship All the words in the box have something to do with friendship. Write those words to finish this note. Use your Spelling Dictionary.

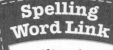

Spelling Word Link

liked

neighbor
share
welcome
invite

Dear Ariana,

Can you come to my house on Sunday? My new __(1)__ moved in next door. I will __(2)__ her to play with us. We can make her feel __(3)__. We can __(4)__ our toys with her.

Sarah

1. ____________
2. ____________
3. ____________
4. ____________

Write a Play Write a short play about two people who are best friends. Tell about some of the things that they do together. Try to use words from the box on this page.

Fact File

Eleanor Roosevelt was a special friend to people who needed help. The wife of a president, she worked to make life better for people all over the world.

36 Review: Units 31–35

1. ____
2. ____
3. ____
4. ____
5. ____
6. ____
7. ____
8. ____
9. ____
10. ____
11. ____
12. ____

Unit 31 Vowel + r Sound in car pages 204–209

ar
car

start	arm	far
barn	hard	party

Spelling Strategy

The vowel + **r** sound in **far** is spelled **ar**.

Write the spelling word that means the opposite.

1. easy **2.** near **3.** stop

Write the missing spelling words.

The doctor took the cast off Maya's **(4)** today. Tomorrow we will have a big **(5)** for her in our **(6)**.

Unit 32 Vowel + r Sound in store pages 210–215

store

store	corn	or
morning	short	story

Spelling Strategy

The vowel + **r** sound in **corn** and **store** is spelled **or** or **ore**.

Write the spelling word that means the same.

7. shop **8.** small

Write the missing spelling words.

Every **(9)** I read a **(10)** as I eat breakfast. I like to eat toast **(11)** a big **(12)** muffin.

Unit 33 Words Ending with er pages 216–221

flower	water	better
sister	father	after

Spelling Strategy The vowel + **r** sound at the end of **flower** is spelled **er**.

Write the spelling word that goes with each word.

13. man **15.** girl
14. garden **16.** river

Write the missing spelling words.

17. We went to the park _______ school.
18. Jill can climb the bars _______ than anyone.

Unit 34 Words with ed or ing pages 222–227

running	clapped	getting
shopping	stepped	pinned

Spelling Strategy run + ing → running
clap + ed → clapped

Change the letters in dark print. Write spelling words.

19. **st**opping **21.** **tr**apped
20. **p**etting **22.** ru**bb**ing

Write the missing spelling words.

23. I stood on a chair as Gram _______ my skirt.
24. Then I _______ down and changed my clothes.

13. ____
14. ____
15. ____
16. ____
17. ____
18. ____
19. ____
20. ____
21. ____
22. ____
23. ____
24. ____

Unit 35 More Words with ed or ing pages 228–233

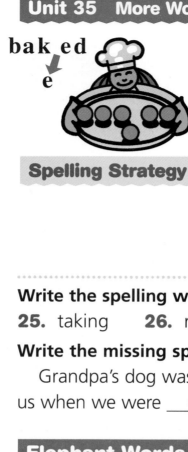

bak ed
e

liked	hoping	chased
making	named	riding

Spelling Strategy

like + ed → liked
name + ed → named
hope + ing → hoping
ride + ing → riding

Write the spelling word that rhymes with each word.

25. taking **26.** roping **27.** hiked

Write the missing spelling words.

Grandpa's dog was ___(**28**)___ Frisky. He always ___(**29**)___ us when we were ___(**30**)___ our bikes.

25. ____________
26. ____________
27. ____________
28. ____________
29. ____________
30. ____________
31. ____________
32. ____________
33. ____________
34. ____________
35. ____________
36. ____________

Elephant Words Units 31–35 pages 204–233

are	warm	four
your	missed	telling

Spelling Strategy Elephant Words have unusual spellings. Check them carefully when you write them.

Write the missing spelling words.

The ___(**31**)___ of us ___(**32**)___ playing tag to keep ___(**33**)___. I just ___(**34**)___ tagging ___(**35**)___ coat with my hand. You keep ___(**36**)___ me that you can run faster than I can, but we will see!

Spelling-Meaning Strategy

Word Families

You know that words in the same family are alike in spelling and meaning. Look at this word family.

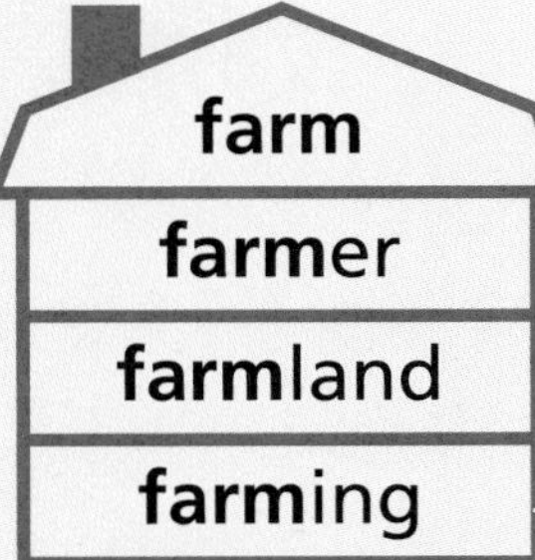

Miss Green lives on a **farm**.
She is a cattle **farmer**.
She owns a lot of **farmland**.
Farming is hard work.

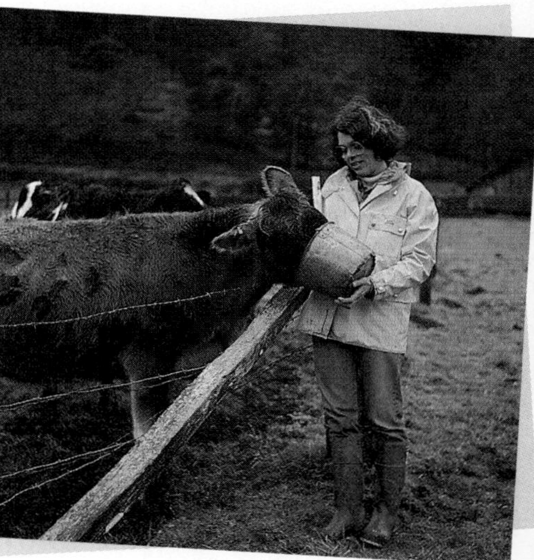

Think How are the words in this family alike in meaning? How are they alike in spelling?

Apply and Extend

Write a word from the farm **family in each sentence.**

1. We visited a big _______ today.
2. There were many miles of _______.
3. The _______ showed us the fields.
4. We learned what hard work _______ is!

1. ____________
2. ____________
3. ____________
4. ____________

With a partner, think of words in these families. Make a list for each family.

Check the Word Families list that begins on page 272. Did you miss any words? Add them to your lists.

UNIT 36

Letters

Literature and Writing

based on

Send Wendell

by Genevieve Gray

In the story, Wendell's Uncle Robert comes for a visit. Wendell might have written this letter after Uncle Robert left. What does this letter tell about?

July 15, 1989

Dear Uncle Robert,

Thank you for coming to visit us. I had fun playing in the park and going to the zoo with you. I can't wait to visit you at your farm in California. Come back and see us soon!

Love,
Wendell

Think and Discuss

1. Why would this letter be interesting to Uncle Robert?
2. What are **five parts** of a letter? You may need to look at the example on page 261 if you need help.
3. What part tells when the letter was written?
4. What part tells who wrote the letter?

The Writing Process

Letters

Who do you think would like to get a letter from you? Write a letter to that person. Follow the guidelines. Use the Writing Process.

1 Prewriting
- Make a list of questions to answer in your letter.

2 Draft
- Pretend that the person you are writing to is sitting next to you. Write your letter as if you were talking to that person.

3 Revise
- Add words or sentences that will make your letter more interesting.
- Remember to use your Thesaurus to find exact words.
- Read your letter to a friend. Make changes.

4 Proofread
- Did you spell each word correctly?
- Did you use commas correctly?

5 Publish
- Copy your letter, and address an envelope. Mail your letter.

Guidelines for Writing a Letter

✓ Be sure to include all five parts of the letter.

✓ Use details that help your reader picture what you are writing about.

Composition Words

are
more
your
mother
missed
liked

Student's Handbook

Extra Practice and Review

Cycle 1

Unit 1 Spelling the Short a Sound pages 24–29

hat	bag	as
bat	sat	bad

Spelling Strategy The short **a** sound may be spelled **a**.

Write the spelling word that goes with each word.

1. chair **2.** ball **3.** head

Write the missing spelling words.

Tilly left the store with a big __(4)__ of food. Just __(5)__ she stepped outside, she tripped. That was a __(6)__ way to start the day!

Unit 2 Spelling the Short e Sound pages 30–35

pet	ten	bed
help	set	went

Spelling Strategy The short **e** sound may be spelled **e**.

Change the letter in dark print. Write a spelling word.

7. **d**en **9.** ba**d**

8. s**a**t **10.** **s**ent

Write the missing spelling words.

Ben and I are going to a special zoo. We can __(11)__ the animals' soft fur. We can even __(12)__ feed the baby sheep and goats!

1. ______
2. ______
3. ______
4. ______
5. ______
6. ______
7. ______
8. ______
9. ______
10. ______
11. ______
12. ______

Unit 3 Spelling the Short i Sound pages 36–41

ĭ pig

win	is	six
hit	pin	dig

Spelling Strategy

The short **i** sound may be spelled **i**.

Write the spelling word that rhymes with each word.

13. sit **14.** mix **15.** big

Write the missing spelling words.

16. Will Joe _______ a prize for his pumpkin?

17. The prize _______ a big blue ribbon.

18. Joe can _______ the ribbon to his shirt.

Unit 4 Spelling the Short o Sound pages 42–47

ŏ top

pot	nod	not
fox	mop	spot

Spelling Strategy

The short **o** sound may be spelled **o**.

Write a spelling word for each clue.

19. You use it to clean.

20. You use it to cook.

21. It has a bushy tail.

22. Your head does this.

Write the missing spelling words.

23. My broken pen left a _______ on my shirt.

24. I could _______ clean the ink off.

Unit 5 Spelling the Short u Sound pages 48–53

sun	mud	bug
bun	nut	bus

Spelling Strategy The short **u** sound may be spelled **u**.

Write the spelling word for each clue.

25. ant **26.** dirt **27.** acorn

Write the missing spelling words.

28. Dad and I ride on the _______ to the beach.
29. The _______ is beginning to shine.
30. I eat a soft _______ from our basket.

Elephant Words Units 1–5 pages 24–53

want	any	said
I	some	from

Spelling Strategy Elephant Words have unusual spellings. Check them carefully when you write them.

Write the missing spelling words.

Mom and __(**31**)__ saw __(**32**)__ people making juice. They made it __(**33**)__ oranges. Mom __(**34**)__ that a machine took out all the seeds. I didn't find __(**35**)__ seeds at all. I __(**36**)__ a machine like that!

25. ______

26. ______

27. ______

28. ______

29. ______

30. ______

31. ______

32. ______

33. ______

34. ______

35. ______

36. ______

1. ______
2. ______
3. ______
4. ______
5. ______
6. ______
7. ______
8. ______
9. ______
10. ______
11. ______
12. ______

Unit 7 Vowel-Consonant-e pages 60–65

ī five

late	nine	made
fine	same	hide

Spelling Strategy The long **a** and the long **i** vowel sounds may be spelled by the vowel-consonant-**e** pattern.

Write a spelling word that means the opposite.

1. different **3.** early
2. find **4.** sick

Write the missing spelling words.

5. We ______ a list of birds that we saw today.
6. I counted ______ different kinds of birds!

Unit 8 More Vowel-Consonant-e pages 66–71

ō bone

use	these	rope
home	close	those

Spelling Strategy The long **o**, **u**, and **e** vowel sounds may be spelled by the vowel-consonant-**e** pattern.

Change the letter in dark print. Write a spelling word.

7. c**h**ose **8.** **r**ole **9.** ho**s**e

Write the missing spelling words.

Do you want to __(**10**)__ any of __(**11**)__ balloons right here? I think __(**12**)__ over there are prettier.

Unit 9 Consonant Clusters pages 72–77

swim	step	nest
brave	glad	lost

sw
swim

Spelling Strategy A **consonant cluster** is two consonant letters whose sounds are blended together.

Write the spelling word that goes with each word.

13. bird **15.** foot
14. smile **16.** pool

Write the missing spelling words.

17. One day I got _______ in the park.
18. I was _______ and did not get scared.

Unit 10 Words Spelled with k or ck pages 78–83

rock	pick	truck
bake	clock	kick

k
lake

Spelling Strategy The final consonant sound in **bake** and **rock** may be spelled **k** or **ck**.

Write the spelling word you see in each longer word.

19. bakery **20.** kickstand **21.** pickle

Write the missing spelling words.

We used a **(22)** to move broken things. A wheel hit a **(23)**, and an old **(24)** began to tick!

13. _______
14. _______
15. _______
16. _______
17. _______
18. _______
19. _______
20. _______
21. _______
22. _______
23. _______
24. _______

Unit 11 Double Consonants pages 84–89

gg
egg

bell	off	dress
will	grass	tell

Spelling Strategy A final consonant sound may be spelled with two letters that are the same.

Write the spelling word that rhymes with each word.

25. pass **26.** mess **27.** fill

Write the missing spelling words.

We heard the __(**28**)__ ring. Then Ms. Day came to __(**29**)__ us it was time to get __(**30**)__ the swings.

Elephant Words Units 7–11 pages 60–89

ONE

give	have
one	goes

Spelling Strategy Elephant Words have unusual spellings. Check them carefully when you write them.

Write the missing words. Use some words two times.

I __(**31**)__ my library card to the man. He __(**32**)__ to check my name. I already __(**33**)__ two books, but I can take __(**34**)__ more. I __(**35**)__ to decide between two books. Which __(**36**)__ should I take?

25. ________

26. ________

27. ________

28. ________

29. ________

30. ________

31. ________

32 ________

33. ________

34. ________

35. ________

36. ________

Cycle 3

Unit 13 More Long a Spellings page 96–101

way	play	trail
sail	hay	nail

Spelling Strategy The long **a** sound may be spelled **ay** or **ai**.

Write the spelling word that is hidden in each box.

1. tshaymle **2.** adlplaymi **3.** osptrailyk

Write the missing spelling words.

The **(4)** on our boat is torn. It ripped on a sharp **(5)** on the **(6)** to our picnic.

Unit 14 More Long e Spellings pages 102–107

keep	please	we
eat	tree	mean

Spelling Strategy The long **e** sound may be spelled **e, ee,** or **ea**.

Write the spelling words that go with the words.

7. food **9.** thank-you

8. save **10.** leaf

Write the missing spelling words.

11. At school _______ are learning about words.

12. The word **bat** can _______ different things.

1. ________
2. ________
3. ________
4. ________
5. ________
6. ________
7. ________
8. ________
9. ________
10. ________
11. ________
12. ________

Unit 15 The Vowel Sound in ball pages 108–113

a ball

paw	call	ball
small	log	fall

Spelling Strategy

The vowel sound in **ball** may be spelled **o, aw,** or **a** before **ll**.

Write the spelling word for each clue.

13. tiny **14.** foot **15.** wood **16.** shout

Write the missing spelling words.

17. Jeff hit the _______ high into the air.

18. We watched it _______ into the bushes.

Unit 16 Words with sh or ch pages 114–119

sh sheep

chase	wish	much
such	wash	ship

Spelling Strategy

the **sh** sound → **ship, wish**
the **ch** sound → **chase, much**

Write the spelling word that rhymes with each word.

19. clip **20.** fish **21.** case

Write the missing spelling words.

Fido splashes too __(**22**)__ soap and water on us. It is __(**23**)__ hard work to __(**24**)__ him!

13. ______
14. ______
15. ______
16. ______
17. ______
18. ______
19. ______
20. ______
21. ______
22. ______
23. ______
24. ______

Unit 17 Words with th or wh pages 120–125

when	then	with
what	while	which

th
teeth

Spelling Strategy the **th** sounds → **with, then**
the **wh** sound → **when**

Change the letters in dark print. Write spelling words.

25. wi**ll** **26.** th**an** **27.** **sm**ile

Write the missing spelling words.

Now __(**28**)__ will I do? I can't tell __(**29**)__ fish is mine __(**30**)__ they all swim together!

Elephant Words Units 13–17 pages 96–125

they	great	the
people	catch	sure

S U R E

Spelling Strategy Elephant Words have unusual spellings. Check them carefully when you write them.

Write the missing spelling words.

Many __(**31**)__ came to __(**32**)__ fishing contest. Everyone was __(**33**)__ that Jill would __(**34**)__ the most fish. Later, we had a cookout. We cooked every fish, and __(**35**)__ all tasted __(**36**)__!

25. ____
26. ____
27. ____
28. ____
29. ____
30. ____
31. ____
32. ____
33. ____
34. ____
35. ____
36. ____

Unit 19 Words with nd, ng, or nk pages 132–137

ng
king

king	thank	hand
think	long	thing

Spelling Strategy Some words end with the consonants **nd, ng,** or **nk**.

Write the spelling word that goes with each word.

1. finger **2.** idea **3.** crown

Write the missing spelling words.

I wrote a ___(**4**)___ letter to ___(**5**)___ Papa. I wish I knew the name of the ___(**6**)___ he sent me!

Unit 20 Words with s or es pages 138–143

bikes
es

dishes	bells	boxes
wishes	things	names

Spelling Strategy

s → bells, names
es → dishes, boxes

Write the spelling word that rhymes with each word.

7. smells **8.** wings **9.** flames

Write the missing spelling words.

Kate took the tops off the ___(**10**)___. Inside were toy cups and ___(**11**)___! Her ___(**12**)___ had come true!

1. ______
2. ______
3. ______
4. ______
5. ______
6. ______
7. ______
8. ______
9. ______
10. ______
11. ______
12. ______

Unit 21 More Long o Spellings pages 144–149

boat	cold	no
coat	grow	show

ō
boat

Spelling Strategy The long **o** sound may be spelled **o, oa,** or **ow.**

Write the spelling word for each meaning.

13. to get big **14.** a ship **15.** to point out

Write the missing spelling words.

Len buttoned his ___(**16**)___. The ___(**17**)___ air made his ears sting. He had ___(**18**)___ hat for his head!

Unit 22 Sounds in moon and book pages 150–155

zoo	food	book
soon	good	foot

o͝o
book

o͞o
moon

Spelling Strategy The vowel sounds in **food** and **book** may be spelled **oo**.

Write the spelling word you see in each longer word.

19. cookbook **20.** football **21.** goodness

Write the missing spelling words.

We visited the seals at the ___(**22**)___. We gave them some ___(**23**)___. I hope we can go back ___(**24**)___!

13. ______
14. ______
15. ______
16. ______
17. ______
18. ______
19. ______
20. ______
21. ______
22. ______
23. ______
24. ______

25. ______
26. ______
27. ______
28. ______
29. ______
30. ______
31. ______
32. ______
33. ______
34. ______
35. ______
36. ______

Unit 23 Homophones pages 156–161

plain plane

plane	plain	rode
road	hole	whole

Spelling Strategy **Homophones** sound alike but do not have the same spelling or the same meaning.

Change the letters in dark print. Write spelling words.

25. **tr**ain **26.** hol**d** **27.** pla**t**e **28.** **st**ole

Write the missing spelling words.

29. We ______ in a special parade car.

30. People by the side of the ______ waved.

Elephant Words Units 19–23 pages 132–161

who

toe	you	who
to	too	two

Spelling Strategy Elephant Words have unusual spellings. Check them carefully when you write them.

I am looking for someone **(31)** can teach me how **(32)** dance. Each time I try, I step on my own **(33)**. I cannot make my **(34)** feet work together! Maybe **(35)** have this problem **(36)**!

Cycle 5

Unit 25 More Long i Spellings pages 168–173

sky	find	night
try	right	kind

Spelling Strategy The long **i** sound may be spelled **y, i,** or **igh.**

Write the spelling word that means the same.

1. evening **2.** correct **3.** friendly

Write the missing spelling words.

Tonight the __(**4**)__ is full of stars. Tina and I will __(**5**)__ to __(**6**)__ the Dog Star.

Unit 26 Final Sound in puppy pages 174–179

puppy	lucky	happy
funny	many	only

Spelling Strategy The long **e** sound at the end of a two-syllable word may be spelled **y**.

Change the letters in the dark print. Write spelling words.

7. **b**unny **8.** ha**nd**y **9.** lu**mp**y

Write the missing spelling words.

The tiny __(**10**)__ was sleepy. It was __(**11**)__ one week old. It had __(**12**)__ things to learn!

1. ______
2. ______
3. ______
4. ______
5. ______
6. ______
7. ______
8. ______
9. ______
10. ______
11. ______
12. ______

13.
14.
15.
16.
17.
18.
19.
20.
21.
22.
23.
24.

Unit 27 The Vowel Sound in cow pages 180–185

ow
cow

town	house	cow
how	mouse	brown

Spelling Strategy The vowel sound in **brown** and **mouse** may be spelled **ow** or **ou**.

Write the spelling word that goes with each word.

13. calf **14.** color **15.** home **16.** city

Write the missing spelling words.

17. I saw a _______ run across the floor.

18. I wonder _______ it got in here!

Unit 28 Compound Words pages 186–191

bathtub

bedtime	myself	maybe
upon	anyone	without

Spelling Strategy A **compound word** is a word that is made up of two shorter words.

Change the word in dark print. Write a spelling word.

19. any**thing** **20.** bed**room** **21.** **your**self

Write the missing spelling words.

Look at the bird sitting __(**22**)__ that branch. Oh, __(**23**)__ you can't see it __(**24**)__ these glasses.

Unit 29 Contractions pages 192–197

I'll	you're	isn't
didn't	I've	we'll

Spelling Strategy

I + will → **I'll**
is + not → **isn't**

Write the contraction for each pair of words.

25. did not **26.** we will **27.** you are

Write the missing spelling words.

I think __(**28**)__ need a new coat soon. The one that __(**29**)__ been wearing __(**30**)__ big enough.

Elephant Words Units 25–29 pages 168–197

eye	buy	cookie
could	should	can't

Spelling Strategy Elephant Words have unusual spellings. Check them carefully when you write them.

Write the missing spelling words.

Mom lets me __(**31**)__ a __(**32**)__ at the bakery. I __(**33**)__ decide which one I want. I wish I __(**34**)__ take them all. Maybe I __(**35**)__ just close one __(**36**)__ and choose without looking!

25. ________
26. ________
27. ________
28. ________
29. ________
30. ________
31. ________
32. ________
33. ________
34. ________
35. ________
36. ________

Unit 31 Vowel + r Sound in car pages 204–209

ar car

car	start	yard
part	barn	farm

Spelling Strategy The vowel + **r** sound in **car** is spelled **ar**.

Change the letter in dark print. Write a spelling word.

1. par**k** **2.** **j**ar **3.** **y**arn **4.** **h**arm

Write the missing spelling words.

5. I have a small garden in my back _______.

6. I will _______ planting seeds there soon.

Unit 32 Vowel + r Sound in store pages 210–215

store

store	for	more
short	born	horn

Spelling Strategy The vowel + **r** sound in **for** and **store** is spelled **or** or **ore**.

Write the spelling word that means the opposite.

7. less **8.** long

Write the missing spelling words.

Jed went to the __(**9**)__ and bought a bike __(**10**)__. He also got a toy __(**11**)__ his newly __(**12**)__ son.

1. ____________
2. ____________
3. ____________
4. ____________
5. ____________
6. ____________
7. ____________
8. ____________
9. ____________
10. ____________
11. ____________
12. ____________

Cycle 6

Unit 33 Words Ending with er pages 216–221

under	over	better
brother	mother	after

Spelling Strategy The vowel + **r** sound at the end of **under** is spelled **er**.

Write the spelling word that means the same.

13. above **14.** below **15.** mom

Write the missing spelling words.

My little __(**16**)__ Zane plays the drums each night __(**17**)__ supper. I hope he plays __(**18**)__ soon!

Unit 34 Words with ed or ing pages 222–227

batted	getting	stopped
hugging	pinned	sitting

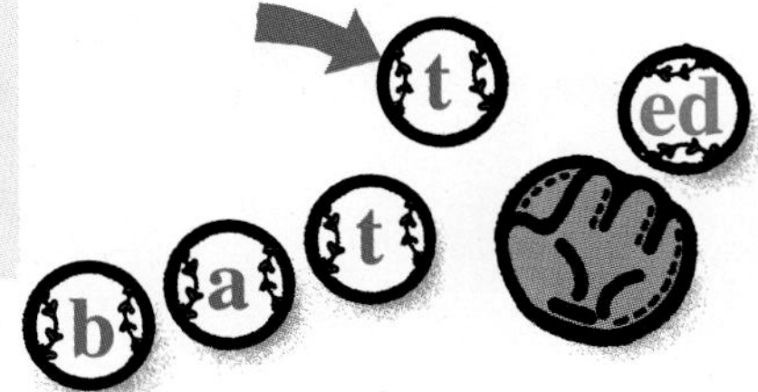

Spelling Strategy

stop + ed → stopped
hug + ing → hugging

Write the spelling word that rhymes.

19. popped **20.** hitting **21.** letting **22.** patted

Write the missing spelling words.

23. The judge ________ a ribbon on Sarah's picture.

24. Then everyone began ________ Sarah.

13. ____________________

14. ____________________

15. ____________________

16. ____________________

17. ____________________

18. ____________________

19. ____________________

20. ____________________

21. ____________________

22. ____________________

23. ____________________

24. ____________________

25.

26.

27.

28.

29.

30.

31.

32.

33.

34.

35.

36.

Unit 35 More Words with ed or ing pages 228–233

bak ed
e

hoping	baked	using
closed	hiding	riding

Spelling Strategy

bake + ed → baked
close + ed → closed
hope + ing → hoping
hide + ing → hiding

Write the spelling word that goes with each word.

25. cake **26.** horse **27.** door

Write the missing spelling words.

Dad was __(**28**)__ his special glasses. He was __(**29**)__ to see Mars, but it was __(**30**)__ behind a cloud.

Elephant Words Units 31–35 pages 204–233

are

are	warm	four
your	missed	telling

Spelling Strategy Elephant Words have unusual spellings. Check them carefully when you write them.

Write the missing spelling words.

The baker was __(**31**)__ us a very long story. Now we have __(**32**)__ the bus. The bakery is __(**33**)__ blocks from __(**34**)__ house. We do not even have coats! How __(**35**)__ we going to stay __(**36**)__?

Writer's Resources

Capitalization and Punctuation Guide

Rules for Capitalization

Sentences	**Begin every sentence with a capital letter.** **T**he girl looked at the picture. **W**hat did the picture show?
People, Places, Pets	**Begin the names of people, places, and pets with capital letters.** My friend **D**ean lives on **E**lm **S**treet in **L**akewood. He has a dog named **W**ags.
I	**Always write the pronoun** I **as a capital letter.** Stan and **I** rode our bikes.
Days	**Begin the names of the days of the week with capital letters.** Is the picnic on **S**aturday?
Holidays	**Begin the names of holidays with capital letters.** There are parades on **C**olumbus **D**ay.
Months	**Begin the names of months with capital letters.** Were you born in **J**anuary?
Titles for People	**Begin titles for people with capital letters. Put a period after most titles.** **M**rs**.** Mann **M**r**.** Chan **D**r**.** Rogers **M**s**.** Willis **M**iss Gomez **The title** Miss **does not end with a period.**

Book Titles	**Begin the first word, the last word, and each important word in a book title with a capital letter. Draw a line under the title.** The book <u>**T**he **C**at in the **H**at</u> is funny. I read <u>**T**he **S**nowy **D**ay</u> yesterday.

Rules for Punctuation

End Marks	**End a telling sentence with a period.** The squirrel is brown**.**
	End a question with a question mark. Does the squirrel see the nut**?**
Apostrophes	**Use an apostrophe in a contraction to show where letters are left out.** do not → don't I have → I've you are → you're we will → we'll
Commas	**Use a comma between the day and the year in a date.** Penny was born on June 21**,** 1982. She started school on August 31**,** 1988.
	Use a comma between the name of a city or a town and the name of a state. We watched fireworks in Tampa**,** Florida. We went to a fair in Carmel**,** California.
	Use a comma after the greeting and after the closing in a letter. Dear Daniel**,** Yours truly**,**

Writer's Resources

Letter Model

Friendly Letter

Remember that a letter has **five** parts.

1. The **date** tells when the letter was written.
2. The **greeting** means "hello."
3. The **body** is the main part of the letter.
4. The **closing** means "good-by."
5. The **name** tells who wrote the letter.

Use all five parts when you write a letter. Put capital letters and commas where they belong.

Study this letter model.

Greeting

May 5, 1998 ← Date

Dear Kim,

Body → Aunt Rose took us to the circus on Saturday. It was the most fun I've ever had! The circus goes to Boston next. Will you get to see it?

Closing → Your friend,

Jessica ← Name

My First Thesaurus

How to Use This Thesaurus

A thesaurus can help you find just the right words to use when you write. Imagine you wrote this sentence:

My birthday gift came in a big box.

You decide that **big** doesn't tell how big the box really was. You need a more exact word.

You can find other words for **big** in this thesaurus. The entry words in a thesaurus are in ABC order, so you turn to the **B** section and find **big**.

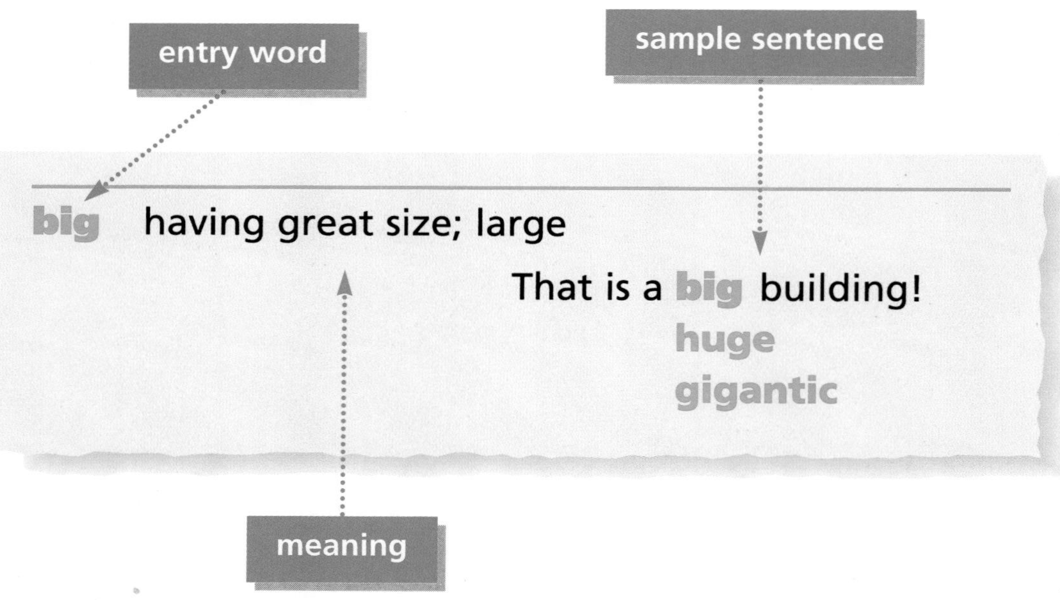

You read the meaning of the word **big**. Then you read the sample sentence. You see that **huge** and **gigantic** are words you could use in place of **big**.

You decide that **huge** is the word that tells how big the box really was. You write your sentence again, using the word **huge** in place of **big**.

My birthday gift came in a huge box.

My First Thesaurus

afraid filled with fear

My dog is **afraid** of water.
scared
frightened

---

argue to fight using words

We **argue** about what to play.
quarrel
disagree

bad not pleasant

The **bad** weather made us sad.
terrible
awful

---

big having great size; large

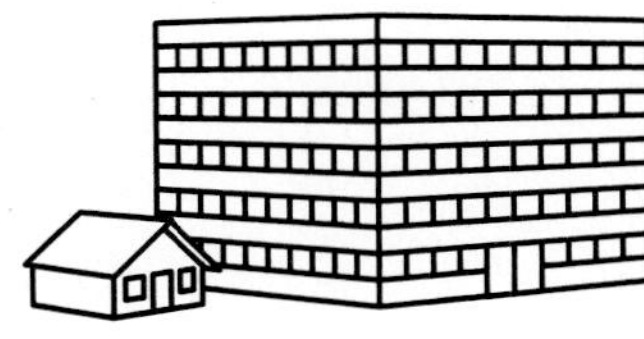

That is a **big** building!
huge
gigantic

---

boat a small craft that floats and moves on water

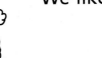

We like to ride on a **boat**.
ship
vessel

(continued)

brave able to face danger or pain without fear

Officer Day is a **brave** woman.
bold
fearless

break to cause to come apart

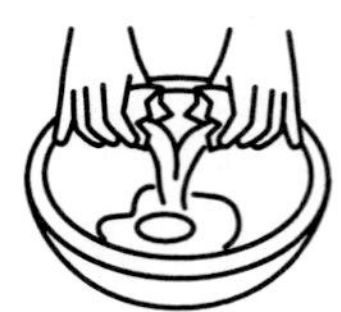

Word Bank

burst	shatter
destroy	tear
split	crush
crack	smash

bright giving off light

Look at Sarah's **bright** new bike!
sparkling
gleaming

close to move something so that it is not open

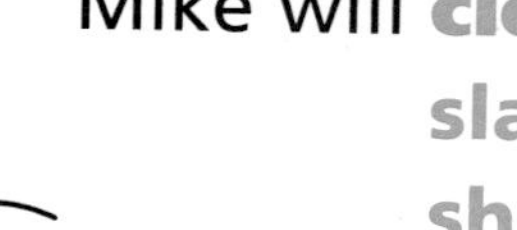

Mike will **close** the car door.
slam
shut

cold having no warmth

The air here is very **cold**.
icy
chilly

cook to use heat to prepare food

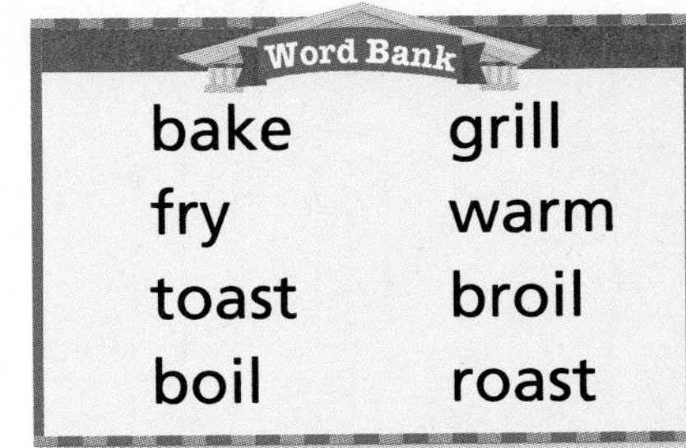

cry to have tears fall from your eyes

The sad movie made me **cry**.

weep

sob

F

fast with great speed

Can you run as **fast** as Tia?

quickly

swiftly

find to look for and discover

We hope to **find** Pablo's keys.

spot

locate

fix to make something work right

Fran will **fix** the zipper.

repair

mend

go to move from one place to another

Is it time to **go** yet?
leave
depart

great very good

You did a **great** job!
wonderful
terrific

happy showing or feeling joy

We were **happy** to see Grandpa.
glad
delighted

help to do what is needed or useful

Will you **help** me?
assist
aid

hot giving off much heat

Dad built a **hot** fire.
sizzling
blazing

job work that needs to be done

Doing the dishes is my **job**!

task
chore

---

jump to spring into the air

Jon will **jump** over the puddle.

hop
leap

---

junk things that are of no use

I threw out all the **junk**!

trash
rubbish

kind a group of things that are alike

This **kind** of fruit is best.

type
variety

---

knock to hit

Word Bank

bang	strike
rap	whack
thump	pound
beat	tap

L

little not big

Gus waved to the **little** girl.
small
tiny

look to watch or see

Dan likes to **look** at flowers.
stare
gaze

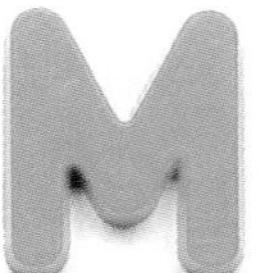

make to put together

Word Bank

build	produce
mold	shape
create	construct
form	assemble

nice pleasant; not mean

My friends are very **nice**.
friendly
kind

old having lived a long time

The **old** man was very helpful.
elderly
aged

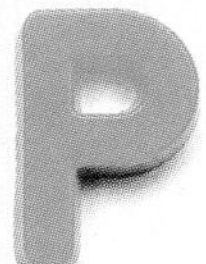

part a bit; not the whole thing

What do you call that **part**?
piece
section

pick to decide on one of a group of things

Which one would you **pick**?
choose
select

pile many objects bunched one on top of another

Look at this **pile** of clothes!
stack
mound

pretty pleasing to look at

The butterfly is **pretty**.
beautiful
lovely

quiet having little or no noise

My favorite place is **quiet**.
calm
peaceful

run to move quickly on foot

bolt	gallop
jog	trot
sprint	dash
dart	race

say to speak aloud

What did the coach **say**?
whisper
shout

shine to give off light

Clara's eyes seemed to **shine**.
twinkle
glow

smart able to learn quickly

Chet is very **smart** in school.
clever
intelligent

strange not usual

Beth's lamp is very **strange**.
odd
unusual

walk to move on foot at a steady pace

Word Bank

hike	pace	march
plod	step	stride
stroll	strut	tramp

wet not dry

Is your coat still **wet**?
soaked
drenched

work to stay in motion; go

Does the tractor **work** at all?
run
operate

Spelling and Meaning

B

bake
- **bake**s
- **bake**d
- **bak**ing
- **bak**er
- **bak**ery

B

bright
- **bright**er
- **bright**est
- **bright**ly
- **bright**en
- **bright**ness

C

care
- **care**s
- **care**d
- **car**ing
- **care**ful
- **care**fully
- **care**less

C

clean
- **clean**s
- **clean**ed
- **clean**ing
- **clean**er
- **clean**est

C

clear
- **clear**s
- **clear**ed
- **clear**ing
- **clear**er
- **clear**est
- **clear**ly

D

dress
- **dress**es
- **dress**ed
- **dress**ing
- **dress**er

F

farm
- **farm**s
- **farm**ed
- **farm**ing
- **farm**er
- **farm**house
- **farm**land

F

fish
- **fish**es
- **fish**ed
- **fish**ing
- **fish**y
- **fish**erman

H

hand
- **hand**s
- **hand**ed
- **hand**ing
- **hand**ful
- **hand**le
- **hand**made

H
happy
happier
happiest
happily
happiness

H
help
helps
helped
helping
helper
helpful
helpless

H
high
higher
highest
highly
highway

H
hope
hopes
hoped
hoping
hopeful
hopeless

K
kind
kinder
kindest
kindly
kindness

L
land
lands
landed
landing
landlord
landmark
landscape

L
light
lights
lighted
lighting
lightning
lighter
lighthouse

O
out
outdoor
outer
outing
outline
outside

P
paint
paints
painted
painting
painter
paintbrush

P

play

- **play**s
- **play**ed
- **play**ing
- **play**er
- **play**ful
- **play**ground

P

please

- **pleas**es
- **pleas**ed
- **pleas**ing
- **pleas**ant
- **pleas**ure

R

race

- **race**s
- **race**d
- **rac**ing
- **race**r
- **race**track

R

rain

- **rain**s
- **rain**ed
- **rain**ing
- **rain**y
- **rain**bow
- **rain**coat

S

sad

- **sad**der
- **sad**dest
- **sad**ly
- **sad**ness

S

sail

- **sail**s
- **sail**ed
- **sail**ing
- **sail**boat
- **sail**or

S

ship

- **ship**s
- **ship**ped
- **ship**ping
- **ship**ment
- **ship**wreck

S

shop

- **shop**s
- **shop**ped
- **shop**ping
- **shop**per
- **shop**keeper

S

slow

- **slow**s
- **slow**ed
- **slow**ing
- **slow**er
- **slow**est
- **slow**ly

S

spot

spots
spotted
spotter
spotless
spotlight

S

stop

stops
stopped
stopping
stopper
stoplight

S

sun

sunflower
sunglasses
sunny
sunrise
sunset
sunshine

T

thank

thanks
thanked
thanking
thankful
thankless

T

time

times
timed
timing
timer
timekeeper

U

use

uses
used
using
user
useful
useless

W

warm

warmed
warming
warmer
warmest
warmly
warmth

W

water

waters
watered
watering
waterfall
waterproof
watery

W

wish

wishes
wished
wishing
wishbone

Spelling Dictionary

How to Use a Dictionary

Finding an Entry Word

Entry Words

A word you look up in a dictionary is called an entry word. Entry words are listed in ABC order.

To find a word that has an ending, like **ed** or **ing**, you usually look up the base word. For example, to find **sailed**, you would look up the entry word **sail**.

Guide Words

At the top of each page in a dictionary, you will see two guide words. The guide words name the first and last entry on the page. Use the guide words and ABC order to find an entry word.

Reading an Entry

Look carefully at the dictionary entry below.

The **entry word** is shown in red.

The numbered **meanings** tell you each meaning of a word.

Sample sentences help to make the meanings clear.

tail

tail **1.** A thin part that sticks out from the back of an animal's body: *Your dog is always wagging its* ***tail.*** **2.** Something that hangs like an animal's tail: *The kite had a* ***tail*** *made of cloth and string.* **tails**

◆ *These sound alike* **tail, tale.**

Other **word forms** are often shown.

Homophones are shown at the end of some entries.

Spelling Dictionary

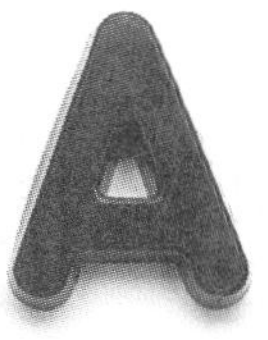

a **1.** One: *I didn't hear **a** word you said.* **2.** Any; each: ***A** circus has clowns and elephants.*

absent Not present in a place or with someone: *Two children are **absent** from school today.*

add **1.** To find the sum of two or more numbers: *If you **add** 6 to 8, you get 14.* **2.** To put on as a new part: *We want to **add** a new deck to the house.* **3.** To put in something more: *I **add** carrots to the soup.* **added, adding**

afford To be able to pay for or spend: *We can **afford** the small car but not the large one.* **afforded, affording**

after **1.** The opposite of **before:** *The children will nap **after** lunch.* **2.** Behind: *The clowns came **after** the elephants in the parade.* **3.** At a time later than: ***After** a few hours, we went home.*

alarm A bell that rings when there is danger: *When we hear the **alarm** for a fire drill, we leave the school.* **alarms**

all **1.** The total number of; every: ***All** five children are good friends.* **2.** Completely: *I was sick, but I'm **all** better now.* **3.** Each and every one: ***All** of us like Marcie.*

am A form of **be:** *I **am** happy.*

an The form of **a** that is used before words beginning with a vowel or with a silent **h:** *I saw **an** elephant and a tiger. Sarah rode a horse for **an** hour.*

and Together with or along with; as well as: *My sister **and** I went to the store and to the park.*

any One or some in a group of three or more: *Take **any** book or books you want.*

anyone Any person; anybody: ***Anyone** in the class may play this game.*

are A form of **be:** *You **are** at home. We **are** coming to your party.*

arm The part of the body that connects the hand and wrist to the shoulder: *Your elbow is part of your **arm**.* **arms**

as **1.** In just the same way: *You'll never meet anyone **as** nice.* **2.** For example: *At the zoo we saw large animals, such **as** tigers and lions.* **3.** At the same time that: *I sang a song **as** I worked.*

ask The opposite of **tell;** to question. *Did you **ask** me what time it is?* **asked, asking**

at Used to show where: *Will you be **at** school?*

ate The past form of **eat:** *We **ate** sandwiches and fruit for lunch.*

baby A very young child or animal: *A duck's **baby** is a duckling.* **babies**

baby ducklings

back 1. The part of the body on the other side from the chest: *I could not scratch my **back** between my shoulders.* 2. The opposite of **front:** *The teacher asked the children in the **back** of the room to stand up.* **backs**

bad Not good; awful: *The apple tasted **bad,** so Jon did not eat it.* **worse, worst**

bag A sack made of paper or cloth: *Mom put a sandwich and an orange in a **bag** for Li's lunch.* **bags**

bake To cook in an oven: *We will bake bread today.* **baked, baking**

baked The past form of **bake:** *We **baked** cookies yesterday.*

baker A person who bakes: *The **baker** made bread and cakes to sell.* **bakers**

baking A form of **bake:** *We like **baking** cakes.*

ball A round object used in a game or sport: *Molly throws the **ball,** and Polly catches it.* **balls**

barn A large building where farm animals live and where grain and hay are kept: *There are cows and horses in the **barn.*** **barns**

barn

bat 1. A strong wooden stick or club used for hitting a ball, as in baseball: *Ben got a new baseball **bat** for his birthday.* **bats** 2. To hit a ball with or as if with a strong wooden stick: *Rosa **batted** the ball across the field.* **batted, batting**

bat A small, furry animal that looks like a mouse with big wings: *A **bat** sleeps during the day and hunts at night.* **bats**

bath The act of washing in water: *Bill gave his muddy dog a **bath.*** **baths**

bathtub A large tub that you sit in to wash yourself: *Nick washed himself in the **bathtub.*** **bathtubs**

be 1. To live: *There once **was** a beautiful princess.* 2. To have a certain place: *Please **be** home in five minutes.* 3. To have a certain feeling: *We **are** glad to see them.* **was, being**
◆ *These sound alike* **be, bee.**

beach The sandy shore of the sea or a lake: *Children built castles of sand on the **beaches.*** **beaches**

bear To give birth to: *Dogs **bear** several puppies at one time.* **bore, born, bearing**

bed A piece of furniture or a place for sleeping: *I put clean sheets on my **bed.*** **beds**

bedpost A post at the corner of a bed: *Each **bedpost** on my brother's bed has one of his hats on it.* **bedposts**

bedroom A room for sleeping: *My dog likes to sleep in my **bedroom.*** **bedrooms**

bedside The space beside a bed: *I have a table with a lamp at my **bedside.***

bedspread A top cover for a bed: *My aunt bought me a new **bedspread** for my birthday.* **bedspreads**

bedtime The time when a person goes to bed: *Dad reads us a story at **bedtime.*** **bedtimes**

bee An insect that has four wings and a hairy body. Most bees have a stinger. *A **bee** may make honey in its hive.* **bees**
◆ *These sound alike* **bee, be.**

been A past form of **be:** *Ollie has **been** to the circus.*

beetle An insect with hard front wings that cover the back wings when the beetle is resting. Some beetles are black: *This kind of **beetle** eats the farmer's crops.* **beetles**

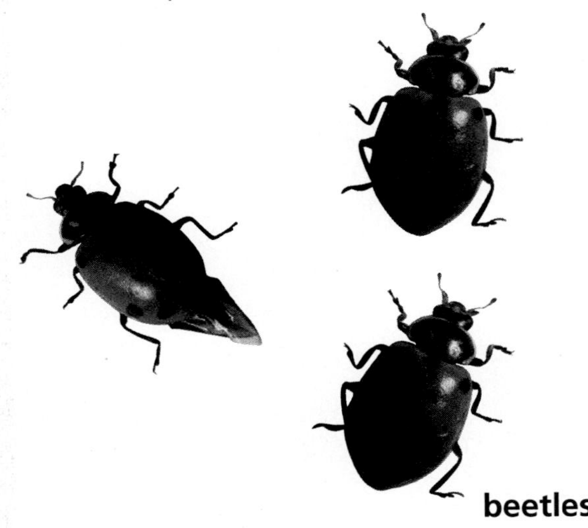

beetles

before 1. Ahead of; earlier than: *My sister got home **before** me.* 2. In the past: *I've heard that **before.***

behind At the back of or in the rear of: *He looked quickly **behind** him.*

bell A piece of metal that makes a sound when it is struck: *After I ring the **bell,** Suki will come to the door.* **bells**

best A form of **good** that compares more than two people or things: *Emily made the **best** picture of all.*

better 1. A form of **good** that compares two people or things: *Caleb is a **better** swimmer than Peter is.* 2. More excellent or higher in quality: *I know that my work will be **better** next year.*

big 1. Large: *Elephants are **big** animals.* 2. Important: *She is a **big** star on TV.* **bigger, biggest**

bike A machine with two wheels, a seat for the rider, and pedals; a bicycle: *Clara and Patrick ride their **bikes** to school.* **bikes**

black The opposite of **white:** ***Black** is the color of the sky at night.* **blacker, blackest**

block 1. A piece of wood, plastic, or stone that is usually shaped like a square or a rectangle: *The baby is playing with a toy **block.*** 2. An area of a city or town that has streets on four sides: *I took a walk around the **block.*** **blocks**

boat A small ship that travels on water: *We rowed a **boat** across the lake.* **boats**

bone One of the many hard pieces inside the body: *Can you feel a **bone** in your elbow?* **bones**

book A set of pages put together and placed between covers: *Allison read a **book** to me.* **books**

booth A small stand or place where things such as tickets are sold: *The woman in the **booth** sold us tickets for the show.* **booths**

born A past form of **bear:** *A new baby was **born.***

box **1.** A container with four sides, a bottom, and a top: *We put the presents in the cardboard **boxes** and tied them with ribbons.* **2.** The amount that this kind of container holds: *We sold a **box** of old books.* **boxes**

braces Wires and bands used for making crooked teeth straight: *Mike will need to wear **braces** on his teeth for two years.*

branch One of the parts that grow out from the trunk of a tree or shrub: *A leaf fell from the **branch** of the tree.* **branches**

brass A kind of metal. Some musical instruments are made out of brass: *Chris plays a trumpet made of **brass.*** **brasses**

brave Not afraid: *I tried to be **brave** when I bumped my toe.* **braver, bravest**

bright Giving off or filled with a lot of light: *The **bright** sun lit up the forest.* **brighter, brightest**

bring To take with or to: *I **bring** a peach to school every day.* **brought, bringing**

brook A small stream: *Children can walk in the **brook** because the water is not deep.* **brooks**

brother A boy or man who has the same mother and father as another person: *My **brother** is two years older than I am.* **brothers**

brown **1.** The color of chocolate: *Zia has long **brown** hair.* **2.** To cook until brown on the outside: *I can **brown** the rolls in the oven.*

bug An insect, such as a cricket or an ant: *A bee is a **bug** that buzzes and has wings.* **bugs**

bun A roll made of bread: *Beth ate a **bun** for breakfast.* **buns**

bus A large machine with a motor, wheels, and many seats used for carrying people from place to place: *Some children ride the **bus** to school.* **buses**

but Even so; just the same; anyhow: *Andrew wore his jacket, **but** he was still cold.*

buy To get by paying money for: *I want to **buy** a new kite, so I am saving my money.* **bought, buying**
◆ *These sound alike* **buy, by.**

by Past, beyond, or near: *The school bus goes **by** my house.*
◆ *These sound alike* **by, buy.**

C

cabin A small, simple house: *The **cabin** in the forest was made of logs.* **cabins**

cabin

caboose A car at the end of a train, where the crew can cook and sleep: *The first car of the train is the engine, and the last car is the **caboose.*** **cabooses**

call **1.** To shout: *When I **call** my dog's name, he comes.* **2.** To send for: *When our parents **call** us, we come in.* **3.** To speak with on the phone: *I **call** Mom at work when I get home from school.* **called, calling**

came The past form of **come:** *Grandma **came** to our house today.*

camper A person who lives outside in a tent or a cabin for a little while: *The **camper** slept in a tent in the woods.* **campers**

can To be able to: *Elmer **can** run faster than his brother.* **could**

can A metal or plastic container: *Paul bought a **can** of tomato soup* at the store. **cans**

cannot Not able to: *The baby **cannot** walk yet.*

can't A short way to write **cannot:** *I **can't** find my lunch!*

cape A warm coat that is worn over the shoulders: *The princess wore a long gold **cape** over her dress.* **capes**

car A machine with a motor and wheels, used for carrying people and things: *The family packed the **car** and went on a trip.* **cars**

careful Taking steps to keep from being hurt: *Be **careful** to look both ways before you cross the street.*

carpet A thick covering for a floor; rug: *The dog loves to lie on the new **carpet.*** **carpets**

cart A container or basket with wheels that is moved by hand: *He pushed the **cart** full of toys to the front of the store.* **carts**

castle A large stone building or fort with high, thick walls and towers: *The king and queen lived in a **castle** with all their servants and friends.* **castles**

cat A soft, furry animal with sharp claws, whiskers, and a long tail: *Our **cat** played with a ball of yarn.* **cats**

catch To get hold of something that is moving: *I'll throw the ball and you **catch** it.* **caught, catching**

cattle Large animals, such as cows, that have hoofs and grow horns: *The rancher gives the **cattle** hay to eat in winter.*

cattle

center **1.** the middle: *They put the flowers in the **center** of the table.* **2.** A place where many activities take place: *The town built a new **center.*** **centers**

change Coins: *Do you need **change** for the bus?*

chase **1.** To run after in order to catch; to follow: *We **chase** our dog every time it runs away.* **2.** To drive away: *A cat **chased** the bird from the tree.* **chased, chasing**

child A young boy or girl: *That game would be a good gift for a **child.*** **children**

children More than one child: *There are twenty **children** in the class.*

chin The part of the face below the mouth: *Dad has whiskers on his **chin.*** **chins**

chop To cut by hitting with a sharp tool, such as an ax: *I **chop** each piece of wood in two.* **chopped, chopping**

chore A small job: *My weekly **chores** are to empty the trash and sweep the stairs.* **chores**

clap To slap hands together: *Do not **clap** until the end of the song.* **clapped, clapping**

class A group of students who learn together: *There are two new children in **class** starting today.* **classes**

claw A sharp, curved nail on the toe of an animal or bird: *The rooster has sharp **claws.*** **claws**

claw

clean **1.** Not dirty: *Please put the dirty clothes in the washer, then fold the **clean** clothes.* **cleaner, cleanest** **2.** To get rid of dirt; to wash: *We **clean** the house every Saturday.* **cleaned, cleaning**

clear Free from clouds, mist, or dust: *Today the sky was **clear.*** **clearer, clearest**

clearing An open place without trees in a forest: *We saw deer in a **clearing** in the woods.* **clearings**

clip To cut: *I **clip** my nails once a week.* **clipped, clipping**

clock A machine that shows time: *Please look at the **clock** and tell me what time it is.* **clocks**

close **1.** Near: *The market is **close** to our house.* **closer, closest** **2.** To shut: *Have you **closed** the door?* **closed, closing**

club A group with members who join together to do special things, such as hiking: *Our **club** went swimming today.* **clubs**

coach A railroad car for people: *We rode in the **coach.*** **coaches**

coast The land touching the sea: *Clams and shrimp are found along the **coast.*** **coasts**

coat **1.** A type of outer clothing with sleeves: *I wore a warm **coat.*** **2.** An outer layer of fur or hair on an animal: *I brushed the horse's **coat.*** **coats**

coin A kind of money: *I found an old **coin** on the sidewalk.* **coins**

cold The opposite of **hot:** *The lake was too **cold** for swimming.* **colder, coldest**

collect To gather or bring together in a group: *Who will **collect** the trash and bring it to the dump?* **collected, collecting**

come To move toward the person who is speaking or toward a certain place: *The children **come** quickly when the teacher calls them.* **came, come, coming**

cookie A small, sweet cake: *You may have a **cookie** after dinner.* **cookies**

corn A tall vegetable grown for its large yellow ears. Corn is used as food or ground up for use in baking: *We ate **corn** and hamburgers for lunch.* **corn**

cottage A small house in the country: *The **cottage** had only three rooms and a garden in the back.* **cottages**

cottage cheese A soft white cheese made from skim milk: *Jane really enjoys **cottage cheese** with fruit.*

couch A sofa: *The cat ran under the **couch.*** **couches**

could The past form of **can:** *We were happy that Uncle Bob **could** come for dinner.*

counter A place in a store where things are paid for: *When you finish shopping, please pay at the **counter.*** **counters**

cow A large animal with horns and hoofs. Cows are raised for milk: *A young **cow** is called a calf.* **cows**

crab An animal from the same group as lobsters and shrimp. Crabs have flat bodies and five pairs of legs. The front pair of legs are large and have claws. Crabs often have hard shells: *We saw a **crab** on the beach.* **crabs**

crab

crawl To move slowly on or as if on the hands and knees: *Ants **crawl** across the picnic table.* **crawled, crawling**

crew The people who work together to sail a ship or fly an airplane: *I asked someone in the **crew** to show me around the ship.* **crews**

crossing A place with flashing lights where railroad tracks may be crossed: *Cars stopped at the **crossing** as the train went by.* **crossings**

crowd To fill with people or things: *We like to **crowd** around the fireplace on cold winter nights.* **crowded, crowding**

crowded The past form of **crowd:** *The children **crowded** into the gym.*

crown A head covering made of gold with jewels. A crown is worn by a king or queen: *The queen wore a **crown** made of gold and bright rubies.* **crowns**

cry To weep: *Babies **cry** when they are hungry.* **cried, crying**

cup A small, open container with a handle. Cups are used for drinking: *Roberto set the table with plates and **cups.*** **cups**

cure **1.** Something that makes a sick person get better: *Rest and good food may be a **cure** for your cold.* **cures** **2.** To bring back to good health: *Doctors and nurses try to **cure** sick people.* **cured, curing**

cut To shorten or trim: *I **cut** the grass every week.* **cut, cutting**

cute Very pretty: *Kate is wearing a **cute** dress with flowers and bows on it.* **cuter, cutest**

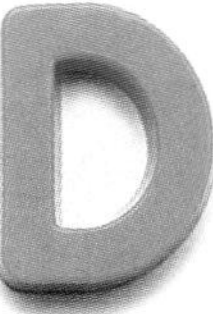

dairy A farm that produces milk: *The store gets milk and cheese from a **dairy.*** **dairies**

day The time between when the sun rises and when it sets: *She begins the **day** with a good breakfast.* **days**

decide To make up one's mind: *She can't **decide** about joining the club.* **decided, deciding**

decided The past form of **decide:** *She **decided** to join the chorus.*

did The past form of **do:** *John **did** his job well.*

didn't The opposite of **did:** a short way to write **did not:** *I **didn't** forget my books.*

diet The usual food and drink taken in by a person or animal every day: *A healthy **diet** has lots of fruits and vegetables in it.* **diets**

dig **1.** To move dirt out of the ground: *Dogs **dig** holes to bury bones.* **2.** To find by looking hard for: *If you **dig** into your desk, you will find crayons.* **dug, digging**

dish **1.** A plate for holding food: *Adam put **dishes** and cups on the table.* **2.** Something held or served in a dish: *I ate two **dishes** of fruit salad.* **dishes**

dish

do **1.** To carry out an act: *I **do** all of my homework.* **2.** Used to make a strong statement: *I **do** want to go.* **did, done, doing, does**

dock A place to tie up a boat: *Lisa ties a rope to her boat when it is at the **dock.*** **docks**

dog An animal with four legs that barks and eats meat. A dog is part of the same group as wolves and foxes; a pet: *Irma teaches her **dog** to sit up and do other tricks.* **dogs**

don't The opposite of **do;** a short way to write **do not:** *I **don't** need help with my homework.*

dot A small round mark, circle, or point: *Do not forget to put a **dot** over the letter **i.*** **dots**

down **1.** From a higher to a lower place: *The cat climbed **down** from the roof.* **2.** In or to a lower point or place: *The teacher told the children to sit **down** in their chairs.*

draw To make pictures with lines: *You may get out your crayons and **draw.*** **drew, drawn, drawing**

dress A piece of clothing with a top and skirt that is worn by women and girls: *Martha, Rosa, and Kim wore pretty **dresses** to my birthday party.* **dresses**

dry **1.** The opposite of **wet:** *Our sneakers were wet, so we put on **dry** ones.* **2.** Having little or no rain: *It was a **dry** summer.* **drier, driest** **3.** To make or become dry: *First we will wash the dishes, then we will **dry** them.* **dried, drying**

dump A special place where trash is taken: *A truck took our old stove to the **dump.*** **dumps**

E

each Every: *Speak to **each** child.*

earn To get by working: *Jason and Rigo **earn** money by taking care of little children.* **earned, earning**

eat **1.** To take food into the body through the mouth: *The children **eat** apples when they are hungry for a snack.* **2.** To have a meal: *We **eat** dinner at six o'clock.* **ate, eaten, eating**

egg The round or oval object laid by a mother bird or fish. A young animal grows inside the shell and later hatches: *We watched a baby chicken hatch from an **egg**.* **eggs**

elk A large deer with very big antlers: *We saw an **elk** while hiking in the woods.* **elk** or **elks**

elk

end **1.** The opposite of **beginning:** *We didn't know what would happen until the **end** of the story.* **2.** The first or last part of something that is long: *Sam sat at one **end** of the table.* **ends**

engine The railroad car that pulls the rest of the train: *The driver of the train always sits in the **engine**.* **engines**

exit A way out: *That door is an **exit** from the room.* **exits**

eye What people and animals see with: *Our puppy closed both **eyes** and went to sleep.* **eyes**
♦ *These sound alike* **eye, I.**

fabric Cloth, such as cotton or wool: *The costume is made of a light, red **fabric**.* **fabrics**

fall **1.** To drop or come down quickly: *The books **fall** off the table.* **fell, fallen, falling** **2.** The act of dropping down quickly, as after tripping or slipping: *Rick hurt his arm in a **fall** on the steps.* **falls** **3.** The season that follows summer: *September, October, and November are months in the **fall**.*

far The opposite of **near;** to or at a great distance: *I walked **far** into the woods.* **farther** or **further, farthest** or **furthest**

farm **1.** A piece of land or a ranch on which crops or animals are raised: *We saw sheep and pigs at the **farm**.* **farms** **2.** To raise crops or animals: *Those families **farm** in the valley.* **farmed, farming**

farmer A person who owns a farm: *The **farmer** raises pigs and sheep.* **farmers**

farming The job of growing crops and raising animals: ***Farming*** *is difficult in places where the soil is rocky.*

farmland Land used for planting and growing vegetables: *Next year my dad plans to buy more* ***farmland.***

fast Moving, acting, or done quickly: *We need* ***fast*** *runners for the race.* **faster, fastest**

father A man who has children: *My friend's* ***father*** *is a carpenter.* **fathers**

feast A big fancy meal: *We made a* ***feast*** *and invited our friends to eat with us.* **feasts**

feet More than one **foot:** *After the long hike, we soaked our* ***feet*** *in the cool water.*

find The opposite of **lose;** to look for and discover: *Could Kip and Alex help me* ***find*** *my lost pen?* **found, finding**

fine **1.** Good: *Thank you for the* ***fine*** *job you did.* **2.** The opposite of **sick;** in good health: *I was sick yesterday, but I feel* ***fine*** *today.* **finer, finest**

fish Any of a large group of water animals that have a backbone, fins, and gills for breathing: *We had tuna, a kind of* ***fish****, for dinner.* **fish** or **fishes**

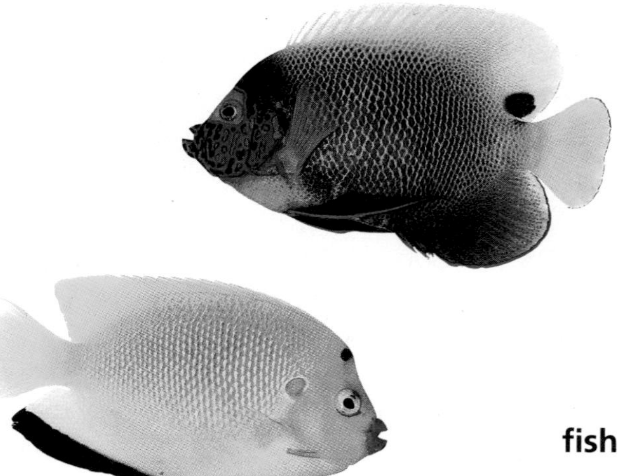

fish

fit Strong and healthy: *Irene stays* ***fit*** *by swimming and eating well.* **fitter, fittest**

five Being one more than four: *I counted* ***five*** *dogs in the park.*

fix The opposite of **break;** to make work again; to mend: *They* ***fix*** *flat tires at the gas station.* **fixed, fixing**

flag A piece of cloth with pictures or stripes that is used to stand for a country or a club: *My dad and I raise the* ***flag*** *to the top of the flagpole every morning.* **flags**

flat Not bumpy; smooth: *We could see for miles across the* ***flat*** *land.* **flatter, flattest**

flea A small, jumping insect with no wings: *A* ***flea*** *jumped off my dog's back.* **fleas**

flight A trip in an airplane or space ship: *Many people would like to be on the first* ***flight*** *to Mars.* **flights**

flip To turn over in the air: *I like to* ***flip*** *the pancakes for breakfast.* **flipped, flipping**

flow To move freely like water in a stream: *The water will* ***flow*** *into the pipe.* **flowed, flowing**

flower A plant that makes seeds and usually has colorful petals: *A rose is a* ***flower.*** **flowers**

fly **1.** To move through the air using wings: *The birds* ***fly*** *to their nests.* **2.** To operate a plane or spacecraft: *Captain Roy will* ***fly*** *the plane.* **3.** To move quickly: *I have to* ***fly,*** *or I will be late for school.* **flew, flown, flying**

food Anything that an animal or person can eat: *We gave our dog his* ***food*** *for dinner.* **foods**

foot **1.** The part of the leg of a person or animal that it stands or walks on: *Julio can hop on one* ***foot.*** **2.** A length equal to 12 inches: *My new ruler is one* ***foot*** *long.* **feet**

for In order to find, get, have, keep, or save: *I was looking* ***for*** *my cat.*
♦ *These sound alike* **for, four.**

fossil The outline or parts left of a plant or animal that lived long ago. Fossils are found in rocks: *A* ***fossil*** *of a dinosaur may show how big the dinosaur was.* **fossils**

fossil

found The past form of **find:** *My lost pen was* ***found*** *at last!*

four **1.** A number written 4 that is equal to the sum of 3 + 1: *We* ***four*** *are best friends.* **2.** Being one more than three: *There are* ***four*** *people in my family.*
♦ *These sound alike* **four, for.**

fox An animal that has a pointed nose, a long, bushy tail, and thick fur. Some foxes are red and live in holes in the ground: *We saw a deer, a rabbit, and a* ***fox*** *in the woods.* **foxes**

frog A small animal with smooth skin, webbed feet, and long back legs. Frogs live in or near water. They swim well and can make long jumps: *We saw two big green* ***frogs*** *on a rock in the pond.* **frogs**

from **1.** Starting at: *We will play* ***from*** *now until two o'clock.* **2.** Beginning in or on: *Those flowers are* ***from*** *our garden.* **3.** Out of: *I took a book* ***from*** *the box.*

fun A good time: *Children have* ***fun*** *at the circus.*

funny Causing laughter: *My friend told me a* ***funny*** *joke.* **funnier, funniest**

furry Covered with fur: *We saw the new,* ***furry*** *puppy.*

game Something done for fun: *Grandma taught us a new* ***game*** *to play.* **games**

gather To come together or put together: *I'll* ***gather*** *the papers together.* **gathered, gathering**

gave The past form of **give:** *I* ***gave*** *my dad the tools he needed.*

gear Things, such as tools or clothes, used for a special job, game, or activity: *Ci put his sneakers, shorts, and other* ***gear*** *for running in his bag.*

get **1.** To become: *Our new puppies* ***get*** *stronger every day.* **2.** To earn: *He's* ***getting*** *a reward for finding the lost bike.* **got, got** or **gotten, getting**

give **1.** To make a gift of: *My sisters **give** me presents.* **2.** To hand over; pass: *Please **give** me the* paper. **3.** To provide; supply: *My friend will **give** us some help.* **gave, given, giving**

glad The opposite of **unhappy;** pleased; happy: *We were really **glad** to be back home again.* **gladder, gladdest**

glide To move smoothly and quietly: *The kites **glide** high in the air.* **glided, gliding**

globe **1.** A map of the world that is shaped like a ball: *We have a **globe** with a light inside it.* **2.** The earth: *Astronauts travel all around the **globe.*** **globes**

go **1.** The opposite of **come;** to leave: *I will **go** now.* **2.** To move from one place to another: *We **go** to the store every day.* **3.** The opposite of **stop;** to begin or continue to move: *The car wouldn't **go.*** **went, gone, going, goes**

goal A score given for driving a ball or puck into a special part of the playing area: *You make a **goal** in soccer by kicking the ball into the net.* **goals**

goal

goes A form of **go:** *This bus **goes** into town.*

good The opposite of **bad:** *Every child wants to read that **good** book.* **better, best**

gown A women's long, fancy dress: *The princess wore a **gown** of silver cloth to the ball.* **gowns**

grand Very large: *The queen lives in a **grand** castle.* **grander, grandest**

grass Ground covered with green plants that have tall, thin leaves: *Dad sits on the **grass** in the yard.*

graze To eat growing grass: *Sheep **graze** in the fields all summer.* **grazed, grazing**

great **1.** Very large in size or number: *A **great** many people watched the game.* **2.** Wonderful: *We all had a **great** time at the zoo.* **greater, greatest**

green The color of most plant leaves and grass: *Peas are **green,** and carrots are orange.* **greener, greenest**

groom To make neat: *Monkeys in the jungle **groom** themselves.* **groomed, grooming**

grow To become bigger in size: *Baby lambs **grow** into big sheep.* **grew, grown, growing**

gym A large room for playing sports: *Jillian, Trisha, and Emily jog around the **gym.*** **gyms**

hamster A small, furry animal with large cheeks and a short tail: *Tom's pet is a soft, furry **hamster.*** **hamsters**

hand The part of the arm that is below the wrist. The hand includes the fingers and thumb: *Dad held Jacob's **hand** when they crossed the street.* **hands**

happy Feeling joy; glad: *I'm **happy** that my birthday is almost here.* **happier, happiest**

hard **1.** The opposite of **soft:** *The glass broke when it hit the **hard** floor.* **2.** The opposite of **easy;** difficult: *That problem is too **hard** for first graders.* **harder, hardest**

harp A musical instrument with strings that are stretched on a frame. A player plucks the strings to make sounds: *Carlos played a beautiful song on the **harp.*** **harps**

harp

has A form of **have;** owns: *Jenny **has** a toy tiger.*

hasn't The opposite of **has;** a short way to write **has not:** *He **hasn't** ever been late for school.*

hat Something worn on the head: *Louis wore a **hat** to keep his ears warm.* **hats**

hatch To come out of an egg: *A hen sits on her eggs until her chicks **hatch.*** **hatched, hatching**

have **1.** To own: *I **have** a bicycle.* **2.** To be in a certain relationship to: *You **have** three sisters and two brothers.* **3.** Used to show that something has already been done: *We **have** eaten all the oranges.* **4.** To be forced; must: *I **have** to go home now.* **had, having, has**

hay Grass and other plants that are cut and dried and used as food for farm animals: *The **hay** is stored in the barn.*

he The man or boy talked about before: *I wrote a letter to my friend, then **he** wrote to me.*

healthy Not sick or hurt: *Good food and lots of sleep help keep us **healthy.*** **healthier, healthiest**

help To give or do what someone needs or can use: *I **help** my little sister pick up her toys.* **helped, helping**

helper Someone who gives help: *The teacher's **helper** will pick up the papers.* **helpers**

helpful Giving help; useful: *Jeb was **helpful** when he showed me how to fix my bike.*

herd A group of animals of one kind, such as cows, that are kept together: *Dogs help the rancher move a **herd** of cows to my barn.* **herds**

hide **1.** The opposite of **find;** to keep or put out of sight: *We **hide** the ball behind a tree.* **2.** To cover up: *Clouds can sometimes **hide** the sun in the sky.* **hid, hidden** or **hid, hiding**

high **1.** The opposite of **low:** *Mountains are **high,** and valleys are low.* **2.** At a great distance above the ground: *The balloon was **high** in the sky.* **higher, highest**

hill A tall, rounded part of the earth. A hill is not as high as a mountain: *Let's fly our kites from the top of the **hill.*** **hills**

his Belonging to him: *Where did he put **his** glasses?*

hit **1.** To strike: *The stone **hit** the water with a splash.* **2.** To move by striking with a bat: *I **hit** the ball over the fence and into the seats.* **hit, hitting**

hoe A tool with a flat blade on a long handle. A hoe is used for breaking up soil and for weeding: *Martha will use a **hoe** to dig weeds out of the garden.* **hoes**

hole An opening into or through something: *I found a **hole** in my shoe.* **holes**
♦ *These sound alike* **hole, whole.**

home **1.** The place where you live: *A **home** may be a house, an apartment, or a room.* **2.** A place outdoors where plants or animals may live: *The forest is the **home** of trees, foxes, and rabbits.* **homes**

home run A hit in baseball that allows the batter to touch all the bases and score a run: *Roberto hit a **home run** in the baseball game yesterday.* **home runs**

hood **1.** A covering for the head and neck, usually on a coat: *The **hood** on my jacket will keep my head warm.* **2.** The metal cover over the motor of a car, bus, or truck: *He lifted the **hood** of the car to look at the motor.* **hoods**

hoof The tough covering on the foot of some animals. Horses, cattle, deer, and pigs have hoofs: *The horse tripped over a rock and hurt his **hoof.*** **hoofs** or **hooves.**

hoof

hop **1.** To move with light, quick leaps: *The children **hop,** skip, and jump on the playground during recess.* **2.** To jump over: *Kimberly **hopped** the fence and ran to the barn.* **hopped, hopping**

hope To wish for something: *I **hope** that I will win this race.* **hoped, hoping**

horn **1.** A musical instrument, such as a trumpet: *Every child got a paper hat and a toy **horn** at the party.* **2.** A signal that makes a loud sound: *The **horn** in Jill's car makes a funny sound.* **horns**

hospital A building where doctors and nurses take care of people who are sick or hurt: *Did you have to stay in the **hospital** when you broke your leg?* **hospitals**

hot Having or giving off great heat: *The sun is **hot.*** **hotter, hottest**

house A building to live in: *My family moved into a new **house** last week.* **houses**

how **1.** In what way; by what means: *I would like to know **how** you did that trick.* **2.** To what extent or amount: ***How** do you like your new bike?*

hug To put your arms around and squeeze: *I was **hugging** the stuffed dog that I love most.* **hugged, hugging**

huge Very big: *Elephants and whales are **huge** animals.* **huger, hugest**

I

I The person who is the speaker or writer: ***I** am a good friend.*
♦ *These sound alike* **I, eye.**

if **1.** On the condition that: I will go only **if** you go. **2.** Whether: *I wonder **if** it is time for lunch.*

igloo A house made from blocks of frozen ice or hard snow: *An **igloo** is often shaped like a dome, or half of a circle.* **igloos**

ill Sick: *Fran's cats were **ill**, and they kept sneezing.*

I'll A short way to write **I will** or **I shall:** ***I'll** color the sky blue.*

injure To hurt: *If I fall off my bike, I could **injure** my knees.* **injured, injuring**

into **1.** To the inside of: *I went **into** the house.* **2.** To that state or form of: *We got **into** a real mess when we gave the dog a bath.*

invite To ask to come somewhere or do something: *How many people did you **invite** to the party?* **invited, inviting**

is A form of **be:** *Molly **is** my sister.*

isn't A short way to write **is not:** *It **isn't** raining out.*

it **1.** The thing or matter talked about before: *I saw a house I liked and bought **it**.* **2.** Used with verbs: ***It** has been snowing since yesterday.*

I've A short way to write **I have:** ***I've** been to the zoo three times.*

jellyfish A sea animal with a soft body. Many jellyfish have long arms that can sting: *We saw a **jellyfish** floating in the sea.* **jellyfish** or **jellyfishes**

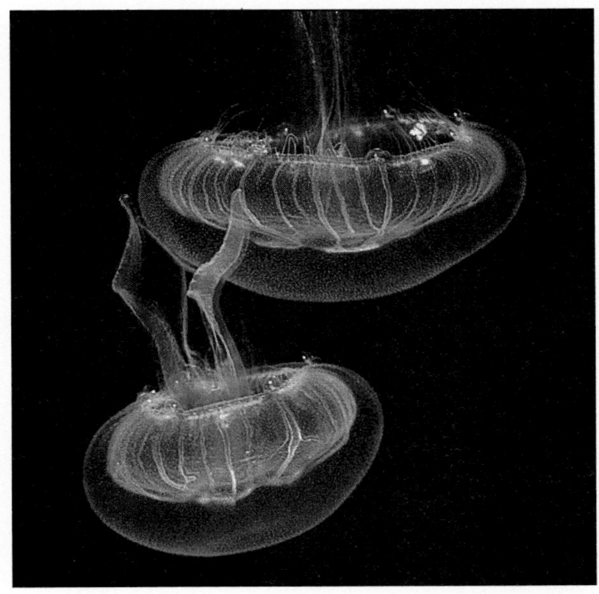

jellyfish

job Work; a task or chore: *Who gets the **job** of sweeping the floor?* **jobs**

jog To run slowly: *I **jog** around the block every morning.* **jogged, jogging**

jogging A form of **jog:** *We went **jogging** this morning.*

judge A person who chooses the winner of a contest or race: *The **judge** gave our cat first prize.* **judges**

keep **1.** To continue in a certain way or place: *Good foods **keep** us healthy.* **2.** To stop: *The fences **keep** the cows from getting on the road.* **kept, keeping**

kick **1.** To hit with the foot: *Ellie can **kick** the ball across the field.* **2.** To move the feet or legs, as in swimming: *The faster you **kick,** the faster you can swim.* **kicked, kicking**

kid A young goat: *The mother goat and her **kid** rubbed their horns on the fence.* **kids**

kind The opposite of **mean;** helpful and friendly: *We are always **kind** to our neighbors.* **kinder, kindest**

kind A sort or type: *I like this **kind** of sandwich.* **kinds**

king A man who rules a country: *When the **king** makes a rule, every person in the land follows it.* **kings**

kite A light frame made of wood and covered with paper. A kite flies in the wind at the end of a long string: *Fly your **kite** high in the sky on a windy day.* **kites**

lady A woman: *A **lady** on the bus gave us directions.* **ladies**

lake A body of water with land all around it: *In the summer, we go sailing on the **lake.*** **lakes**

lake

land To come down or bring to rest on the ground: *Planes **land** at the airport.* **landed, landing**

large Big; not small: *The chair came in a **large** box.* **larger, largest**

late **1.** The opposite of **early;** not on time: *Please don't be **late** for dinner.* **2.** After the right time: *The train arrived **late.*** **later, latest**

leg The part of the body between the hip and the foot: *Timmy can hop on one **leg.*** **legs**

light **1.** Something bright that you can see: *Those points of **light** in the sky are the stars.* **2.** The light of day: *We got up before **light.*** **lights** **3.** The opposite of **dark:** *Sunshine coming in the windows made the room **light.*** **lighter, lightest** **4.** To make or become bright with light: *We **light** the room with candles.* **5.** To guide or show with a light: *The lamps along the path will **light** our way.* **lighted** or **lit, lighting**

lighted A past form of **light:** *Lamps **lighted** the room.*

lighthouse A tower with a powerful light at the top that is used to guide ships away from dangerous shores: *The ship saw the **lighthouse** and sailed away from the rocky shore.* **lighthouses**

lights A form of **light:** *We saw the **lights** of the city.*

like To enjoy; to think someone or something is nice: *I **like** playing the drums.* **liked, liking**

line **1.** A long, thin mark, such as those on a piece of writing paper: *Please write your name on the top **line** of your paper.* **2.** A row of people or things: *The children stood in a **line.*** **lines** **3.** To form a row: *People **lined** up to get tickets.* **lined, lining**

lizard An animal from the same group as turtles and snakes. Lizards have scales, four legs, and a long tail: *A **lizard** eats lots of bugs.* **lizards**

lizard

locker A small closet for locking up clothes and other things: *I keep my sneakers, my jacket, and my books in my **locker** at school.* **lockers**

log A cut piece of tree trunk, used for building or for burning: *We burned the **log** in the fire.* **logs**

long The opposite of **short:** *An elephant has a **long** trunk and a short tail.* **longer, longest**

look To see with your eyes: *I **look** at the pictures in my book.* **looked, looking**

lost **1.** The opposite of **found:** *I looked everywhere for my **lost** sock, but I did not find it.* **2.** Not able to find your way: *We took a wrong turn and got **lost.***

lucky Having good luck: *A **lucky** person won the contest.* **luckier, luckiest**

lunch A meal eaten in the middle of the day: *We have **lunch** every day at noon.* **lunches**

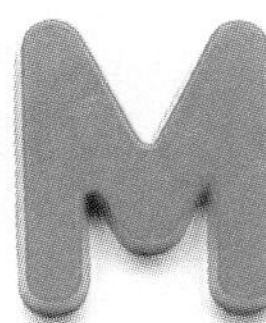

made The past form of **make:** *The children **made** little animals out of clay.*

mail Letters and packages sent through the post office: *I got a card from Gil in the **mail.***

make **1.** To form, shape, or put together: *They **make** masks out of paper bags and colored paper.* **2.** To cause to be or become: *Those songs **make** me happy.* **3.** To carry out or do: *We **make** a trip to visit our uncle every summer.* **made, making**

man A fully grown male human being: *A boy will grow up to be a **man.*** **men**

many The opposite of **few;** adding up to a large number: *There are **many** stars in the sky.* **more, most**

Mars The red planet that is fourth in distance from the sun: ***Mars** is next to the planet Earth.*

mask Something that covers and hides the face: *The clown had a funny **mask** on her face.* **masks**

masks

match A sports contest: *The whole family saw the famous tennis player win the **match.*** **matches**

maybe Perhaps: ***Maybe** we can go shopping tomorrow.*

me A form of **I:** *They sent **me** a book for my birthday.*

mean **1.** To have as its meaning: *What does this word **mean?*** **2.** To be important: *His friends **mean** a great deal to Robby.* **meant, meaning**

mean Not kind or good: *Hurting someone's feelings is **mean.*** **meaner, meanest**

men More than one **man:** *Three **men** were fixing the street.*

miss **1.** To fail to hit, reach, catch, meet, or get: *Harry **missed** the train.* **2.** To fail to be present for: *I **missed** one day of school.* **missed, missing**

mistake Something that was not done the right way: *Some of the children made a **mistake** on the last spelling test.* **mistakes**

moon The body in the sky that goes around the earth: *When the **moon** is full, it looks like a flat white disk in the sky.* **moons**

moose A large animal that is part of the same group as a deer: *A **moose** came out of the woods.* **moose**

mop **1.** A cleaning tool with a long handle, used for washing or dusting floors: *Sweep the floor with a broom and wash it with a **mop.*** **mops** **2.** To clean or wipe with a mop: *Peter will **mop** the floor because he spilled glue on it.* **mopped, mopping**

more The opposite of **less;** greater in number: *There are **more** children in that class than in our class.*

morning The early part of the day: *We woke up in the **morning.*** **mornings**

moth A flying insect that looks like a butterfly. A moth has soft wings and a body that is fatter than a butterfly's body: *A **moth** ate a hole in my wool shirt.* **moths**

mother A woman who has children: *He lives with his **mother** and his brothers.* **mothers**

motor A machine that gives the power to make something move or run; an engine: *Pam fixed the **motor** in my truck and it runs better.* **motors**

mouse A small, furry animal with a thin tail. Some mice live in holes in or near houses: *Does a **mouse** like to eat cheese?* **mice**

mouth The part of the body through which an animal takes in food: *How many teeth do you have in your **mouth?*** **mouths**

much **1.** Greatly; a lot: *This test was **much** harder than the last one.* **more, most** **2.** A great amount: ***Much** of my work is done.*

mud Wet, sticky, soft dirt: *The soil in the garden turned to **mud** after the rain.*

mule An animal that looks like a horse but has longer ears and a tail like a donkey's: *The **mule** carried all of the packs along the hiking trail.* **mules**

muscle A part of your body that is under the skin. You use more than one muscle when you move: *Did you know that you use almost every **muscle** in your body when you swim?* **muscles**

must Used to show that something is necessary: *If you want good marks, you **must** work hard.*

myself My own self: *I can clean my room all by **myself.***

N

nail **1.** A thin, sharp piece of metal. People hammer nails into pieces of wood to hold them together: *He pounded the **nail** with the hammer from the toolbox.* **nails** **2.** To put together with nails: *We **nail** the boards together to make a bed.* **nailed, nailing**

name **1.** A word or words by which a person, animal, thing, or place is known: *Their **names** are Seth and Carrie.* **names** **2.** To give a name to; to call: *We **named** our cat Cleo.* **named, naming**

neighbor A person who lives next door to or near another: *Our **neighbor** lets us play in her yard.* **neighbors**

nest A home shaped like a bowl that is made by birds. Birds lay eggs and take care of their young in the nest: *The robin made a **nest** of twigs.* **nests**

nest

next Coming right after: *Monday was rainy, but the **next** day was sunny.*

night The opposite of **day;** evening; the time between when the sun sets and when it rises: *The sky is dark at **night.*** **nights**

nine Being one more than eight: *The dog had **nine** puppies.*

no **1.** The opposite of **yes:** ***No,** I'm not going.* **2.** Not any: *There are **no** apples left.*

nobody No person: ***Nobody*** *was looking.*

nod To move the head down and up quickly to say yes or greet someone: *The teacher asks if the children want to draw, and they* ***nod.*** **nodded, nodding**

noisy Making a lot of noise: *The school yard is* ***noisy*** *during the day.* **noisier, noisiest**

nose The part of the head that a person or an animal smells with: *The puppy sniffs my shoes with its* ***nose.*** **noses**

not Used to make a word or words mean **no:** *I will* ***not*** *go.*

now At this time: *He's eating and can't answer the phone* ***now.***

nut A fruit or seed with a hard shell, such as a peanut or acorn: *The squirrel carried a* ***nut*** *to its nest in the oak tree.* **nuts**

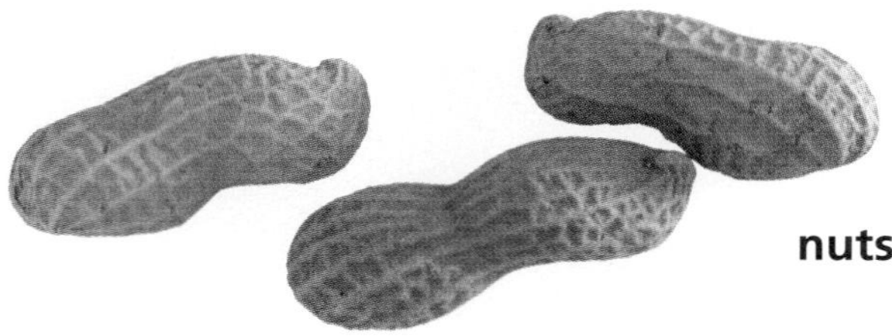

nuts

ocean The great body of salt water that covers most of the earth and moves in waves: *Whales and fish live in the* ***ocean.*** **oceans**

of **1.** Belonging to: *The walls* ***of*** *the room are white.* **2.** From the group making up: *Most* ***of*** *the children are here.* **3.** Holding; containing: *We carried the bag* ***of*** *food home.* **4.** From: *We hopped out* ***of*** *the car quickly.*

off **1.** Away from a place: *The car drove* ***off.*** **2.** The opposite of **on:** *Turn the radio* ***off.*** **3.** So as to be no longer on: *Take your coat* ***off.***

old **1.** Having lived for a long time: ***Old*** *people know a lot about life.* **2.** The opposite of **new;** showing signs of age or use: *We bought a new rug because our* ***old*** *one had holes in it.* **older, oldest**

on The opposite of **off;** in or into action: *Turn the television* ***on.***

one **1.** A single person or thing: ***One*** *of us is taller than Jamie.* **ones** **2.** Being a single person or thing: *You may have just* ***one*** *apple, not two.* **3.** Some: ***One*** *day I would like to travel.*

only Just; and nothing more: *She's* ***only*** *three years old.*

or Used between words to show a choice: *I don't know whether to laugh* ***or*** *cry.*

out **1.** Not in; outside: *Dad is* ***out*** *in the garden.* **2.** Not here; away: *The doctor is* ***out*** *right now.* **3.** No longer working: *Our power was* ***out*** *during the storm.* **4.** Into view: *The moon came* ***out*** *from behind a cloud.*

over **1.** Higher than; above: *A sign hung* ***over*** *the door.* **2.** Upon: *Put paint* ***over*** *those walls.*

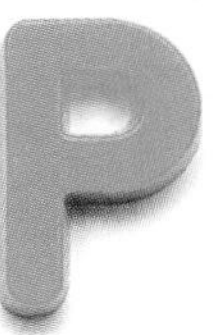

page One side of a printed sheet of paper, as in a book: *Please turn to the next **page.*** **pages**

page A child who delivers messages and runs errands in a castle: *A **page** brought news that the queen was sick.* **pages**

palace A king's or queen's big, fancy house: *The **palace** had more than one hundred rooms.* **palaces**

parrot A bird with brightly colored feathers: *A **parrot** can learn to say funny things.* **parrots**

part **1.** A piece of a whole: *John gave me **part** of his apple.* **2.** A piece in a machine: *I need a new **part** for my radio.* **3.** A role played by an actor: *Mike has a small **part** in the school play.* **parts**

party A gathering of people for fun: *I had a big **party.*** **parties**

paw The foot of a four-footed animal that has claws: *My dog stuck her **paw** in the mud.* **paws**

pay To give money for things or for work done: *I **pay** for my lunch at school.* **paid, paying**

pen Something used for writing: *Grandpa signed his name with a **pen.*** **pens**

pen A small place with a fence around it where animals are kept: *The cows are in the barn, and the pigs are in the **pen.*** **pens**

penguin A bird that lives by the ocean. Penguins have white feathers in front and black feathers on the back. Penguins cannot fly, but they can use their wings to swim: *The **penguin** ate a large fish.* **penguins**

penguin

people Human beings: *The **people** on the bus sang songs and played games.* **people**

perch To rest or sit on a branch or rod: *Birds **perch** on the branches of the tree.* **perched, perching**

pet **1.** A tame animal that lives with people: *A dog, cat, or fish can be a **pet.*** **pets** **2.** To stroke or pat in a gentle manner: *We like to **pet** the baby animals at the farm.* **petted, petting**

petal One of the brightly colored parts of a flower: *A daisy might have white, yellow, or pink **petals.*** **petals**

pick To choose: *I **pick** this book to read.* **picked, picking**

picnic A meal that people eat outdoors: *On Monday my class had a **picnic** in the park.* **picnics**

pig A farm animal that has short legs, a fat body, and a flat nose: *In the barn, a **pig** and her baby piglets say, "Oink, oink."* **pigs**

piglet

piglet A young pig: *The pink **piglet** that we saw at the farm had a little, curly tail.* **piglets**

pilot A person who runs the plane while it is flying: *The **pilot** was not on the plane, so we could not take off.* **pilots**

pin **1.** A short, stiff piece of wire used to hold things together: *Mom used a **pin** to put a flower on Jenny's shirt.* **pins** **2.** To put together or attach with a pin: *Eric **pinned** these pieces of cloth together.* **pinned, pinning**

pit The place in front of a stage where people playing musical instruments sit. The pit is lower than the stage: *We carried our instruments into the **pit** and began to play our music.* **pits**

plain **1.** Simple; not fancy: *He wore his **plain** white shirt instead of the one with stripes.* **plainer, plainest** **2.** A large, flat piece of land without any trees: *We could see for miles across the grassy **plain.*** **plains**
♦ *These sound alike* **plain, plane.**

plane A machine with wings that can fly through the air; an airplane: *On Monday, we will fly across the country in a **plane.*** **planes**
♦ *These sound alike* **plane, plain.**

planet A body that moves around a star, such as the sun: *Earth is a **planet.*** **planets**

play **1.** To have fun: *The children went out to **play.*** **2.** To take part in a game of: *Let's **play** tag after school.* **played, playing** **3.** A story acted out on stage: *Every child has a part in our **play.*** **plays**

played The past form of **play:** *We **played** a game.*

player A person who plays a game or sport: *She is a great hockey **player.*** **players**

playful Lively; liking to play: *The **playful** kitten rolled and tumbled on the rug.*

playground An outdoor area for play, sports, and games: *The class met in the **playground** after school.* **playgrounds**

please To be willing to: ***Please** tell us a story.* **pleased, pleasing**

Pluto The planet that is farthest from the sun: ***Pluto** is a cold, tiny planet.*

pot A deep, round container that is used for cooking: *After dinner we washed three dishes, a **pot,** a pan, and a bowl.* **pots**

price The amount of money asked or paid for something: *The **price** of the tent was $79.00.* **prices**

puddle A small amount of water that is collected in one place: *We splashed through the mud **puddle.*** **puddles**

pupil A young person who goes to school: *Our teacher has twenty **pupils** in his class.* **pupils**

puppy A young dog: *Our **puppy** likes to sleep on an old blanket.* **puppies**

queen **1.** A woman who is the ruler of a country: *The **queen** hoped that all people in her land would be happy.* **2.** The wife of a king: *The king and **queen** planned a huge feast for all of their friends.* **queens**

quiet The opposite of **noisy;** silent; having little or no noise: *The children in the library were very **quiet** today.* **quieter, quietest**

quilt A covering for a bed: *The **quilt** my grandmother made me keeps me warm at night.* **quilts**

railroad The metal track that trains ride on: *The **railroad** goes through our town.* **railroads**

rain **1.** Water that falls from clouds to the earth in drops: *The **rain,** sleet, and snow made our bus late for school.* **2.** A fall of rain: *The streets flood during a heavy **rain.*** **rains**

rainbow Colored light across the sky: *When the rain stopped, we saw a **rainbow.*** **rainbows**

ran The past form of **run;** raced; jogged: *The children **ran** around the park.*

read To understand the meaning of printed words: *In our class, we **read** many good stories.* **read, reading**

red The color of most apples and fire trucks: *We mixed **red** paint and blue paint to make purple paint.* **redder, reddest.**

reptile Any one of a group of animals that creep or crawl on the ground. Reptiles have backbones and are usually covered with scales. The body of a reptile gets as warm or cold as the air around it. Snakes, turtles, and lizards are reptiles: *A **reptile** does not have fur on its body.* **reptiles**

reptile

ribbon A strip of cloth given as a prize in a contest: *The judge gave our dog Buddy first prize, a blue* ***ribbon.*** **ribbons**

ride **1.** To sit on and make an object move: *I* ***ride*** *my bicycle to school.* **2.** To be carried in a car, bus, or plane: *I'll drive the car, and you can* ***ride*** *with me.* **rode, ridden, riding** **3.** A trip in a car, bus, or plane: *Dad and I went on a bus* ***ride.*** **rides**

right **1.** The side or direction opposite of **left:** *The number 3 is on the* ***right*** *side of a clock face.* **2.** The opposite of **wrong;** correct: *I tried to think of the* ***right*** *answer.*

ring A place where shows or contests take place: *The dogs in the show walk around the* ***ring.*** **rings**

rinse To clear out or off with water: ***Rinse*** *your mouth after you brush your teeth.* **rinsed, rinsing**

road A street: *The car drove along the* ***road*** *near the beach.* **roads**
◆ *These sound alike* **road, rode.**

rock A stone: *He tripped on a* ***rock*** *and fell down.* **rocks**

rode The past form of **ride:** *She* ***rode*** *her bike to the park.*
◆ *These sound alike* **rode, road.**

room **1.** Space that is or may be used: *There's* ***room*** *in our car for five people.* **2.** A part of a building that has four walls: *The* ***room*** *where we cook is the kitchen.* **rooms**

root **1.** The part of a tooth that is in the gums: *Brushing your teeth helps keep the* ***roots*** *healthy.* **2.** The part of a plant that grows down into the soil: *A tree's* ***roots*** *grow deep into the earth.* **roots**

rope **1.** A strong, thick cord: *Dad made a swing for my baby brother, using* ***rope*** *and a piece of wood.* **ropes** **2.** To set off with ropes: *The coaches* ***rope*** *off the playing field.* **roped, roping**

rope

rug A piece of thick, heavy cloth used to cover a floor: *We sat on the* ***rug*** *and played a game.* **rugs**

run **1.** To move quickly on foot: *My mother asked me not to* ***run*** *down the stairs.* **2.** To flow: *If the paints spill, they will* ***run*** *all over the floor.* **ran, run, running**

sad Unhappy: *Keesha was* ***sad*** *when Grandma went home.* **sadder, saddest**

said The past form of **say:** *Mom* ***said*** *we could go out and play.*

sail **1.** A piece of strong cloth that is stretched out to catch the wind and move a ship or boat through the water: *The **sail** on Rico's boat is red and green.* **sails** **2.** To travel on a ship or boat that moves by catching the wind with large pieces of strong cloth: *They **sail** down the river on a raft made of logs.* **sailed, sailing**
◆ *These sound alike* **sail, sale.**

sale **1.** The act of selling: *We hope to earn lots of money at our clothing **sale.*** **2.** A selling of goods at reduced prices: *Goodman's Store is having a shirt **sale.*** **sales**
◆ *These sound alike* ***sale, sail.***

same The opposite of **different;** alike: *These two books are the **same** size and shape.*

sat The past form of **sit:** *Everyone **sat** quietly and listened to me.*

saw A tool that has a thin metal blade with sharp teeth for cutting hard things: *We used a **saw** to cut the wood.* **saws**

saw The past form of **see:** *I **saw** many stars in the sky last night.*

say To speak; talk: *"What did you **say?**" Joseph asked.* **said, saying**

score A record of points made by each person or team in a game or contest: *You may keep the **score** this time.* **scores**

sea The body of salt water that covers most of the earth; ocean: *I sit by the **sea** and watch the boats.* **seas**
◆ *These sound alike* **sea, see.**

sea horse A small ocean fish with a head that looks like the head of a horse: *The **sea horse** was hiding behind some plants.* **sea horses**

seashell The hard shell of a snail, clam, oyster, or other sea animal: *I found a yellow **seashell** in the sand.* **seashells**

seashells

seashore The land at the edge of or near the ocean: *We always rent a house by the **seashore** during the summer.* **seashores**

season One of the four parts of the year. The seasons are spring, summer, autumn, and winter: *The **season** of autumn is also called fall.* **seasons**

see To look at and take in with the eyes: *Can you **see** the writing on the board?* **saw, seen, seeing**
◆ *These sound alike* **see, sea.**

seeing A form of **see:** *I'll be **seeing** you soon.*

seen A past form of **see:** *Have you **seen** my mittens?*

set **1.** To put; place: *I **set** the package on the table.* **2.** To place in order for proper use; arrange: *Please help me **set** the table for dinner.* **set, setting**

sewer A drain built to carry away dirty water: *When a pipe in the **sewer** breaks, workers must dig up the street to fix it.* **sewers**

shall **1.** Used to show something will take place in the future: *We **shall** eat dinner at six.* **2.** Used to show something that must be done: *You **shall** clean your room today.* **should**

shape Good working order; good health: *Runners must stay in **shape.***

share To have, use, or do with another or others: *Would you like to **share** this last orange?* **shared, sharing**

sharp Pointed or having an edge that cuts: *A bear's claws and teeth are quite large and very **sharp.*** **sharper, sharpest**

she The woman or girl talked about before: *My mother told me that **she** would return soon.*

sheep An animal with hoofs and a thick coat of wool. Sheep are raised for their wool, skin, or meat: *A baby **sheep** is a lamb.* **sheep**

sheep

ship A boat that can travel in deep water. A ship has a motor or sails: *People can go across the ocean on a **ship.*** **ships**

shoot A plant that has just begun to grow: *The first tulip **shoot** has come up in the garden.* **shoots**

shop **1.** A place where things are sold; a store: *We buy our shoes at that **shop.*** **shops** **2.** To visit stores to look or buy: *They are **shopping** for new clothes.* **shopped, shopping**

shore The land along the edge of a body of water: *Children play near the rocks along the **shore** of the lake.* **shores**

short **1.** The opposite of **tall;** small: *Beth is tall, but her brother is **short.*** **2.** The opposite of **long;** covering a small distance: *We took a **short** walk.* **shorter, shortest**

should The past form of **shall:** *You **should** send them a note. We **should** arrive at noon.*

shout To say something in a loud voice; yell: *I had to **shout** to get my dog to come away from the street.* **shouted, shouting**

show **1.** To cause or allow to be seen: *I **show** Mom my school papers.* **2.** To point out; to explain: ***Show** me how to do that dance, please.* **showed, shown** or **showed, showing**

shrimp A small animal with a shell and a tail shaped like a fan. Shrimp live in the ocean. They are part of the same group as lobsters and crabs: *Some people earn money by fishing for **shrimp.*** **shrimp** or **shrimps**

side 1. A line that forms an edge: *We will plant tulips along this **side** of the garden.* 2. The space next to someone or something: *Horses stood by the side of the barn.* **sides**

sightseeing The act of visiting and touring interesting places: *We went **sightseeing** during our vacation in Maine.*

silly 1. Not showing good sense; foolish: *Forgetting my socks was a **silly** mistake.* 2. Not serious: *We watched the clowns acting **silly.*** **sillier, silliest**

sing To perform a song: *Our teacher plays music, and we **sing** songs.* **sang, sung, singing**

sister A girl or woman who has the same mother and father as another person. *My friend has a **sister** and a brother.* **sisters**

sit To rest on the lower part of the body where the hips and legs join: *Tyrone and Kevin **sit** on the bench at the game.* **sat, sitting**

six Being one more than five: *I picked **six** apples.*

skill Ability to do something well: *That model car has been made with great **skill**.* **skills**

sky The part of the air that seems to be over the earth: *There is an airplane up in the **sky!*** **skies**

sleep To be not awake: *I **sleep** during long rides in the car.* **slept, sleeping**

slip To lose your balance and fall or start to fall: *It is easy to **slip** on ice.* **slipped, slipping**

slow The opposite of **fast;** moving or going at a low speed: *The bus was so **slow** that we were late for school.* **slower, slowest**

small Little in size or amount: *An elephant is big, but a mouse is **small.*** **smaller, smallest**

snail A land or water animal with a soft body and a hard shell: *The **snail** moves very slowly across the rocks in the fish tank.* **snails**

snail

snake A reptile that has a long, narrow body and no legs. *We saw a **snake** in the field.* **snakes**

so Very; a lot: *You are always **so** friendly to everyone.*

soil The loose top layer of dirt in which plant life can grow: *We dug holes in the **soil** and planted tomato* seeds. **soils**

some A few or a little: *Dad gave us **some** oranges. **Some** snow fell, but mostly it rained.*

someone Somebody; some person: ***Someone*** *called, but I don't know who it was.*

son A male child: *Ray's parents have one* ***son.*** **sons**
◆ These sound alike **son, sun.**

soon In a short time from now: *Dinner is almost ready, so we'll eat* ***soon.*** **sooner, soonest**

space The huge place around the earth where the stars, sun, and planets are: *We use rockets to send people into* ***space.***

spot **1.** A small mark: *Amy got a* ***spot*** *of red paint on her shirt.* **spots** **2.** To find or locate: *It was hard to* ***spot*** *you in the crowd.* **spotted, spotting**

dog with spots

stall A space that is closed in on all sides. Many barns and stables have stalls: *The horse tried to get out of its* ***stall.*** **stalls**

start **1.** To set up: *Ellen and Kate want to* ***start*** *a soccer club.* **2.** To get a machine going: *Mom could not* ***start*** *her truck today.* **3.** To begin to do; the opposite of stop: *Dad will* ***start*** *cooking dinner now.* **started, starting**

stay To remain in one place: *Let's* ***stay*** *here and play another game.* **stayed, staying**

step **1.** A movement made by lifting one foot and putting it down in another spot: *The baby took one* ***step*** *this morning.* **2.** A way of walking: *Please watch your* ***step*** *going across these rocks.* **steps** **3.** To move by taking steps; to walk: *She* ***stepped*** *up to the teacher's desk.* **stepped, stepping**

stone A rock: *Kara stopped walking because she had a* ***stone*** *in her shoe.* **stones**

stop To end or cause to end the moving or acting of something: *The cars* ***stop*** *to let the children cross the street.* **stopped, stopping**

store A place where things are sold; shop: *We can buy clothes at the* ***store.*** **stores**

storm A strong wind with rain, sleet, hail, or snow: *The campers hurried back to camp when they felt a* ***storm*** *coming.* **storms**

story A tale you may read or hear: *I just read a great* ***story.*** **stories**

stray **1.** An animal that has gone away from a group or the place it is supposed to stay: *The rancher looked all day for the* ***stray.*** **strays** **2.** Having gone away from a group or from a place: *The* ***stray*** *cat was cold and hungry.*

stream A narrow path of water that moves in one direction: *That* ***stream*** *runs into the river.* **streams**

stream

street A road in a city or town: *Our* ***street*** *is the longest one in the town.* **streets**

subway A train that travels through tunnels underground: *Taking the* ***subway*** *is a good way to travel in the city.* **subways**

such So much or so great: *You read with* ***such*** *speed!*

summer The hottest season of the year, between spring and fall: *We can swim and play outdoors in the* ***summer.*** **summers**

sun The star around which the earth moves: *The* ***sun*** *shines and gives light and heat to the earth.* **suns**
♦ *These sound alike* **sun, son.**

sure Certain: *I checked the spelling in the dictionary, so I'm* ***sure*** *it's right.* **surer, surest**

swim To move through the water by moving the arms, legs, or fins: *Fish* ***swim*** *in the tank of water.* **swam, swum, swimming**

tadpole A young frog that lives in water and has a tail: *A* ***tadpole*** *will lose its tail when it grows into a frog.* **tadpoles**

tail **1.** A thin part that sticks out from the back of an animal's body: *Your dog is always wagging its* ***tail.*** **2.** Something that hangs like an animal's tail: *The kite had a* ***tail*** *made of cloth and string.* **tails**
♦ *These sound alike* **tail, tale.**

take **1.** To hold: *We* ***take*** *the brushes and start to paint.* **2.** To do: *I will* ***take*** *a bath after dinner.* **3.** To carry or cause to go along with one: *Franz and Mark* ***take*** *their little brother to school.* **took, taken, taking**

tale A story: *Luis told us a funny* ***tale*** *about going to camp.* **tales**
♦ *These sound alike* **tale, tail.**

tame Used to living with people: *We had a* ***tame*** *deer in our yard.* **tamer, tamest**

tease To annoy or bother by making fun of: *I don't like my brother to* ***tease*** *me.* **teased, teasing**

teasing A form of **tease:** *The children shouldn't be* ***teasing*** *the dog.*

teeth More than one **tooth:** *When your baby* ***teeth*** *fall out, new ones grow in.*

tell **1.** The opposite of **ask:** *If you ask a question, I'll* ***tell*** *you the answer.* **2.** To say in words: *I'm going to* ***tell*** *you a story.* **told, telling**

ten Being one more than nine: *Little Paul counted his **ten** toes.*

than Compared to: *Mountains are bigger **than** hills.*

thank To say that you are grateful that you were given something: *I **thank** my friends for the new books.* **thanked, thanking**

thanked The past form of **thank:** *We **thanked** Aunt Millie for the gift.*

thankful Grateful; full of thanks: *They were **thankful** when Tim found their lost cat.*

thanks A showing or saying that you are grateful or thankful: *She gave **thanks** for her good health.*

that **1.** The one farther away or at a distance: *This is a robin, and **that** is a sparrow.* **2.** The one just talked about: ***That** animal we saw in the forest was a fox.* **those**

the Used to show that a word stands for certain persons or things: ***The** dogs have black tails.*

them A form of **they:** *Did you see **them?** The letter was from **them.***

then **1.** At the time: *We lived in the city **then.*** **2.** After that; next: *One more game, and **then** we should go home.*

these A form of **this:** *This is my hat. Are **these** your gloves?*

they The people, animals, or things last talked about; those ones: *Elephants are large, but **they** move quickly.*

they're A short way to write **they are:** ***They're** coming to visit next week.*

thing An object or animal that is not named: *What are those **things** on the table?* **things**

think **1.** To use your mind to form ideas: *Can you **think** of a gift to make for Miss Marble?* **2.** To believe: *I **think** the storm is over.* **thought, thinking**

this **1.** The one that is present, nearby, or that was just talked about: ***This** house is mine.* **2.** The one nearer than another: ***This** is an oak tree, and that is a pine tree.* **these**

those A form of **that:** *That sock is mine. **Those** are your socks.*

threw The past form of **throw:** *She **threw** the ball well.*
♦ *These sound alike* **threw, through.**

throne The special chair that a king or queen sits on: *The king sat on a **throne** made of gold.* **thrones**

throne

through **1.** In one side and out the other: *We walked **through** the parking lot.* **2.** Among or between: *She walked **through** the flowers.*
♦ *These sound alike* **through, threw.**

throw To send through the air with a quick motion of the arm: *Most dogs like people to **throw** a ball for them to chase.* **threw, thrown, throwing**

thunder The rumbling or crashing noise that comes after a flash of lightning: *The **thunder** was so loud that everyone jumped.*

tie A game or contest that ends with the same score for both sides: *Both teams scored six points, so the game was a **tie.*** **ties**

time A certain point in the past, present, or future, as shown on a clock: *The **time** right now is 3:30 in the afternoon.* **times**

to **1.** Toward: *I sang a song as I walked **to** school.* **2.** So as to reach: *They came **to** my house.* **3.** On or in contact with: *Tie a bow **to** the package.* **4.** Used with action words: *I would like **to** play with that game.*
◆ *These sound alike* **to, too, two.**

toe One of the parts that stick out from the foot. *There was a hole in Ann's sock, and her big **toe** was cold!* **toes**
◆ *These sound alike* ***toe, tow.***

told The past form of **tell:** *Grandpa **told** us how to make a kite.*

too **1.** Also: *I want to go **too.***
2. More than enough: *Don't hold your pen **too** tightly.*
◆ *These sound alike* **too, to, two.**

took The past form of **take**: *Sam took his jacket from the closet.*

tooth One of the set of hard parts in the mouth used for chewing and biting: *His front **tooth** is loose.* **teeth**

toothbrush A small brush that is used to clean the teeth: *Beth picked up her new, orange **toothbrush** and brushed her teeth.* **toothbrushes**

top **1.** The opposite of **bottom;** the highest part: *I stood on the **top** of the hill.* **2.** A lid; a cover: *Please put the **top** on the box.* **tops**

tow To pull along behind with a chain, rope, or cable: *They had to **tow** our car to the garage.* **towed, towing**
◆ *These sound alike* **tow, toe.**

town A place where people live that is larger than a village but smaller than a city: *The family lived in a **town** just a few miles from the city.* **towns**

traffic The number of cars, buses, and trucks moving along roads and streets: *I see lots of **traffic** in the morning when people are driving to work.*

trail An outdoor path or track: *I hiked along the **trail** through the woods.* **trails**

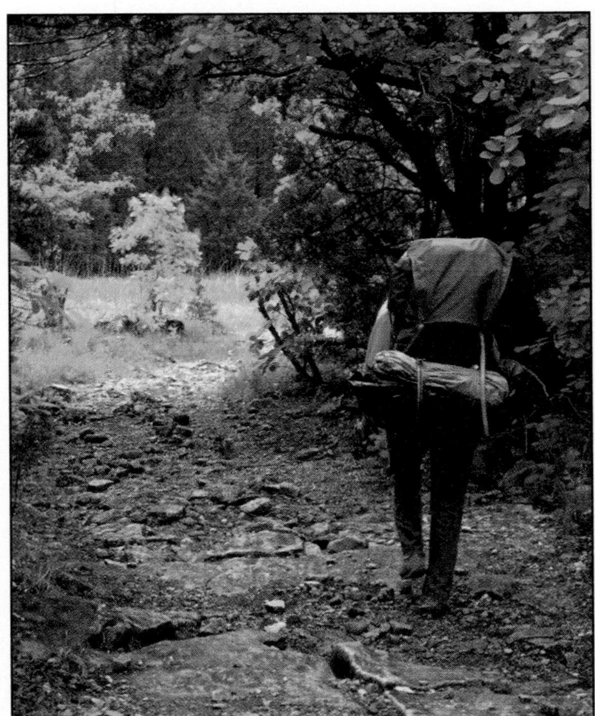

trail

trailer A house with wheels that can be pulled by a car or truck. A trailer can be used as a home when it is parked or put up on cement blocks: *Our **trailer** has a kitchen, a bathroom, and three beds.* **trailers**

train A string of railroad cars used to move people or things. The cars are connected together and pulled by an engine: *The **train** stopped at our station and we began our trip.* **trains**

train

trash Things to be thrown away: *We put all the **trash** in a large bag and took it to the dump.*

tree A tall plant with branches and one main stem of wood: *The **tree** has many branches and leaves.* **trees**

trip A passing from one place to another; a journey: *We rode in a bus on our **trip** across the country.* **trips**

truck A large machine with wheels and a motor that is used to carry big or heavy loads: *The movers put the tables and chairs in a **truck** and took them to our new house.* **trucks**

trunk **1.** The covered, back part of a car, used for storage: *We put all of our camping gear in the **trunk.*** **2.** The long nose of an elephant, used for holding and feeding: *The elephant used its **trunk** to pick up the log.* **trunks**

try To make an effort: *The children **try** to stay quiet during the story.* **tried, trying**

tuba A large brass wind instrument with a full, rich sound: *You need a lot of air in your lungs to play the **tuba!*** **tubas**

tune A group of musical notes that make up a simple song: *David whistled a **tune** as he worked on his model airplane.* **tunes**

two Being one more than one: *She has **two** sisters.*
♦ *These sound alike* **two, to, too.**

under The opposite of **above;** below: *A boat was passing **under** the bridge.*

up From a lower to a higher place: *I threw the ball **up.***

upon On: *We stopped and sat down **upon** a flat rock.*

us A form of **we:** *They told **us** the latest news.*

use To do something with an object: *Did you **use** soap to wash your hands?* **used, using**

very A lot; really: *I am **very** happy that Liz is my friend.*

vest A jacket without sleeves that is worn over a shirt: *Dad wears a warm **vest** under his coat in the winter.* **vests**

wade To walk into or through something, such as water or mud, that keeps the feet from moving quickly: *On our hike we had to **wade** across a stream.* **waded, wading**

want To wish: *We **want** to play outdoors.* **wanted, wanting**

warm Somewhat hot: *I took a bath in **warm** water.* **warmer, warmest**

was A past form of **be:** *Bobby **was** the winner of that race.*

wash To clean using water and soap: *Whose turn is it to **wash** the dishes?* **washed, washing**

water That which falls from the sky as rain and forms rivers, oceans, and lakes: *I hope it rains soon because the trees need **water.***

way **1.** How you do something: *I like the **way** you kick a ball.* **2.** Travel along a road or path: *Lead the **way** home.* **ways**

we The people who are speaking or writing: ***We** went to the circus.*

weather The way it is outdoors. The weather may be hot or cold, sunny or cloudy, or wet or dry: *The **weather** is warm and cloudy.*

welcome **1.** To greet warmly: *We will **welcome** our friend by giving him a hug.* **welcomed, welcoming** **2.** Greeted or accepted warmly: *You are always a **welcome** visitor.*

well A deep hole that is dug into the ground to get water: *We pump water from the **well** into a pail.* **wells**

well **1.** In a way that is good: *My dog behaves **well.*** **2.** The opposite of sick; in good health: *I had a cold last week, but now I'm **well** again.*

we'll A short way to write **we will** or **we shall:** ***We'll** help you fix lunch tomorrow.*

went The past form of **go:** *We **went** to the store before we came home.*

wet Being soaked with water: *Brad went out in the rain and got **wet.*** **wetter, wettest**

we've A short way to write **we have:** ***We've** had fun at the park.*

what That which; the thing that: *I saw **what** you did.*

wheel **1.** A round thing that can turn. Cars, trucks, and buses move on wheels: *The front **wheel** of my bicycle is bent, so I can't ride it.* **2.** Something that is shaped like a wheel: *The driver uses a steering **wheel** to turn the car.* **wheels**

wheel

when **1.** At what time: ***When** did you leave?* **2.** At or during the time that: *Jason will get off the school bus **when** it stops.*

which **1.** The one or ones talked about: *They bought the car,* ***which*** *was blue.* **2.** Being what one or ones: ***Which*** *coat is yours?*

while **1.** Some amount of time: *Please stay for a* ***while.*** **2.** During the time that: *Our vacation was great* ***while*** *it lasted.*

whistle To make a clear, high sound by forcing air through the teeth or lips: *Can you* ***whistle*** *a song?* **whistled, whistling**

white The opposite of **black;** the color of snow: *The moon looks* ***white*** *in the dark sky.* **whiter, whitest**

who The person or group that: *The friend* ***who*** *was here has left.*

whole Complete: *The* ***whole*** *class laughed at the joke.*
◆ *These sound alike* **whole, hole.**

why For what reason: ***Why*** *did you say that?*

will Used to show something that is going to take place in the future: *Mom* ***will*** *drive tomorrow.* **would**

win **1.** The opposite of **lose;** to be first in a game or contest: *Maria and Sara want to* ***win*** *the race.* **2.** To receive as a prize: *We may* ***win*** *a trip to New York.* **won, winning**

winter The coldest season of the year, between fall and spring: *This* ***winter*** *was very snowy.* **winters**

wish **1.** A strong hope for something: *I hope I get one of my three* ***wishes.*** **wishes** **2.** To hope for; want: *I* ***wish*** *to be a teacher when I grow up.* **wished, wishing**

with **1.** In the company of: *Come* ***with*** *me.* **2.** By means of; using: *We washed the clothes* ***with*** *soap.*

without Not having: *I painted that picture* ***without*** *help.*

would The past form of **will:** *You said that you* ***would*** *help me dry the dishes.*

wouldn't A short way to write **would not:** *He* ***wouldn't*** *play with us.*

write **1.** To form letters or words on a piece of paper with a pen or pencil: ***Write*** *your name on the top of your paper.* **2.** To make up a story, a poem, or a play for someone to read: *I like to* ***write*** *stories for my family and friends.* **wrote, written, writing**

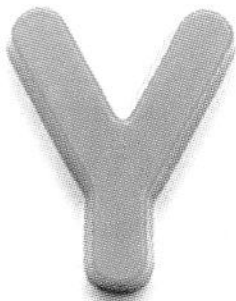

yard A length equal to 3 feet or 36 inches: *A* ***yard*** *is less than a meter.* **yards**

yard A piece of ground near a building: *I raked the grass in the* ***yard.*** **yards**

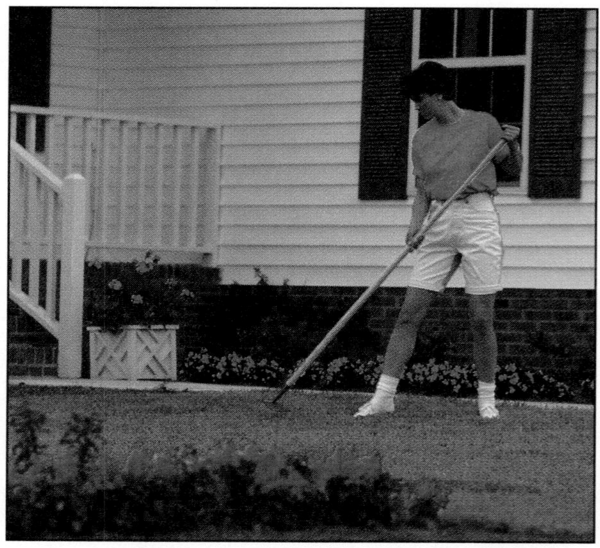

yard

yes **1.** It is true: ***Yes,*** *Sue is home from work.* **2.** An answer that shows something is all right or okay: *Our teacher said* ***yes*** *when we asked if we could stay inside.*

you The one or ones spoken or written to: *This package is addressed to* ***you.***

you'll A short way to write **you will** or **you shall:** *I hope* ***you'll*** *come to my party next week.*

young Not old or fully grown: *The* ***young*** *prince hoped to become a knight.* **younger, youngest**

your Belonging to you: *Where did you put* ***your*** *books?*
◆ *These sound alike* **your, you're.**

you're A short way to write **you are:** ***You're*** *my best friend.*
◆ *These sound alike* **you're, your.**

Z

zoo A large place where living animals are kept. People can go to a zoo and see the animals: *I saw tigers at the* ***zoo.*** **zoos**

zoo

Content Index

Numbers in **boldface** indicate pages on which a skill is introduced as well as references to the Capitalization and Punctuation Guide.

Spelling Across the Curriculum

Spelling and Meaning

Thinking Skills

Vocabulary

Content Index

Writing

Credits

Illustrations **100** Annie Gusman **101** Lehner & Whyte **107** Lehner & Whyte **118** Jennifer Harris **134** Annie Gusman **153** Lehner & Whyte **172** Linda Davick **177** Lehner & Whyte **178** Mary Lynn Carson **190** Lehner & Whyte **209** Fred Schrier **215** Marina Thompson **220** Lehner & Whyte

Assignment Photography **61** (b), **82** (tl), **85** (b), **97** (m), **98** (b),**133, 139, 140** (bl) (br), **148** (b), **152** (b), **172** (b), **181** Allan Landau **167** (br), **206** (mr), **217** Parker/Boone Productions **57** (tr), **64** (t), **76** (tr) (tl), **113** (t), **115** (b), **166–167, 187** (b), **202, 238–239** Tony Scarpetta **25** (b), **31** (b), **37** (b), **43, 93** (tr) Tracey Wheeler

Photography **3** Rich Iwasaki/Allstock/PNI **8, 16** (dog) Images Copyright © 1997 PhotoDisc, Inc. **16** (web) © Archive Photos/PNI **29, 35** Images Copyright © 1997 PhotoDisc, Inc. **38** Larry Lefever/Grant Heilman Photography **41** Grandma Moses: Country Fair Copyright ©1996, Grandma Moses Properties Co., New York. **49** Rich Iwasaki/Allstock/PNI **53** T. Nakajima/Photonica **65** Free Library of Philadelphia **71** (t) David J. Sams/Tony Stone Images **71** (br) Image Copyright © 1997 PhotoDisc, Inc. **71** (bl) Chris Butler/Science Photo Library/Photo Researchers **77** Andre Jebby/Stock South/PNI **82** (bl) Image Copyright © 1997 PhotoDisc, Inc. **83** NASA/Mark Marten/Science Source/Photo Researchers **89** The Granger Collection **95** Lawrence Migdale/Tony Stone Images **100** David Epperson/Allstock/PNI **101** Corbis-Bettmann **103** Joe McDonald/Bruce Coleman/PNI **109** Image Copyright © 1997 PhotoDisc, Inc. **113** AKG Photo London **116** Image Copyright © 1997 PhotoDisc, Inc. **119, 125** (b) Corbis-Bettmann **129** Strauss & Curtis/The Stock Market **137** AKG Photo London **143** Jack Fields/Corbis **149** (t) Peter Scoones/Masterfile **149** (b), **151** (r) Images Copyright © 1997 PhotoDisc, Inc. **155** Jerald P. Fish/Tony Stone Images **161** The Granger Collection **165** Robert Daemmrich/Tony Stone Images **169** H. Heyn/Milon/Photo Researchers, Inc. **171** NASA **173** Frank Zullo/Science Source/Photo Researchers, Inc. **175** Kathi Lamm/Allstock/PNI **177, 178** (tl) (br) Images Copyright © 1997 PhotoDisc, Inc. **178** John Scheiber/The Stock Market **179** Patrice Ceisel/Stock, Boston/PNI **185** (tl) Dave Bartruff/Corbis **185** (tr) Martin Jones/Corbis **185** (ml) Dave Rosenberg/Tony Stone Images **185** (mr) © Cs. Rafael, 1994/Sovfoto/Eastfoto/PNI **185** (b) Michael Fogden/Oxford Scientific Films/Earth Scenes **191** (r) David Madison/Tony Stone Images **191** (m) Robert E. Daemmrich/Tony Stone Images **191** (r) Jess Stock/Tony Stone Images **197** (tr) (b) Images Copyright © 1997 PhotoDisc, Inc. **203** (t) Peter Cade/Tony Stone Images **203** (m) Lawrence Migdale/Tony Stone Images **203** (b) Peter Beck/The Stock Market **209** (b) Joe Sohm/Chromosohm/Stock Connection **215** Don Smetzer/Tony Stone Images **221** (b) Darryl Torckler/Tony Stone Images **223** Zigy Kaluzny/Tony Stone Images **225** Image Copyright © 1997 PhotoDisc, Inc. **226** Merlin D. Tuttle/Bat Conservation International **227** (m) Image Copyright © 1997 PhotoDisc, Inc. **227** (b) Karl Weatherly/Corbis **229** DeWitt Jones/Corbis **232** Images Copyright © 1997 PhotoDisc, Inc. **233** Schomburg Center, NYPL **237** Roseanne Olson/Allstock/PNI **239** Richard Hutchings/Photo Researchers, Inc. **277** Image Copyright © 1997 PhotoDisc, Inc. **278** Thomas Braise/The Stock Market **279** Image Copyright © 1997 PhotoDisc, Inc. **280** Tony Stone Images **281** Ted Mahieu/The Stock Market **282, 283** Images Copyright © 1997 PhotoDisc, Inc. **285** Tom Brakefield/The Stock Market **286** Steve Grubman **287** James Amos/Corbis **288** Michael Hart/FPG International **289** Frank Fournier/Contact Press Images/PNI **290** Image Copyright © 1997 PhotoDisc, Inc. **291** Robert Brons/BPS/Tony Stone Images **292** Alese & Mort Pechter/The Stock Market **293, 295** Images Copyright © 1997 PhotoDisc, Inc. **297** Art Wolfe/Tony Stone Images **298** Renne Lynn/Tony Stone Images **299, 300, 301, 302, 303, 304** Images Copyright © 1997 PhotoDisc, Inc. **305** James Randkley/Tony Stone Images **306** © Christie's Images, 1995/PNI **307** David Ulmer/Stock, Boston/PNI **308** John Elk/Tony Stone Images **310** H.L. Miller/Stock South/PNI **311** Tom & Michelle Grimm/Tony Stone Images

Handwriting Models

a b c d e f g h i
j k l m n o p q r
s t u v w x y z

A B C D E F G H I
J K L M N O P Q R
S T U V W X Y Z

a b c d e f g h i
j k l m n o p q r
s t u v w x y z

A B C D E F G H I
J K L M N O P Q R
S T U V W X Y Z

Words Often Misspelled

You use many of the words on this page in your writing. Check this list if you cannot think of the spelling for a word you need. The words are in ABC order.

A
again
always
am
and
are

B
because
before

C
cannot
coming
could

D
down

F
family
for
friend
from

G
getting
girl
goes
going

H
have
here
how

I
I'm
it
it's

K
knew
know

L
letter
little

N
name
new
now

O
on
other
our
outside

P
pretty

R
really
right

S
said
school
some
something
started

T
that's
their
there
through
time
tried

V
very

W
want
was
went
were
where
would
write

Y
you
your